UNDERSTANDING HUMAN BEHAVIOR FOR EFFECTIVE POLICE WORK

UNDERSTANDING HUMAN BEHAVIOR FOR EFFECTIVE POLICE WORK

*

HAROLD E. RUSSELL

and

ALLAN BEIGEL

Second Edition

Basic Books, Inc., Publishers

NEW YORK

Library of Congress Cataloging in Publication Data

Russell, Harold E., 1918–
   Understanding human behavior for effective police
work.

   Includes bibliographies and index.
   1. Criminal psychology. 2. Deviant behavior.
3. Crisis intervention (Psychiatry) 4. Mental illness.
5. Police—Job Stress. I. Beigel, Allan. II. Title.
HV6080.R88   1982   157'.0243632   81–66981
ISBN 0–465–08862–7   AACR2

Contents

PART III

Understanding Mental Illness

PART IV

Assessing and Managing Abnormal Behavior in the Field

PART V

Behavioral Aspects of Crisis Situations

PART VI

The Stresses of Police Work

PART VII

Conclusion

Foreword

THE new edition of *Understanding Human Behavior for Effective Police Work* by Doctors Russell and Beigel represents an important updating of an already excellent text. With a continuing emphasis on the provision of practical information to police officers that was so vividly displayed in the first edition, the authors have produced a text which enhances the understanding of, and effective response to, those forms of human behavior so often encountered by police officers.

A number of important and substantive changes have been made in the second edition. In addition to the clarifying organizational changes which have been made in the text, six new chapters covering timely and significant subjects have been added. These chapters addressing stress, hostage and conflict situations, and crisis intervention with victims represent important additions which are consistent with what is happening today in police work. In the presence of expanded involvement of mental health practitioners in law enforcement and other components of the criminal justice system, the last chapter on the role of the mental health professional in police work is indeed very appropriate.

Clearly, the new edition represents far more than perfunctory changes. Each of the chapters has been revised, including new and relevant bibliographic material. The reference sources utilized in the new chapters are excellent. Collectively, over 100 new and current reference materials have been added to the revised text.

From the perspective of one who as a psychologist has taught police officers, and as a police officer has been taught by mental health professionals, this new edition by Doctors Russell and Beigel represents a significant contribution to the management of human behavior in police settings.

Terry Eisenberg, Ph,D.
President
Personnel Performance, Inc.
Los Gatos, California

Preface

THE recognition that the understanding of human behavior is an important component of professional police work has continued to grow. Not only was this responsible for our decision to prepare the original edition of *Understanding Human Behavior for Effective Police Work,* but it has also been a major factor in our determination to prepare this revision.

As the sensitivity of law enforcement officers to issues of human behavior has increased, new areas of interest to police officers and administrators have emerged, and these are reflected in the new chapters contained in this volume.

Specifically, many police administrators have begun to focus on the job-related stresses of police work. Studies have begun to indicate alarming rates of divorce, suicide, and stress-related illnesses, such as ulcers and heart disease, among police officers. As a result, two of the new chapters prepared for this volume address this subject.

In the first edition, the principal focus of the chapters on handling abnormal behavior in the field was on those individuals with a variety of behavior emanating from significant mental disorders. Less attention was given to crisis situations, although chapters on handling riots and disasters were included. In this volume, recognizing the increased attention that crisis situations have received in both law enforcement and mental health circles, we have prepared new chapters on hostages, conflict intervention, and understanding the reactions of victims.

When our first edition was published, mental health professionals were involved in law enforcement agencies only in a limited way, and there was scant knowledge or understanding of the experiences of the mental health professional in police work. During the last seven years, the involvement of mental health professionals in police work has expanded considerably, leading to the creation of a whole cadre of police mental health professionals. As a result, we felt that it was important to include here a chapter delineating the proper roles and responsibilities of police mental health professionals.

In addition to the six new chapters in this revised edition, we have updated much of the previous material. Specifically, recent research in several areas, most notably deviant sexual behavior, has been included. Recognition has also been given to the new third edition of the *Diagnostic and Statistical Manual* of the American Psychiatric Association, published in 1980, which adopts a more behavior-oriented approach to the diagnosis and assessment of mental disorders. This modification should be welcomed by all law enforcement officers and should help to reduce some of the communication problems between law enforcement and mental health professionals.

Finally, we want to assure the reader that our continued use of masculine pronouns to refer to police officers in no way indicates that we are not aware of the ever-increasing number of competent women police officers. We have retained the male pronoun for consistency and to avoid awkward and repetitive usage.

In this text, we have retained our goal of meeting the needs of today's officers by describing clearly those areas involved in the behavioral aspects of police work and by providing helpful hints that can be useful to the police officer in the field. Again, we have directed the text primarily to the officer on the street, the recruit in the academy, and the student in police science academic programs. We hope that all will welcome this revised edition.

Harold E. Russell, Ph.D., Sm. Hyg.
Allan Beigel, M.D.

Acknowledgments

DURING the preparation of the first edition of *Understanding Human Behavior for Effective Police Work,* we were able to call upon only a few law enforcement and mental health professionals who had significant experience in training law enforcement officers for behavioral intervention. It is perhaps a measure of the progress during the past seven years that the list of people to whom we were able to turn has expanded greatly. In this brief space, it is not possible to acknowledge all the people with whom we have come in contact and whose suggestions are reflected in this volume. However, we do want to give special recognition to those individuals who read portions of the manuscript and contributed significantly to our work. They include: Sergeant Scott Chestnut of the Arizona Department of Public Safety; Chief Don Daniel of the Creve Coeur, Missouri, Police Department; Bruce L. Danto, M.D., a Detroit psychiatrist and well-known suicidologist; Sergeant Ed Donovan, President of the International Law Enforcement Stress Association; Professor Charles Druding of Phoenix College; Gary M. Farkas, Ph.D., a psychologist with the Honolulu Police Department; Kevin Gilmartin, Ph.D., psychologist to the Pima County Sheriff's Office; A. Nicholas Groth, Ph.D., Director of the Sex Offender Program for the State of Connecticut Department of Corrections; Sheriff Travis McPherson of Deaf Smith County, Texas; Chaplain John A. Price of the Albuquerque Police Department; James Reese of the Federal Bureau of Investigation; Peter Ronstadt, Chief of the Tucson Police Department; Donald Rossi, Ph.D., Director of the Behavioral Science Section of the Michigan State Police; Jose Santiago, M.D., Chief of Psychiatry at Kino Community Hospital in Tucson; Donald T. Shanahan, Director of the Southwestern Law Enforcement Institute in Richardson, Texas; Dave Smith, Ph.D., of the Washington State Patrol; John H. Smith. M.D., of the Ministry of the Solicitor General in Toronto, Ontario; S. A. Somodevilla, Ph.D., Staff Psychologist to the Dallas, Texas, Police Department; Victor G. Strecher, Ph.D., Director of the Institute of Contemporary Corrections and the Behavioral Sciences at Sam Houston State University; Deputy Chief Marion Talbert of the San Antonio Police Department; and Professor Robert B. Tegarden, Director of the Florida Institute for Law Enforcement in St. Petersburg.

A special acknowledgment is due to Chief William J. Gilkinson of the Tucson Police Department. Chief Gilkinson recently retired after more than twenty years with the Department and more than ten years as its police chief. His continuing support of our work during the past eleven years has been primarily responsible for our ability to develop both the original and revised versions of this text. His sensitivity to the importance of police officers being able to assess and manage abnormal behavior in the field is not only a credit to the police department that he ably headed for so many years, but to his own psychological understanding of police work.

The revision of the chapters from the first edition contained in this volume as well as the preparation of the new chapters could not have been possible without the significant editorial and library assistance of numerous people, including Marge Crago, Mark Floor, Betty Hansen, Joan Hauze, Regina May, and Mary Schmidt.

Working under the pressure of a deadline is difficult at best. In that situation, a cooperative secretary and typist is essential. We were extremely fortunate throughout the preparation of this manuscript to have had the most able assistance of Miss Judith Smith. There is no question that this volume could not have been ready for publication as soon as it was without her active participation.

We would like to express our appreciation to Jo Ann Miller of Basic Books for guiding us in the preparation of this edition and once again to acknowledge Herb Reich for his support of our original idea which led to the publication of the first edition.

Finally, as in the first edition, we want once again to express our sincere thanks to the many policemen and policewomen by whom and for whom this book is written. Without their positive response to the first edition and their many helpful suggestions, this second edition would not have been either possible or appropriate.

PART I

Introduction

Chapter 1

The Changing Role of the Police Officer

Police Work—1880

"Killers watched every move the ranger ace made. Slade [the Ranger] knew it. So he tensed to alertness as two shadowy figures approached in the poorly lit Juarez street. They wore hoods and the flowing robes of brothers of the mission. But under the shorter robe of one, Slade spotted a pair of rangeland boots. Slade's guns streaked from their holsters as the 'brothers' wheeled to face him. The quiet street exploded with gunfire. A slug ripped the crown of his hat. Then a stunning blow to his midriff sent him reeling—but both his guns pumped their lethal hail in the last few seconds of a duel to death!" (Scott 1973).

Police Work—1980

"They had worked for more than two weeks tailing people in a numbers operation. Finally, the pick-up man who took the work into the bank where the office crew would run the adding machine was 'put' there.

It was a three-story building in a neighborhood that was hotter than a pistol; a plainclothes cop couldn't hang around ten minutes without being spotted and the alarm going out through the entire area. They knew the building but that wasn't enough. Which of the three floors or basement was being used for the numbers bank was still a question. The lieutenant had one of the team bring his five-year-old boy to work with him so he would look like a father on his day off, an ordinary guy who would not be suspected of being a cop. He slipped into the building when the toot of a horn signaled that the numbers courier was coming up the street. That gave him time to get to the top floor and see the guy coming up the stairs go into the second-floor apartment. Each floor looked like a railroad flat of five rooms running one into the other in a row.

"Feeling rather good about the whole thing, Lt. Scaffardi had had search warrants sworn out. The Chief Inspector's Squad raided the place and came up with the runner and two bookkeepers, plus all of the day's slips. The oldest bookkeeper, a fifty-year-old who looked like a minister, asked the captain if he could 'talk' to him. When the captain said he 'was listening,' the bookkeeper offered $5,000 to forget the whole thing. When the captain asked 'What $5,000?' the guy said, 'The five my brother will be here with in thirty minutes.' A phone call was made and the brother showed up with five big ones. So he got arrested for bribery and the other three for numbers" (Salerno and Tompkins 1969).

Newspapers, magazines, radio, television, movies, and drama perpetuate the idea that the police are "a body of men engaged in the exciting, dangerous, and competitive enterprise of apprehending criminals. Emphasis on this one aspect of police functioning has led to a tendency on the part of both the public and the police to underestimate the range and complexity of the total police task" (President's Commission 1967, p. 13). The apprehension of criminals has been and will continue to be an integral part of police work. But there is also a growing awareness among law enforcement officers and agencies that this is not their only function.

As we shall see, the daily experiences of many police officers provide evidence that their role as law enforcers is changing rapidly and extensively. There are some who do not regard this change as progressive and who are reluctant to turn from the methods and philosophies of the "good old days."

The "Good Old Days"

People who speak of the "good old days" of police work are recalling the past, when often the only things a police officer needed were a badge, a gun, and plenty of guts. Actually, it is doubtful if these alone ever did suffice; more likely then, as now, good police officers possessed other equipment and human attributes that contributed much to their ability to fulfill their assigned tasks.

Even back in the "good old days," police officers performed many social services, including distributing charity to the poor, helping the unemployed to find jobs, visiting the sick to check on communicable diseases, and escorting drunks safely home. Whitehouse concludes: "It would appear that police traditionalists have not read their police history closely enough. The police officer's dual function of performing law enforcement duties and peacekeeping community services has apparently been present as long as there have been municipal police departments" (Whitehouse 1973, p. 92).

Nevertheless, the police officer was perceived by the community primarily as an enforcer of the law. He detected and apprehended criminals, and his presence deterred others from engaging in criminal acts. Emphasis was on the physical and mechanical aspects of police work. The officer was usually selected according to size and general toughness. He received little, if any, formal training and had a low status in the community and even lower pay.

The common viewpoint of those days concerning crime and criminals might well be described by the old saying, "There is more justice in the end of a nightstick [or a gun] than in all the courts of the land." Crime was fairly rigidly defined as a function of the individual's will, and its complexity as a social, economic, political, and psychological problem was appreciated very little by the general public. The officer was neither given nor expected to have flexibility in determining the enforceability of certain laws. Criminals were considered to be those who, with malice aforethought and free choice, elected to engage in criminal activity. With this philosophy in vogue, enforcement of the law assumed first priority over other legal concepts such as civil rights, liberty, and sometimes even freedom. As far as law enforcement practices were concerned, the end justified the means.

The Changing Role

Today, a police officer patrolling a district in a large city is confronted with a variety of problems, few of which involve serious criminal activity. He probably recognizes criminal activity as the essence of police work and may even succeed in convincing himself that this is really why he is there. But most of his duty hours will involve such activities as helping a drunk, finding a lost child, settling a family dispute, giving a traffic citation, preventing a suicide, taking a mentally disturbed person into protective custody, or helping a confused senior citizen. During one recent typical tour of duty in a medium-sized city, two police officers handled the following calls:

Officer #1

TYPE OF CALL	TIME SPENT
Accident (auto)	32 minutes
Family disturbance	17 minutes
Neighbor problem (noncriminal)	14 minutes
Juvenile problem (noncriminal)	7 minutes
Burglary	20 minutes
Disturbance (noncriminal)	29 minutes
Armed robbery	26 minutes
Traffic warrant	36 minutes
Accident (auto)	8 minutes

Officer #2

TYPE OF CALL	TIME SPENT
Silent alarm	12 minutes
Accident (auto)	60 minutes
Family disturbance	19 minutes
Disturbance (knife fight)	7 minutes
Disturbance (noncriminal)	11 minutes
Lost child	14 minutes
Alarm (robbery)	11 minutes
Man down (noncriminal)	5 minutes

While these data and other studies indicate that most of a police officer's duty hours are spent in noncriminal, social service tasks, many officers do not feel that this is really police work and argue that these services should be someone else's responsibility. Yet, none can deny the relationship between these services and at least the preventive aspects of crime. Family disturbances may result in homicides and assaults; the drunk may be robbed and/or assaulted; and suicidal behavior on many occasions can lead to homicide. Besides, there is no one else to perform these services—at least no one that is on the job twenty-four hours a day, seven days a week.

Furthermore, people in the lower socioeconomic classes are accustomed to calling the police for assistance in dealing with a variety of problems. The police are seen as their first, and sometimes only, resource. Often specialized agencies and personnel are unavailable to handle these situations, and police officers have to function as social workers, psychologists, and family counselors. Unfortunately, new police officers are, for the most part, rarely more prepared to handle these events than the average citizen.

Police officers must not only deal with a broad range of tasks but are also expected to exhibit an equally wide range of skills in performing them, further complicating their job. As a careful observer of the police role has noted:

Reviewing the tasks we expect of our law enforcement officers, it is my impression that their complexity is perhaps greater than that of any other profession. On the one hand, we expect our law enforcement officers to possess the nurturing, caretaking, sympathetic, empathizing, gentle characteristics of physician, nurse, teacher, and social worker as he deals with school traffic, acute illness and injury, juvenile delinquency, suicidal threats and gestures, and missing persons. On the other hand, we expect him to command respect, demonstrate courage, control hostile impulses, and meet great physical hazards. . . . He is to control crowds, prevent riots, apprehend criminals, and chase after speeding vehicles. I can think of no other profession which constantly demands such seemingly opposite characteristics (Levy 1966).

Increased complexity is but one aspect of the new reality which confronts police officers in their changing role. Society itself is also changing and no longer appears to present the solid front against unlawful behavior that it once did. What one segment of society may consider a serious crime, another may not.

Today, the general public takes less responsibility in dealing with serious criminal activity. There is little desire to get involved. In contrast to the "good old days," police officers now feel more alone in enforcing the law. They must perform in the midst of usually apathetic, indifferent, and often hostile surroundings. They must face situations in which emotions are high and danger is a constant threat, in which they must rely upon every personal resource they possess and not merely upon a nightstick or weapon. In an oversimplified way, this is a measure of how the role of police officers has changed.

The Core Element

Although the police officer's role is increasingly complex, this is not to suggest that he must now function in endless confusion. There remains a single, basic element in the police officer's role.

The one thing a police officer deals with—not just during duty hours, but during the entire waking day—is human behavior. This includes the behavior of criminals, of citizens, of fellow officers, and last, but by no means least, his own behavior. Some of the behavior is criminal, some is not; some is sick, some is not; some is conscious, some is unconscious; some is simple, some is complex. Furthermore, he often deals with this behavior during conditions of emotional stress and in situations involving life-and-death decisions and personal danger.

Therefore, the officer must be like the psychologist, a devoted student of human behavior. But he must practice his psychology on the street rather than in a clinic office or university classroom. He must make in a minimum of time (sometimes in only a few minutes or seconds) decisions that might baffle the academic behaviorist, decisions whose ultimate resolution may involve months or even years of debate and legal consideration. More important, errors in the psychologist's decisions are seldom critical; errors in the cop's judgment can be deadly.

The authors often tell recruits that they have a far tougher job than either of us. No one expects psychologists to be police officers, but police officer are expected to be psychologists—practical, street-level psychologists.

Today's police officer must know as much as possible about human behavior. He can no longer regard this subject as the sole province of the psychologist. "The man who goes into our streets in hopes of regulating, directing, and controlling human behavior must be armed with more than a gun and the ability to perform mechanical movements in response to a situation. Such men as these engage in the difficult, complex, and important business of human behavior. Their intellectual armament—so long restricted to the minimum—must be no less than their physical prowess and protection" (President's Commission 1967, p. x).

Bruce Terris, in his article "The Role of the Police," commented:

The situations in which police officers most frequently find themselves do not require the expert aim of a marksman, the cunningness of a private eye, or the

8

toughness of the stereotyped Irish policeman. Instead, they demand knowledge of human beings and the personal, as opposed to official, authority to influence people without the use or even threat of force (Terris 1967, p. 10).

Many now support a greater emphasis on the behavioral sciences in recruit training. For example, in *Changes in Role Concepts of Police Officers,* Sterling has stated:

This knowledge can be of limitless value to police officers as they face a perplexing array of interpersonal problems which are always accompanied by confusion, distress, danger, and heightened emotions. . . . The police must act quickly, decisively, and lawfully, often with only a partial knowledge of the circumstances. However, their action orientation does not in any sense obviate the need for understanding behavior. Rather, it reinforces the necessity for a greater understanding of the self and others (Sterling 1972, pp. 294–295).

Knowledge of human behavior is essential to the police officer not only to insure maximum effectiveness in his role but also for his safety. Statistics have indicated that approximately 20 percent of police officers killed in the line of duty were answering a family disturbance call. Another 40 percent of police officers' injuries occur on such assignments. Yet a group of policemen trained in certain basic psychological techniques managed to handle over two thousand calls involving over a thousand different families in a tough ghetto area without suffering even a scratch. With proper training in certain psychological principles and techniques, police officers can perform *more effectively and safely* and can make a significant contribution to the care of others who live in their community.

In addition, a knowledge of deviant behavior will be of great value to the police officer in preventing and detecting certain types of crimes. For example, a knowledge of suicidal behavior will provide the police officer with an investigative tool to aid in determining whether the deceased was actually a suicide or met death by accident or through the violence of others. A sadistic sex murder may indicate either a psychopath or a paranoid schizophrenic. Knowing about these two disorders may significantly help the officer's investigation. With a knowledge of alcoholism and drug addiction, the police officer may realize how alcohol can mask more serious neurological and psychiatric conditions which may bring death in a jail cell to a prisoner considered to be only drunk and disorderly. We will discuss these and other aspects of deviant behavior, as well as certain principles applicable to police investigations in the subsequent chapters.

Summary

We have just described the differences between the police officer's role in the late nineteenth century and his present role, and the characteristics required of the officer in each. We have spoken of the changes in society itself and how these changes have affected the role of the police officer. Finally, we have argued that, regardless of the complexity of this role, the officer deals basically with human behavior and thus must be competently prepared in this area of knowledge.

The role of the police officer in our society is changing. In the "good old days" that role focused on apprehending criminals, while in the present-day it centers on controlling, directing, and regulating human behavior. In other words, the *kind* of activity described has changed— from apprehending to acts of control, direction, and regulation.

Further, the *object* of this kind of activity has changed from criminal to human behavior. Today's officers must function in relation to a more general objective than in the past, widening their concern from criminal activity to the larger area of human behavior. The greater complexity of the job facing police officers today can be handled successfully by those who recognize in themselves a greater complexity. They must aim to be as well-trained mentally as physically, as capable of using their minds as their hands. For these people, a knowledge of how human beings, including themselves, behave is essential.

BIBLIOGRAPHY

ARCHER, PETER. 1978. *The Role of the Law Officer.* London: Fabian Society.

BARD, M. 1970. "Training Police as Specialists in Family Crisis Intervention." In *Proceedings of National Institute of Law Enforcement and Criminal Justice.* Washington, D.C.: U.S. Government Printing Office.

GARNER, GERALD W. 1979. *The Police Role in Alcohol-Related Crises.* Springfield, Ill.: Charles C Thomas.

LEVY, R. 1966. Quoted in *Proceedings of Conference for Police Professions.* April 6–8. Lansing: Michigan State University.

SALERNO, R., and TOMPKINS, J. S. 1969. *The Crime Confederation.* New York: Popular Library.

SCOTT, B. 1973. *Killer's Doom.* New York: Pyramid Books.

STERLING, J. W. 1972. *Changes in Role Concepts of Police Officers.* Gaithersberg, Md.: International Association of Chiefs of Police.

PRESIDENT'S COMMISSION ON LAW ENFORCEMENT AND THE ADMINISTRATION OF JUS-

TICE. 1967. *Task Force on the Police.* Washington, D.C.: U.S. Government Printing Office.

TERRIS, B. 1967. "The Role of the Police." *The Annals.* p. 10.

WHITEHOUSE, J. E. 1973. "Historical Perspectives on the Police Community Function." *Journal of Police Science and Administration.* Chicago: Northwestern University School of Law 1(1): 187–192.

Chapter 2

Foundations of a Professional Attitude Toward Human Behavior

IN chapter 1 we suggested that a police officer must perform as a street-level psychologist to function effectively as a professional. Before proceeding in the next section to a discussion of several fundamental psychological concepts and theories, we will consider the topic of a professional attitude toward human behavior.

The Professional Attitude and Personal Involvement

The professional police officer must learn to view behavior from a perspective similar to the behavioral scientist's in order to insure maximal efficiency in handling the many complex situations he faces. Although the recruit may interpret this as an admonition to avoid involvement with others, this attitude is not desirable, especially toward the noncriminal public.

For example, one police department received a citizen's complaint from a woman whose car had been stopped by an officer for speeding on a deserted street late at night. She was returning from a hospital emergency room where she had taken her sick baby. Her complaint was not that the officer had stopped her unjustifiably, but rather that he had shown no concern for the condition of her baby. As she said in her complaint, "He might have at least asked how the baby was."

The image of the aloof police officer runs contrary to practice. The police officer is involved each moment he is in contact with the public or with a criminal offender. He is certainly personally involved when his life is in danger and when his action or decision can avert a crisis or solve a problem. However, this kind of personal involvement must be contrasted sharply with the behavior of an officer who takes a situation personally and then reacts emotionally to it.

To further explore this distinction, the following analogy is pertinent. The psychiatrist does not get angry at the mental patient who calls him a pot bellied quack, but rather accepts the remark as evidence of the patient's anger and hostility. He then directs his attention to the reason for the anger. Is it because the patient feels neglected on the ward or because his wife failed to visit him that afternoon? The doctor tries to understand the patient's behavior by searching for the reasons behind it. Only with this understanding will he be able to alter or control it. As a professional, the police officer must also try to understand the behavior he encounters so that he may also have the opportunity to alter or control it.

Personal involvement in another sense is inevitable for the police officer. He will often see behavior which is shocking, immoral, or degenerate. For example, he may encounter a father who has just beaten his four-year-old son to death, a rapist who has just violated and tortured a seven-year-old, or an armed robber who has beaten an old man and left him to die in the streets. In these situations and many others like them, the police officer cannot avoid experiencing feelings of anger, frustration, revenge, or disgust. The police officer is a human being with normal human reactions to deviant behavior. He cannot and should not stifle these personal reactions but should develop ways of handling them and turning them to good use. The police officer who learns to anticipate his reactions to offensive and difficult situations and who has developed ways of dealing with them not only has removed a serious barrier to the effective performance of his duty but also has taken a first step toward the acquisition of a professional attitude toward behavior.

He has discovered that, although personal involvement is unavoidable, emotional involvement is controllable.

As pointed out in chapter 1, the contemporary police officer has as his primary task the regulation, direction, and control of human behavior. Usually this is understood to refer only to the behavior of those persons, criminal and noncriminal, with whom he comes in contact during the performance of his duties. But the officer's own behavior must also be under his control. He must handle his own feelings, whatever they are and in whatever situation he encounters them.

Consider, as an example, the feeling of fear. During World War II, much was learned about the emotions experienced under conditions of stress and danger. Prior to that time, soldiers were taught that the feeling of fear was an indication of cowardice and that cowardice was despicable. This attitude was exemplified by General George Patton when he scolded and slapped an enlisted man who had been hospitalized for combat exhaustion. In what was perhaps an overzealous attempt to spur the man to greater effort, Patton accused the soldier of cowardice and demanded that he not be treated (Farago 1963). General Patton was apparently unable to understand or admit the existence of the normal emotion of fear. The alternative, though entirely out of character for the General, would have been for him to have openly recognized the emotions experienced by the soldier and to have assisted him in finding ways to cope with them.

General Patton's attitude was not shared by all American military authorities. Army psychiatrists and field commanders know that, in combat, fear is a constant companion. Everyone is afraid. The important thing is not whether the soldier is afraid but how he handles his fear. If he can admit to his fear and use it positively (for example, fear can make one more alert or lead to a better effort), he can then perform effectively.

One study which compared military units where it was possible to admit and talk about fear with those where it was never admitted or discussed showed that the former experienced fewer casualties, both physical and mental, than the latter (Russell 1965). The professional police officer, like the professional soldier, cannot let feelings of fear interfere with effectiveness. The officer with a professional view of behavior who acknowledges fear and learns how to deal with it, will perform more effectively under conditions of emotional stress.

Thus, the first element in the foundation of a professional attitude toward behavior is the realization that, in all stress situations, every human being will experience certain normal emotional reactions. This is as true for the professional police officer as for the ordinary citizen. What, then, differentiates the professional from the citizen?

The professional enters into these situations not only anticipating his own emotional reactions but also those of the person or persons with whom he is dealing. By anticipating what he and others may be feeling, the professional police officer has reduced the number of unknowns inherent in the situation. This will enable him to direct his attention to other factors and enhance his effectiveness.

As an added benefit, his knowledge of what to expect from his own emotions and those of others will permit him to achieve the second element of a professional attitude, the ability to control his own behavior. He will see that recognition and control of his own fear will contribute to his efforts to cope with a hostile crowd.

The Professional Attitude in Operation

As described thus far, a professional attitude toward behavior rests upon several fundamental principles. The professional who deals with human behavior must maintain control of his own emotional involvement in any situation. He must seek with scientific interest the motivations for that behavior, and he must strive objectively to understand how it was learned before attempting to change it.

Unfortunately, this is easily discussed in the pages of a book, but difficult to put into practice. A personal example many make this clearer.

Several years ago, one of the authors (H. E. R.) was requested to perform a psychological evaluation on a young man who had spent an entire evening torturing a small boy (his stepson) to death. He was very angry because the boy's mother had gone away with another man that afternoon, leaving him with the children. In his extreme frustration and anger, he started drinking and, after becoming intoxicated, took both children in the bathroom where he slowly and methodically tortured the little boy to death while the ten-year-old girl was forced to watch. As part of the team ordered by the court to examine this man to determine if he was sane and could stand trial, the author could easily have allowed his own personal feelings of disgust and anger to interfere with the important task of establishing the good rapport with the prisoner necessary to complete the psychological testing. Had he allowed his personal feelings to take control of his behavior, the author would have lost his professional attitude.

The police officer will face situations like this daily. If he has to arrest a man for setting drunks on fire, he cannot judge and condemn him, he cannot allow his feelings to permit him to strike out or to handle him roughly. To do so would not only detract from his performance as a professional police officer but might also provide the offender's lawyer with a means of achieving the release of his client because of a violation of his civil rights.

It is helpful to the police officer in these situations to remember that people *learn* to be the way they are and that in all probability the offender who beats and tortures his victim was himself subjected to similar treatment while growing up. This understanding will enable the police officer to be professionally more tolerant and accepting of behavior which would otherwise alienate him if he did not have the appropriate professional attitude toward behavior.

Summary

This chapter has discussed some basic principles in the development of a professional attitude toward human behavior. It has pointed out that since personal involvement is unavoidable, it must be recognized, accepted, and handled.

In the next chapters, we will present a more detailed discussion of personality development, function, and malfunction and their relationship to human behavior.

BIBLIOGRAPHY

BANTON, M. 1964. *The Policeman in the Community.* New York: Basic Books.
FARAGO, L. 1963. *Patton: Ordeal and Triumph.* New York: Dell.
KELLY, J. A. 1973. "An Appraisal of the Attitudes of Police Officers Toward the Concept of Police-Community Relations." *Journal of Police Science and Administration* 1(2): 224–231.
PECKHAM, MORSE. 1979. *Explanation and Power: The Control of Human Behavior.* New York: Seabury Press.
RUSSELL, H. E. 1965. *Combat Psychiatry.* Fort Sam Houston, Texas: U.S. Army Medical Field Service School, Brooke Army Medical Center.

PART II

The Origins
and Complexities
of Human Behavior

Chapter 3

Normal Personality Development

TO THIS POINT we have spoken about behavior—the police officer's concern with it and the professional attitude toward it. We will now focus on personality—its basic structure, course of development, manner of function and malfunction, and its relationship to behavior.

The professional police officer who constantly encounters both normal and abnormal behavior must have some understanding of how personality normally develops. There are three major influences on normal personality development: constitutional or hereditary factors; situational factors which arise from the interaction between people and their environment; and developmental factors within people themselves.

Constitutional Factors

Constitutional factors exist at birth and represent heredity's part in personality development. They include, among others, potential for growth in terms of height and weight, color of hair, intellectual potential, and sex. Less commonly, hereditary factors can include a predisposition toward various diseases such as diabetes or a variety of anatomical defects such as harelip.

Each of these features or conditions may influence the development of personality, helping in some ways and hindering in others. For example, whether one is born a male or a female has profound implications for personality development. Or, a serious anatomical birth defect can pose problems with which the developing personality may or may not successfully cope. Will the person become too dependent or feel inferior as a result of the defect, or will he or she adjust to the situation and even compensate by a greater effort in other areas?

Hereditary factors can, therefore, be considered as the *physical* foundation for all subsequent personality development. They determine the outer boundaries of the personality's development. For the most part, they do not change in the course of life, although many congenital defects can be corrected surgically.

Situational and Environmental Factors

Although the Constitution states that all men are created equal, reality can be very different. Even in the uterus, the yet-to-be-born baby is affected by social, economic, and environmental conditions. If his mother lives in a ghetto, she may not receive adequate prenatal care. Her diet may greatly affect her unborn baby's development. The incidence of complications at delivery may increase, and the baby may suffer some type of brain or physical damage.

After birth, environmental forces are also influential. Studies have shown that prejudice and discrimination adversely affect the development of the personality. They may lead to a very negative self-image.

The theories of Erik Erikson are helpful in understanding the influence of social and environmental factors on personality development. Erikson postulates that the first stage of personality development involves the formation of a basic *sense of trust*. He emphasizes the importance of adequate mothering during the first year of life and claims that, to be effective, it must move beyond the satisfaction of only physiological needs. Psychological needs must also be met—to be rocked, cuddled, sung to, comforted, and loved. If the mother adequately fulfills these needs during the first year of life, the infant will develop a basic sense of trust. If he does not receive this mothering—if his cries go unattended for long periods, if he is not cuddled—then this basic sense of trust will not develop, and the infant will perceive the world as hostile and ungratifying.

In Erikson's conceptual framework, the second stage of personality development is the time of the growth of a *sense of autonomy*. This begins at approximately twelve to fifteen months of age. For the next two years, the child's energies are centered on proving that he is a separate person with a will of his own. In this stage, the child must be allowed to make choices in order to develop a sense of self-reliance. At the same time, he must be protected from exceeding the boundaries of self-determination of which he is capable. The interaction between child and parents will again determine the success or failure of the development of this sense of autonomy.

In Erikson's third stage, at four years, the child begins to want to find out what kind of person he can be, to develop a *sense of initiative.* He observes others, especially his parents, and tries to imitate their behavior. At no other time in life will he be as avid to learn and to do. Parents should always encourage and support this initiative of the child, but it is especially important that they do so during this time of life.

Very soon, the child moves into the fourth stage. He wants to be engaged in tasks which will give him a *sense of accomplishment.* During this period, the child acquires not only knowledge and skills but also the ability to cooperate and to interact positively with others. If he encounters situations in which he is labeled too often as a failure, he will develop a sense of inadequacy rather than accomplishment. At this time in his life, the school and its personnel play an important interactional role with the child. Positive or negative reinforcement in school can influence the development of a healthy or unhealthy personality.

The fifth stage occurs as the child enters adolescence. At this time, the central problem becomes the establishment of a *sense of identity.* Who is he? What will his role in society be? What job or profession will he seek? When or will he marry? Can he make it even though he's part of a minority? Will he be a success or failure? He worries about his acceptance by his peer group. He worries about his future. He becomes fearful of developing sexual desires and of the whole world of heterosexual relationships.

As the adolescent matures into adulthood, he must also be capable of developing a *sense of intimacy* with others (Erikson's sixth stage). This sense of intimacy is necessary for the mature emotional give-and-take essential to a successful marriage. Some people, because of inadequacies in previous stages of emotional development, can never get close enough to others to achieve this sense of intimacy. They tend to retire into psychological isolation and maintain interpersonal contacts on a formal level which is lacking in true warmth and spontaneity.

Positive movement through these stages is, in Erikson's view, the basis for normal personality development. As will be pointed out later, the kind of interaction between a person and his environment can be negative at any point in this process, leading to a variety of emotional problems, both minor and major.

Developmental Factors

One of the earliest and most influential students of personality development, Sigmund Freud, constructed a theory based on an assessment of those mental functions and malfunctions which he encountered in his adult patients. In his theory, Freud postulated a series of concepts concerning the workings of mental processes which, through their interaction, influence personality development. His concepts of the id, ego, and superego represent interdependent aspects of mental functioning which relate dynamically to influence personality and behavior.

The Id

From birth, and through almost the entire first year of life, according to Freud, the newborn's mental processes are influenced entirely by the id. The id may be conceptualized as a mental inheritance, a complex of biological urges and needs (instincts). Examples include hunger and the instinct for self-preservation.

The newborn baby does not learn to be hungry. He is hungry because his biological need for food makes his stomach uncomfortable, leading to a behavior pattern which can be altered by providing food. Likewise, the instinct for self-preservation is common to all living things, ranging from the plant which turns to face the sun and sends down roots deep into the soil for water to the infant who reacts with a startle-withdrawal pattern to a painful stimulus.

Libido is a term which refers to the energy of the id. It may be compared to electricity flowing through a wire. Just as turning on an electric switch sends current through the bulb, so the libido finds expression when a "connection" is made between the needs of the id and a suitable fulfillment for them in the environment. Psychologists call this process "need gratification."

The Ego

The ego, Freud's second basic mental concept, first makes its influence felt on mental processes toward the end of the first year of life. Until then, the newborn baby's psychological functions are influenced entirely by biological urges and needs (id) and the desire to gratify them. He is not aware of any distinction between himself, his needs, and the world outside. Nipple, breast, bottle, mother, and self are all mentally fused into one unit and experienced as such.

However, as he begins to grow older, he becomes aware that, unlike the situation which was present when he was in the womb, he is no longer protected from all outside stimulation. His hunger and elimination needs are no longer being automatically and immediately taken care of. Now when he is hungry, he begins to recognize that there is a delay when the mother gets ready to feed him while she warms the bottle taken from the refrigerator. Bright lights and noises intrude and elimination can produce uncomfortable, even painful, results if he is not changed promptly.

He slowly begins to realize that something outside of himself exists and that his own well-being depends on this outside person, usually mother, for gratification. As his recognition of her increases, he also becomes more aware of himself as a separate person. As this awareness of individuation grows, the ego begins to form and assumes a role in the mental processes.

The ego functions somewhat analogously to a corporation executive. Just as the executive gathers information about all aspects of the company and its place in the total economy and then makes decisions on what corporate actions should be taken, the ego gathers information about the body, its needs, and its relation to the environment and then decides which courses of action to take. The ego acts as the mediator or negotiator between the basic desires of the id and the outside world.

The ego should not be viewed as totally antagonistic to the id. Rather, the ego and id should be conceptualized as partners, since it is the function of the ego to find realistic ways of gratifying the id's desires. To return to the analogy, the corporation executive acts within the economy as a whole to serve the best interests of the corporation's stockholders.

23

Not only does the ego function to mediate the influences of the inner world through contact with the outer world but it also serves a protective function to the individual. Should the ego fail in its protective and executive function, serious mental illness will ensue.

Thus an important function of the ego is to maintain a tolerable state of psychological equilibrium, or balance. Psychologists refer to this equilibrium as *homeostasis*. First coined by the physiologist Walter Cannon, this term was first used to describe the system of physical checks and balances existing within the body helping to maintain a physiological equilibrium. For example, if a man goes out into the hot sun from a cool room, his body temperature does not change because there is a temperature-regulating mechanism in the body which maintains constant body temperature regardless of the outside environment, thereby preserving physiological homeostasis. This concept can also refer to the psychological state. The ego is analogous to the physiological temperature-regulating mechanism and helps keep the individual in psychological homeostasis.

The Superego

In Freud's postulates, the third aspect of mental functioning is the superego, a psychological construct closely related to the concept of conscience. As the child grows up, he acquires from his parents a system of values—things he should do and things he should not do. At first, these are forced upon him from the outside (for example, by parents, church, school), but eventually they become internalized so that, even in the absence of his parents or other authorities, he will follow them.

The values which he first learns from his parents form a rather primitive superego which judges right and wrong in absolute terms. As he later comes into contact with the moral and social code derived from policemen, teachers, clergy, scout leaders, and other authority figures, a more mature social superego develops. Finally, he becomes acquainted with the formalized laws and regulations of society. This superego is reinforced and strengthened throughout his whole life.

However, some people fail to internalize these positive social values. Consequently, lacking the "policeman from within," they respond only to the "policeman from without." As an example, a common response by those arrested to the question "Why is it wrong to steal?" is "Because you get caught." They do not recognize that stealing in itself is wrong because they lack the "policeman from within."

The don'ts internalized by the child represent the conscience. However, Freud also described another part of the superego which he called the *ego ideal.* This represents the positive values and ideals with which the individual identifies. R. W. White defined the ego ideal as "the self that one wants to become." It may be an ideal of personal conduct (an upright citizen, a charming woman, a successful executive), or an ideal of desired accomplishments (to stand for honest city government or to protect the consumer).

When this ego ideal is threatened, anxiety, fear, and/or anger can occur. While some people may have a very poor ego ideal which is easily threatened, others may possess an exaggeratedly superior one. The latter is often a defense against hidden powerful feelings of inferiority and inadequacy which would overpower the ego ideal if recognized openly.

The Three Levels of Mental Activity

Closely associated with Freud's functional approach to understanding developmental factors is his structural approach, which introduces the concepts of consciousness, preconsciousness, and unconsciousness. He described these three layers of mental activity as follows: (1) the *conscious*—our immediate experience; (2) the *preconscious*—that which is presently outside consciousness but which can be immediately recalled into consciousness; and (3) the *unconscious*—that which is made up of events and feelings which cannot readily enter into consciousness or the preconsciousness.

The following analogy is useful in understanding these concepts. In the center of a room stands a person with a flashlight. That portion of the room within the beam of the flashlight is the conscious (what he is now thinking, seeing, hearing); he swings the flashlight to another portion of the room and stops it on a portion of the room previously darkened (the preconscious). The unconscious is that portion of the room which is beyond the capability of the flashlight to reach either because of distance, objects which block portions of the room, or the inadequacy of the flashlight's capacity.

Of all behavior, that which is unconsciously motivated is perhaps the most powerful and significant. Although Freud postulated this concept in a new framework in this century, it actually reaches far back into history. Socrates, the early Greek philosopher, said, "In all of us, even in good men, there is a lawless, wild beast nature which peers out in our sleep" (Mezer 1960, p. 33). Other philosophers often warned that a devil lurks within each of us, awaiting the opportunity to destroy our souls.

Nevertheless, it was Freud who first formulated a clinically workable theory to explain the *dynamic* nature of the unconscious. He demonstrated that the unconscious is not merely a jumbled collection of past experiences, memories, and feelings but rather a dynamic system of primitive needs and urges constantly seeking immediate gratification through entry into consciousness. Some of these unconscious thoughts are allowed expression only under certain conditions; others are never allowed into conscious expression.

Evidence of unconscious activity include dreams, sleepwalking, symbolism, and the processes of remembering and forgetting. Freud called these behaviors "the psychopathology of everyday life" and gave many examples from clinical histories to illustrate how some feelings of guilt, jealousy, and hostility which are usually unconscious can find expression in consciousness through these mechanisms.

For example, in one case a woman may not want to go out with her husband and another couple because she is unconsciously afraid and jealous of the other woman. She develops a severe headache, forcing cancellation of the evening's plans. In another case, a worker hostile to a co-worker may "accidentally" let a pipe slip through his fingers which strikes and injures the other worker.

Slips of the tongue are also examples of unconscious motivation. For example, the fellow at the bus depot who approaches the buxom ticket seller and says "Two pickets to Tittsburgh" does not need a psychologist to interpret his slip.

As we shall see in the chapter on suicide, some people who "accidentally" fall from windows, are hit by cars, or fail to make the curve on a lonely highway may be satisfying an unconscious urge to do away with themselves. They may not consciously intend to commit suicide, but their unconscious urges interfere with their ability to avoid such situations or to take counteractions which might save them.

Summary

The police officer with a professional attitude toward behavior must be able to assess and understand the behavior with which he is dealing.

Why is the adolescent running away from home? Why are some people more violent than others? What causes abnormal sexual behavior? Why do some offenders always get caught so easily?

To answer these and similar questions, the officer must possess a frame of reference which includes an appreciation of what is necessary for healthy personality development. Comparing the background of an offender with the known needs for healthy personality development will enable the officer to evaluate more effectively the motivation of that offender.

The basic psychological terms and theories presented in this chapter are part of the knowledge necessary to appreciate the complexity of human behavior and personality development. In the next chapter we will continue our discussion of basic psychological principles by exploring the development of defense mechanisms and the part they play in both conscious and unconscious behavior.

BIBLIOGRAPHY

CAMERON, N. 1963. *Personality Development and Psychopathology.* Boston: Houghton-Mifflin.

ERIKSON, E. H. 1964. *Childhood and Society.* New York: Norton.

KISKER, G. W. 1972. *The Disorganized Personality.* New York: McGraw-Hill.

MARBURG, GALEN SANFORD. 1977. *The Development of the Healthy and Unhealthy Personality: A Comparison of Those Developmental Processes That Facilitate Optimal Growth, Openness, and Integration with Those That Culminate in Ultimate Constriction, Closure, and Disorganization.* Washington, D.C.: University Press of America.

MEZER, R. R. 1960. *Dynamic Psychiatry.* New York: Springer.

MOHR, D. M. 1978. "Development of Attributes of Personality Identity." *Developmental Psychology* 14:427–428.

STAUB, ERVIN, ed. 1980. *Personality: Basic Aspects and Current Research.* Englewood Cliffs, N.J.: Prentice-Hall.

WHITE, R. W. 1968. *The Abnormal Personality.* New York: Ronald Press.

Chapter 4

The Normal Personality in Operation: Conflicts and the Mechanisms of Defense

IN THE previous chapter, we discussed normal personality development and some of the factors which influence it. Ideally, the id, ego, and superego work together to maintain a psychological balance which maximizes functioning. Before this discussion of the normal personality is complete, it is important to understand how daily stresses are handled by the ego. Upsetting events, nagging problems, both small and great, dreams which never materialize and plans which go astray are experiences encountered by all. To insure that they do not disturb the balance between the id, ego, and superego, the ego employs psychological defense mechanisms to handle these stresses. The failure of these defense mechanisms to work effectively often leads to emotional problems and mental illness. A complete understanding of defense mechanisms requires a knowledge of other psychological concepts including conflict and frustration. An unsuccessful resolution of frustration and conflict can lead to the presence of anxiety or guilt.

Frustration and Conflict

The definition of the id in chapter 3 referred to a group of biological urges and needs. These needs can also be called *motives* or *drives* because they supply the power which motivates or drives the earliest forms of behavior exhibited by the personality. Psychologists refer to these early drives as *primary drives* because they are the basic inherited constituents of behavior; those which appear later in development are *secondary* or *learned* drives. These include love and a need for acceptance. Behavior is the result of the operation of either primary or secondary drives or a combination of both.

Within the scope of these two types of drives falls a vast number of biological, psychological, and social needs, all seeking fulfillment. Not all of them can be fulfilled. Everyone experiences the frustration of his drives. This experience of frustration can be represented by a diagram which shows the individual (I) striving toward some goal or objective (G) with a barrier (B) intervening (Kisker 1972).

$$I \longrightarrow B \qquad G$$

The barrier may be *physical* (time, distance, space, confinement), *biological* (lack of intellectual ability, physical deformities, lack of strength), *psychological* (personality factors, feelings of fear, guilt, or anxiety), or *cultural* (group norms, pressures, and demands). At each barrier a solution must be found or an adaptation made.

Related to this concept of frustration is the concept of conflict. In this situation the individual must choose between two alternative, incompatible goals, (G_1 and G_2).

$$G_1 \longleftarrow \text{---} I \longrightarrow G_2$$

He is torn between two goals of equal, or near equal, repulsion or desirability. He has difficulty in choosing. If the choice is of great importance, the conflict can be very disrupting to his psychological, and even physical, balance. If he resolves the conflict successfully, the probability of personality disturbance is slight; if not, some form of personality breakdown is likely to occur.

Reactions to Frustration and Conflict: Guilt and Anxiety

No one is immune or insensitive to frustration and conflict. If each frustration could be easily overcome and every conflict quickly resolved, there would be no inner turmoil. Anxiety and guilt, the common reactions to frustration and conflict, arise when problems in any area of daily living cannot be quickly resolved. These feelings of anxiety and guilt seem to operate as signals, warning the ego that the psychological balance is being threatened.

Anxiety

Anxiety is an emotion with which everyone is familiar. If it is *normal* anxiety, the reasons for feeling anxious are probably obvious and the anxiety is in proportion to the cause. However, anxiety can also appear when there seems to be no obvious reasons for it or can be manifested out of proportion to the cause. This is known as *pathological* anxiety.

Doctors first thought that anxiety occurred secondary to a physical dysfunction of the nervous system. Freud, however, postulated that anxiety is psychogenic, occurring secondary to mental processes rather than physical dysfunction. Erikson viewed anxiety as being secondary to the conflicts which the child, adolescent, or adult encounters in each stage of life. This is not to suggest that anxiety has no physiological components when it occurs. On the contrary, one of the ways in which anxiety is often noted is through changes in body functions.

Freud also pointed out the usefulness of anxiety. He claimed that anxiety can also act as a signal to the ego, informing it of impending or present danger. With this signal, the ego is better able to anticipate or recognize situations which threaten the psychological balance.

How does anxiety differ from fear? Fear is a relatively well-defined response connected to a specific object, event, or person while anxiety is a vague, diffuse response whose relationship to any specific object, event, or person can be ill-defined. Sometimes it is difficult to make the distinction. Fear and anxiety usually go together.

Anxiety-producing situations, or stress situations, have physiological effects which manifest themselves through the autonomic nervous system and the endocrine system. When a person's security is threatened, physiological changes occur and help prepare him to meet the danger. Thus anxiety, uncomfortable as it is, is useful to the healthy person; it puts him on the alert physically by heightening his perceptions and reactions.

These physical changes vary. The heart may beat faster, blood pressure may go up, pain in the chest may occur, and respiration may increase. Digestion can also be disturbed with a loss of appetite, nausea, vomiting, or diarrhea. Shaking, or a sudden feeling of weakness, can occur. Reactions may range from profuse sweating to cold and clammy hands and feet.

Psychologically, the expression of anxiety may also vary greatly from mild worry or a vague uneasiness to dread, apprehension, or panic. Associated feelings of gloom, depression, pessimism, inadequacy, helplessness, or hopelessness may also occur. The person may be unable to sleep, have nightmares, or awaken easily.

In summary, anxiety may be both a normal signal of impending or present danger or a symptom of psychological imbalance. As a signal, it can serve the useful function of alerting the organism and getting it ready to fight or flee. As a symptom, it represents a reaction to frustration or conflict which, if not dealt with, can impair functioning and lead to more serious emotional problems.

Guilt

Like anxiety, guilt is also a possible reaction to frustration and conflict. It may be conscious or unconscious. A person faced with two unacceptable alternatives, who must choose one, may feel guilty about his reluctant decision.

Guilt feelings are first instilled in the child by the parents, either as an aid in setting limits on behavior, as a form of punishment for misdeeds, or perhaps for not living up to their expectations. Even if they have no conscious intent to create guilt, the child may still feel guilty because of his own interpretation. Guilt is often associated with id strivings, particularly sexual and aggressive urges. In our society, the creation of guilt feelings is also used to control the "base" nature of man. Kierkegaard, the noted Danish philosopher of the nineteenth century, stated that guilt "guides the individual and keeps the more violent tendencies of the personality in check" (Kierkegaard 1944; quoted in Kisker 1972).

When someone feels guilty for something he did not do, it may be because he had an unconscious wish to do it, but the superego would not permit that wish into consciousness. For example, a woman who has had to care for an invalid mother for many years blamed herself for her mother's death. In treatment, it became apparent that her guilt feelings resulted not from any lack of care which she gave her mother while alive, but rather to her wish, at first unconscious, that her mother would die so that she would be freed from her responsibility.

Guilt feelings also vary in intensity. One person may feel little guilt in a specific situation while another may feel very guilty. Some may even worry for years about something which others would easily forget. For example, it is not unusual for the Internal Revenue Service to receive guilt payments for tax omissions or evasions committed many years ago.

Police officers are also familiar with some of the variations of guilt. All have encountered the criminal who seems to want to be caught. The authors know of a burglar who broke into the snack bar at police department headquarters and was easily apprehended. The police may also encounter guilt in unusual ways. In the famous Black Dahlia murder, it was publicized that the police had no clues. In response, more than twenty-five men and women confessed to the crime.

Defense Mechanisms

To this point, we have described (1) how a person strives to achieve certain goals either for conscious or unconscious reasons; (2) how these goals are frequently not achieved because of some barrier or because they are competitive, leading to frustration and conflict; and (3) how frustration and conflict can lead to anxiety and guilt.

We will now describe how the ego attempts to deal with these feelings of anxiety and guilt and maintain psychological balance. Of the techniques used by the ego, two are overt, physical, and always employed consciously. The others are internal and dynamic, representing a psychological process which may be conscious or unconscious.

Fight and Flight

The two overt and physical mechanisms are fight and flight. When a person resorts to fighting, he is trying to overcome his anxiety and guilt by aggressive behavior. This behavior is intended to destroy the source of danger, thus protecting him. However, when aggressive, hostile behavior is allowed direct expression, it may arouse more guilt and anxiety which, in turn, may intensify the aggressive, hostile behavior and create a vicious cycle.

Choosing to flee rather than to fight may also be damaging. The person who constantly makes this choice may become passive and withdrawn or even resort to drugs or alcohol as a means of flight.

Internal Defense Mechanisms

It is the internal psychological mechanisms, however, which are of the greatest importance. Among these are: (1) displacement; (2) rationalization; (3) compensation; (4) projection; (5) reaction formation; (6) denial; (7) repression; (8) identification; (9) substitution; (10) fantasy; (11) regression; and (12) sublimation. These mechanisms are usually employed unconsciously. Just as the body does not need to be told to evoke certain physiological mechanisms of defense, such as temperature regulation, when the physical equilibrium is disturbed, the mind does not need to be told to activate these psychological defense mechanisms when the psychological balance is threatened. However, occasionally these mechanisms may become conscious through increased self-awareness or treatment.

With the possible exception of repression, none of these processes is necessarily pathological or harmful to the individual. All of us use these psychological defense mechanisms daily to protect us against guilt, tension, anxiety, inferiority, and other uncomfortable feelings. It is only when these mechanisms are employed indiscriminately and inappropriately or are not adequately developed that they become pathological.

DISPLACEMENT

In displacement, a strong emotion (such as anger) is displaced onto a person or object other than the one which originally aroused the emotion.

Case Example. Officer Hunt is sitting on his motorcycle observing traffic when he notices a car approaching the corner of First Avenue from Salina Street. There is a stop sign, but the car merely slows down before turning right onto First Avenue. Hunt pursues the vehicle and makes the stop. He intends to give the middle-aged driver a warning rather than a citation. However, when he approaches the driver, he is greeted with violent verbal abuse which ends with the driver's suggestion that he take the ticket and "shove it."

Officer Hunt was a victim of displacement. The motorist's wife had announced, just before he left home, that her mother, whom he disliked intensely, was coming for a three-week visit. Although Officer Hunt may never know the reason for the displacement, he does not need to. He should be aware that a defense mechanism may be operating in this situation and recognize that the motorist is not really angry with him. In this way, he can avoid losing his own temper and responding to the motorist's hostility and aggression with his own. Knowledge of this mechanism may also help Officer Hunt become more introspective about his own behavior in situations where he loses control of his anger without sufficient cause.

RATIONALIZATION

Rationalization is the defense mechanism which enables individuals to justify their behavior to themselves and others by making excuses or formulating fictitious, socially approved arguments to convince themselves and others that their behavior is logical and acceptable.

Case Example. Sergeant Maloney is overweight. The Chief has personally told him to lose pounds or face dismissal for physical unfitness. His own physician has advised him that his health is seriously threatened by his obesity. He is fully aware of his need to diet and has been trying to follow his doctor's orders. His wife nags him about losing weight but continues to cook many fattening foods because she feels the rest of the family shouldn't have to diet just because he has a problem.

The sergeant had been losing weight, but one night after a particularly exhausting and frustrating tour of duty, he opens the refrigerator door and notices a single piece of apple pie (his favorite) left over from supper and eats it.

However, Maloney could not have eaten that pie without feeling guilty or anxious (since his doctor told him dieting was necessary) unless he had first found a way to justify his actions. This was possible through rationalization.

How did he rationalize this action? He might have convinced himself that: (1) it is a fact that many people all over the world are hungry; (2) it is a sin to waste food; (3) if someone doesn't eat this piece of pie tonight, it will be too dried out by morning and will have to be thrown away; or (4) it is, therefore, not only excusable for him to eat the pie and thus avoid wasting food, but it is also his duty to do so even if he sacrifices his own welfare to do it.

With these rationalizations, Maloney can avoid feelings of guilt and anxiety. He is able to eat the pie, as he wanted to, and has justified his behavior to himself (and to others), thereby avoiding feeling anxious and guilty.

COMPENSATION

Compensation is the defense mechanism through which people attempt to overcome the anxiety associated with feelings of inferiority and inadequacy in one area of personality or body image by concentrating on another area where they can excel.

Case Example. Recruit Thomas is the lowman in his class as far as scholastic work is concerned, but he is the top marksman and judo man. He spends every available extra hour either on the range or in the gym perfecting these two skills in which he is already more than qualified even though his classwork continues to suffer.

Compensatory behavior may be healthy and constructive. For example, Recruit Thomas compensates for his academic inferiority by concentrating on judo and marksmanship, in which he already excels. His excellence in these two skills helps his ego cope with the anxiety generated by his marginal performance in the classroom.

PROJECTION

In projection, a person ascribes feelings and ideas, unacceptable to the ego or the superego, to others so that they seem to have these feelings or ideas. The person thus frees himself from the guilt and anxiety associated with them. This process is analogous to that of a motion picture projector. There is a picture on the screen, but the real image is on a small piece of film inside the projector.

Case Example. Sergeant Bucko is one of the first motorcycle officers in the department. He is not too smart and lacks a high school diploma. Things go well enough for him until a new lieutenant takes charge of the squad. The sergeant has never had any trouble with lieutenants in command. This new lieutenant, however, places demands on the sergeant that have made his life miserable. Sergeant Bucko informs the chief that he can't continue to serve under his new lieutenant because he thinks that the new man does not like him. Although he has made no plans for retirement and could continue on the force for another ten years, and even though the chief urges him to reconsider, Sergeant Bucko resigns.

Sergeant Bucko has been confronted with duties that he cannot perform. He feels inadequate and inferior and harbors unconscious dislike and anger towards the lieutenant. He avoids dealing with these feelings and emotions by projecting his anger and dislike onto the lieutenant. Thus, it appears to Bucko that the lieutenant is angry with him and also dislikes him.

REACTION FORMATION

This defense mechanism refers to the development of a trait or traits which are the opposite of tendencies that we do not want to recognize. The individual is motivated to act in a certain way but behaves in the opposite way. Consequently, he is able to keep his urges and impulses under control.

Case Example. Ms. Brewster is a middle-aged librarian who was raised in a strict Catholic family. She has never had a real date and considers sexual activity sinful and animalistic. She constantly calls her local police department with complaints about the goings on in lovers' lane, urging patrol of the area twenty-four hours a day. She is the loudest voice in the community against indecency, advocating strict moral censorship of all movies, plays, and books.

If Ms. Brewster's personal history was carefully examined, it could be learned that she was reared by strict, religious parents who regarded sexual activities as dirty and disgusting. However, they considered sex to be acceptable between married people, although they never explained how Ms. Brewster could change her attitudes and emotions if she did marry. Even in marriage, her mother strongly implied that sexual relations were a duty a wife had to endure. The idea that a woman might even enjoy sex was beyond her mother's comprehension.

Ms. Brewster grew up to be a physically healthy woman with a normal amount of sex drive. She cannot entirely repress these urges. They emerge in dreams, threatening to break forth into consciousness. Her strict superego does not permit any direct expression of these drives.

Ms. Brewster seeks to reduce her own anxieties arising from her personal conflict by becoming overly concerned about the morals of the community. By badgering her local police department with complaints about pornographic movie houses and lovers' lane parkers, she can be preoccupied with sexual matters in a way that quiets her own inner, unacceptable sexual urges and also supports her superego.

DENIAL

When a person uses this mechanism, he refuses to recognize and deal with reality because of strong inner needs.

Case Example. Patrolman Click has been experiencing shortness of breath and occasional chest pains, but he tells himself that these symptoms are probably muscular and of minor importance. One day, while riding in a patrol car with his partner, he suddenly experiences crushing chest pain. His partner rushes him to the nearest hospital where he remains for a week for tests. The doctor tells him that he has heart trouble, but that it is not too serious. He will have to lose some weight, give up smoking, and take medication. He will also have to leave patrol duty and transfer to a desk job. Officer Click doesn't believe the doctor and insists on returning to full patrol duty. He even goes to another doctor, at his own expense and without telling anyone. When he receives a similar evaluation, it does not alter his thinking and he persists in demanding a return to full patrol duty.

Click refuses to believe that he has heart trouble because it is too threatening to his self-image as an active patrolman. He loves the duties of a patrolman and can't see himself in a desk job. To him, being on the streets is real police work. Therefore, he persists in his denial of the medical reality presented to him by two different and competent authorities.

REPRESSION

Repression is an unconscious process whereby unacceptable urges and/or painful, traumatic experiences are completely prevented from entering consciousness. Suppression, which is sometimes confused with repression, is a *conscious* activity by which an individual attempts to forget emotionally disturbing thoughts and experiences by pushing them out of his mind (for example, a person may attempt to forget grief by losing himself in his work).

Case Example. Helen Troy was brought to the police substation by a motorist who found her wandering, dazed and confused, on the highway. Her clothes were torn and she obviously had been beaten. A medical examination indicated probable rape. Helen could give no account of what happened and was hysterical. Investigation revealed that she had left a local bar with a man, later identified as a habitual sex offender who has served time for rape and assault. Days later, Helen could still not recall details of the incident and met all attempts to gather information with "I don't know. . . . I can't remember."

Helen has apparently repressed the entire rape incident. Perhaps the experience was too frightening for her to assimilate and deal with consciously. Possibly she also feels some guilt. Perhaps she led her assailant on, thinking she could control his passion and not imagining he would resort to force. The physical pain of the beating, the terror of her experience, and her possible guilty feelings create a traumatic experience which she can deal with only through repression. She is neither lying when she says she can't remember nor trying to protect anyone.

IDENTIFICATION

In this defense mechanism, a person seeks to overcome feelings of inadequacy, loneliness, or inferiority by taking on the characteristics of someone who is important to him. For example, the child identifies with his parents whom he sees as models of strength and competence.

Case Example. Police were called when the body of an unidentified man was found in a local swimming pool with his feet tied together. Investigation established his identity and also that his wife had died by drowning a few days before while both were on a fishing trip.

In this case, we have a specialized form of identification, introjection. People have an unconscious tendency to assume (introject) characteristics of someone close to them who has died recently. When this man's wife died by accidental drowning, his grief and despondency drove him to employ introjection in his suicidal behavior (Kisker 1972). A knowledge that this behavior exists could be of great value to the officer assigned to investigate whether this man's death was homicide or suicide.

SUBSTITUTION

Through substitution, the individual seeks to overcome feelings of frustration and anxiety by achieving alternate goals and gratifications. Unrequited loves, unfulfilled longings, unattainable plans and ambitions, and unacceptable urges and impulses will create feelings of anxiety and guilt unless the person finds some substitute gratification.

Case Example. Fifteen-year-old Marie Smith is arrested again as a runaway juvenile. She is found living with a thirty-eight-year-old man. This is the fourth time in two years that this has happened, each time with a different man. Each time she promises that it will not happen again. However, when it does, she is at a loss to explain why.

It is likely that Marie is trying to find the love and affection she lacks at home by having sexual relationships with older men. If her father had given her normal love and affection, she would not have to seek it by running away and engaging in promiscuous behavior with a father substitute. The officer who finds Marie Smith might be more helpful if he understood the reasons behind her behavior.

FANTASY

Fantasy is one of the most useful defense mechanisms. Its content is determined by unfulfilled ambitions and unconscious drives.

Case Example. Officer Jeffers sometimes has trouble keeping his mind on the academy lectures. He finds himself daydreaming that he will become the Dirty Harry of the department and imagines himself overcoming all sorts of obstacles in solving the case of the century. Occasionally these fantasies lead to inappropriate behavior, such as the time he tried to arrest a dangerous criminal by himself.

REGRESSION

A person who regresses reverts to a pattern of feeling, thinking, or behavior appropriate to an earlier stage of development.

Case Example. To most people, Officer Riley's wife seems mature. However, whenever she is denied something she really wants (like a new dress for a department party), she throws a temper tantrum. Riley, even though he can't really afford it, finally agrees to her demands in order to stop her tantrum.

Mrs. Riley never learned, while growing up, to deal maturely with denied gratification. She never had to learn because her father and mother gave in immediately whenever she started having a temper tantrum. Today, when denied something by her husband, she is only repeating the successful behavior learned in childhood.

SUBLIMATION

Sublimation is the diversion of unacceptable id impulses into socially and culturally acceptable channels.

Case Example. Charlie Smith has always been hostile. Since early childhood, he has had frequent daydreams of hurting or killing someone. When he entered high school, Charlie did not enjoy regular sports, such as baseball and basketball. One day, a friend took him down to the

local gym and Charlie soon realized that he had found what he wanted
—to become a boxer.

Boxing allowed Charlie to release his aggressions with social approval
and possible financial reward. His sublimation proved a positive and
constructive mechanism for defending against otherwise unacceptable
impulses and needs.

Summary

This chapter has pointed out that the dynamic interaction of the id, ego,
and superego, occurring on both a conscious and unconscious level, can
often lead to frustration and conflict, creating feelings of anxiety and
guilt.

Psychological defense mechanisms, such as displacement, rationalization, and compensation may operate automatically to protect individuals from these unpleasant feelings and to maintain psychological balance (homeostasis). When someone uses these defense mechanisms
constructively and positively, he is acting in a healthy way; when he
employs them indiscriminately and inappropriately, he is heading towards ill health. When they break down completely or have not been
adequately developed, the person is likely to become mentally ill.

The discussion in this chapter should once again impress upon the
professional who must deal with human behavior that there is some
motivation for every action and that, most likely, the person is not
necessarily aware immediately of the reason for his behavior.

However, these basic concepts are only the starting point for understanding specific behaviors. Therefore, the professional must be cau-
tious in drawing any conclusions regarding the underlying causes of a
person's action. If the person himself is unaware of why he acts in a
certain way, the professional will come to understand this behavior only
after thorough investigation and study.

The police officer should also not make instant diagnoses of the behavior he encounters. However, he may legitimately use his knowledge
of psychology to assist him in forming preliminary judgments which will
guide his actions, recognizing that all may not be what appears on the
surface.

In addition, knowledge of psychological defense mechanisms should encourage the police officer to examine the effect of his own presence upon the behavior of others. In many instances, people may view his presence as a barrier to their desires, or as another factor they must consider before deciding upon further action. With this knowledge, the police officer can better anticipate the behavior he is likely to see and, by anticipating it, control his own reactions and increase his effectiveness.

BIBLIOGRAPHY

CRAMER, P. 1979. "Defense Mechanisms in Adolescence." *Developmental Psychology* 15:476–477.

FREUD, A. 1946. *The Ego and The Mechanisms of Defense.* New York: International Universities Press.

FREUD, S. 1961. "Inhibitions, Symptoms and Anxiety." In *Standard Edition,* vol. 20, ed. J. Strachey. London: Hogarth Press, pp. 87–172.

KISKER, G. W. 1972. *The Disorganized Personality.* New York: McGraw-Hill.

MARTIN, DAVID G. 1976. *Personality: Effective and Ineffective.* Monterey, Calif.: Brasks/-Cole.

Chapter 5

Abnormal Behavior:
What It Is and What to Do

THE preceding two chapters have presented concepts of normal personality development and functioning. This body of knowledge is basic to understanding the complexities of human behavior. It is now appropriate to consider some aspects of abnormal behavior based on these concepts.

What Is Abnormal Behavior?

Since *ab* means "away from," abnormal behavior is behavior which is away from or deviating from normal behavior. However, to define normal behavior is not as easy a task as may first appear, since many variables are involved.

Some people regard their own behavior as quite normal and, therefore, conclude that people who behave as they do are normal, while those who do not behave similarly are abnormal. This personal standard of definition is illustrated by the old Quaker proverb:

> Everyone is queer
> Save thee and me
> And sometimes I think
> Thee a bit queer too.

Normal behavior can also be defined as the embodiment of an ideal (the ideal soldier, the ideal husband). If normal behavior is that which emulates an ideal model, then abnormal behavior is that which deviates from it.

Normality can also be conceptualized statistically. Here the average (mean) is considered normal. The more one's score deviates from the mean, the more abnormal one is. The deviation can be in a positive or a negative direction (for example, a child may be exceptionally dull or exceptionally bright depending on whether his IQ score is far below or far above the mean IQ). However, this approach does not lend itself particularly well to the study of the individual because there are always exceptions to the rule and because human behavior is too complex to be reduced to a curve or sets of curves.

Culture also plays in important role in determining what is normal or abnormal. One culture may approve of sex play among children; another may strongly disapprove. One culture condones homosexuality; another condemns it. Otto Klineberg, a social psychologist, has stated (1954): "Abnormality is embedded in the very structure of our society and can only be understood against the background of the culture in which it occurs." In this view, no behavior is intrinsically abnormal; it becomes abnormal only in relation to the whole range of social and cultural preferences.

In our own society, the professional judgment as to whether behavior is significantly abnormal is dependent on the presence of certain symptoms characteristic of mental illness. For example, is the patient hearing voices which do not really exist (hallucinations)? Does he cling strongly to false beliefs despite all tests of reality (delusions)? Is he depressed?

In judging the seriousness of the illness, the professional also looks at the degree of noneffectiveness of the individual's behavior. Is he or she able to continue working, or does his or her behavior interfere to such a degree that work is impossible? Is he or she able to fulfill the role as husband or wife, father or mother? In this view, behavior which is ineffective, self-defeating, self-destructive, and which alienates the individual from those who are important to him is regarded as abnormal.

Common Misconceptions about Abnormal Behavior

Regardless of these definitions of abnormal behavior, it is usually associated by most people with the strange, the alien, the unknown. Consequently, abnormal behavior and mental illness frequently cause fear, repugnance, and misunderstanding. Attitudes toward them are shaped more often by rumor and popular stereotypes than by direct experience and sound information. The following misconceptions are common:

1. *There is something evil about mental illness, and people who suffer from it are themselves evil, violent, and homicidal.* This misconception is a carry-over from the days when the mentally ill were regarded as possessed by evil spirits or as having willingly made a pact with the devil in return for certain favors. Many stories, plays, and movies have perpetuated this belief through tales about mad scientists, witches, maniacal killers, and sex fiends. A typical opening scene in many horror movies shows a state hospital or insane asylum set forlornly in the middle of nowhere. A violent thunderstorm is raging and, as the camera moves inside the institution, a Boris Karloff-type character is pacing to and fro along a darkened, eerie corridor. Is it any wonder that many people are afraid of mental institutions and of the people within them?

The truth is that there is nothing at all evil about mental illness. Most of the mentally ill are neither violent nor dangerous. A better word to describe them is *afraid.* They are afraid of many things—of what is happening to them, of the people around them, and of the world in which they live. This is true even of the person who is brandishing a knife and threatening to kill whomever comes near. If the police officer recognizes this fear, he can use it to his advantage when taking this person into custody by offering his help and protection instead of fighting him.

2. *Mental illness is an "all or nothing" affair.* The concept of mental illness is easily dichotomized. A person is often regarded as insane or normal. Nothing could be farther from the truth. Mental illness, like physical illness, is both a matter of kind and of degree.

Years ago, the Army made a training film whose purpose was to acquaint line commanders with different types of psychiatric casualties and how and why such casualties occurred. The title of the film was *Shades of Gray,* and it opened with vignettes about various types of psychiatric disorders. The film begins something like this:

"It's a big day for the recruits on the grenade range. For the first time

44

they are throwing live grenades. Suddenly, something goes wrong in pit number 5. Private Smith pulls the pin on the grenade and then freezes with the grenade clutched tightly in his hands. The sergeant grabs the grenade from the recruit and throws it just in time." "What went wrong?" the narrator asks.

Another scene begins: "This soldier has been acting strangely recently, keeping more and more to himself. He seems suspicious of his buddies. Suddenly, while eating in the mess hall, he grabs the soldier next to him and accuses him of poisoning his food." The scene ends with the soldier being forcibly taken from the mess hall to the Mental Hygiene Consultation Center.

Another vignette depicts a soldier walking guard on a lonely, desolate post in the far North. "Suddenly," the narrator tells us, "this soldier is overcome by a wave of depression." He drops his weapon and leans against a stunted tree, staring blankly into the distance with tears in his eyes.

The film then goes into a discussion of mental health and mental illness. It points out that if physical examinations were given to every soldier in one of the most elite units, not one man in that platoon would be rated perfect. For example, a few might be coming down with a cold; others may have a minor stomach upset; and hardly anyone would have a perfect set of teeth. On the other hand, there would also be no one who would merit a completely negative physical rating. All would be a "shade of gray."

The same is true of mental illness. As no one is perfectly healthy, so no one is perfectly adjusted. Some may be too sensitive to what others say; some may worry too much about an overdue letter from home or unpaid bills; others may feel without justification that they are not up to the standards of their peers and are inferior or inadequate. Even the chronic mental patient will have some area, no matter how small, of health. Mental health, like physical health, is not a dichotomy; it is not an "all or nothing" affair. It is a matter of degree.

It is also a matter of kind. For example, someone who has a common cold is not suffering from the same disease as the one suffering from strep throat, even though both are ill. Neither of them is suffering from the same kind of disease as the person who has terminal cancer.

In mental health, the person who experiences mild feelings of inadequacy and tension at social gatherings is not suffering from the same type of illness as the individual who has a strong and unrelenting fear (phobia) of crowds. Neither of them is suffering from the same type of illness as the acutely disturbed person who locks himself in a room all day to avoid all contact with people. Variations in kind are as critical as variations in degree.

3. *If a person is mentally ill, he will always be mentally ill and his condition will not vary significantly from day to day.* Illness, mental or physical, is like health. It is dynamic and does not remain constant. A person may show signs of emotional disturbance one day and not another. Even the sickest person in the state hospital has good days and bad days, just like all of us. Those with mental illness can be treated and become functional again. Like physically ill patients, they may also get sick again, receive appropriate treatment, and re-cover.

4. *The feelings and behavior of the mentally ill have no relationship to the feelings and behavior of the mentally healthy.* Nothing could be further from the truth. Have you ever had a day when you were down in the dumps, when everything around you made you feel more depressed? The manic-depressive patient experiences similar feelings. The difference is that your feelings of ups and downs are usually connected with things that are actually happening, while the manic-depressive patient is more often responding to inner feelings and thoughts unrelated to reality. While your depression could be immediately lifted if you were told that you had won $10,000 in a sweepstakes, the manic-depressive is not necessarily cheered by such news. He may even interpret his winning as another example of how unworthy he really is.

Consider another example. Some mentally ill patients experience delusions. A delusion is a false belief which is strongly held despite all tests of reality. All of us have experienced beliefs that later turn out to be false. The difference is that the mentally healthy person is able to check his beliefs against reality and to modify his thinking based on the evidence presented. The delusions of the mentally ill person are not subject to the challenge of reality. Any attempt to convince him, for example, that his belief that all Masons are out to kill him is not true may turn him against you. He may conclude, because of his disturbed thinking, that you are either a fool for not believing him or that you are in league with those plotting against him.

These are some of the popular misconceptions about mental illness and the emotionally disturbed. Understanding these misconceptions is important because they tend to bias people against those who are mentally ill and prevent them from dealing with such persons in a more accepting, human, and professional manner.

Guidelines for Judging Abnormal Behavior

The officer on the street will often have to decide whether a person's behavior is or is not abnormal. If it is abnormal, he will have to decide whether it can be handled without police action or whether official intervention is necessary. He must judge how serious the abnormal behavior is, and whether it is dangerous to the person himself and/or others.

To the trained law enforcement officer, the recognition and handling of abnormal behavior is critical to the effective execution of his duties. We will now turn to those general and specific characteristics of behavior which the police officer will assess in helping him reach his conclusion about that behavior as well as how to handle it.

Appropriateness

Normal behavior tends to be appropriate to the situation; abnormal behavior tends to be inappropriate. The judgment of a behavior's appropriateness involves an assessment of not only the behavior itself, but also the situation in which it is occurring.

For example, suppose you are standing in the foyer of a Catholic church during a noon Mass. Mr. Smith enters the church, comes up beside you, kneels, makes the sign of the cross and starts to pray. This is appropriate behavior since it is taking place in a Catholic church during Mass.

However, suppose the locale, but not the behavior, is changed. It is Sunday noon at a busy intersection. You are in the center of the street directing heavy traffic. Suddenly, Mr. Smith appears, kneels by your side, crosses himself and starts to pray. Not only is the behavior now inappropriate in this different setting, but it is also dangerous. Note that the behavior itself has not changed; only its appropriateness has changed.

Similarly most of the time, emotions are directly related to what is happening or what has happened. If an individual experiences great emotion after a major tragedy, that is appropriate. If, on the other hand, he comes apart following minor frustrations and conflicts, it may not be as appropriate. Perhaps you can recall a relative or acquaintance who became greatly upset under conditions which surprised you. Or, if you have been in military services, you may have noted some recruits who broke down and cried or went AWOL after only a minor reprimand.

In most instances, the degree of sadness or happiness is usually related to what is actually happening. The emotionally disturbed person, however, may be so depressed that he may want to kill himself even though another person with the same problems is neither as depressed or suicidal. Other kinds of mental illness may also show marked discrepancies between the degree or type of emotional response expected in a particular situation and the actual degree or type of emotion demonstrated.

Flexibility

Normal behavior tends to be flexible; abnormal behavior tends to be inflexible. Normal behavior, regardless of setting, tends to be flexible in that it is altered to fit the situation. As an example, the police officer's behavior toward the Chief of Police is flexible if he adopts a different approach when he is talking to him in the office on an official matter in comparison to a department picnic where they are both dressed in sport clothes and drinking beer together.

These criteria for examining behavior are closely related to appropriateness. However, while a person's behavior may be appropriate, it may lack the flexibility characteristic of healthy behavior.

Impulsivity

Since abnormal behavior is related in part to uncontrolled or partially controlled needs and drives, it tends to be impulsive. A person with normal behavior is more likely to consider its consequences and gives important decisions careful thought before implementation.

One of the authors (H. E. R.) recalls a young man who was referred to the Mental Hygiene Consultation Service shortly after he entered basic training. He sat weeping in a chair, crying out with dismay and desperation how he could not cope with the Army and how he had to get out. Asked when he was drafted, he replied he had enlisted. When asked why he enlisted if he hated it so much, he related the following story.

He had never wanted to go into the service. He had been under the care of a psychiatrist for some time and had prevailed upon his doctor to write a letter which he could take to his draft board declaring that he was unfit for military service. He took the letter to his draft board expecting to be told that he would never be called. Instead, the board told him that, when his number came up, this letter would be considered in determining whether to call him up. This made him so angry that he went across the hall to the Army Recruiting Office and enlisted for four years. This man acted impulsively.

Not all abnormal behavior indicates mental illness. As we stressed earlier, there are degrees of mental health and illness, just as there are degrees of physical health and illness. If, however, a person's behavior is abnormal according to one or more of the three general characteristics discussed earlier, we should analyze further the necessity for additional action. In their book *How to Recognize and Handle Abnormal People,* Matthews and Rowland suggest the following specific criteria (Matthews and Rowland 1974).

Big Changes in Behavior

Since behavior is dynamic, not static, everyone's behavior changes over time. However, one should be especially alert for sudden, big changes in an individual's life-style. For example, if a man who always stays at home during his leisure hours, loves his wife and children, never quarrels with his neighbors, and works faithfully at his job suddenly becomes quarrelsome, misses work, spends his time in bars, starts drinking excessively and abuses his wife and children, it is likely that he is suffering from a serious mental disorder. The officer should inquire about the individual's present behavior as contrasted to his past actions. Has he behaved this way before? If so, when, and under what circumstances? When was this current change in behavior first noticed?

Losses of Memory

All of us have losses of memory at one time or another. We may forget dental appointments, miss birthdays and anniversaries, or fail to recall material studied the night before. These memory losses are normal. However, if a person cannot remember who he is, where he is, or the day, month, or year; if a woman has been raped and cannot recall any of the details; or if a man who has been in an auto accident cannot remember anything after the crash, the possibility of brain injury or a psychological dysfunction based on serious conflict should be considered.

Feelings of Persecution

Policemen know that people do plot against other people. A person who is realistically worried about being killed usually will be able to tell the officer who might want to kill him and offer plausible reasons why. The abnormal person, however, *imagines* that someone (or some group) is planning to kill him. He may specify that group but his choice is usually unrealistic. Furthermore, his reasons, if he is able to offer any, are likely to be bizarre and not readily understood by the officer. For example, he may say that "the communists" want to kill him because "they know my message to the President will end the war and dissolve the international conspiracy of communism."

Grandiose Ideas

An individual may claim that he represents the second coming of Christ or that she is the Virgin Mary. In other situations, he may indicate how important he is by telling you that everybody is plotting against him. One must really be an important person if everyone is after him.

Or, he may believe that he has committed the world's worst sin and that he is the most miserable and unworthy human who has ever been born. Even in these negative statements, he is emphasizing his importance.

On the other hand, some seemingly grandiose ideas may turn out to be true after investigation. For example, a soldier, suspected of being somewhat paranoid, was speaking about his father. He told the doctor that his father, who was retired, had been a German Intelligence Agent in World War I and that, during World War II, after immigrating to America, he had parachuted behind German lines for the OSS to make contact with and to escort to freedom a famous Dutch scientist who was being forced by the Nazis to work on V2 bombs. His story sounded like a James Bond novel. The doctor calculated that the patient's father would have been in his sixties during World War II and considered the whole story as delusional. However, later interviews with the father revealed that the boy's story was true.

Talks to Himself

All of us occasionally talk to ourselves, especially if we are angry or emotionally upset. Mentally ill adults, however, can carry on entire conversations with imaginary people or animals for considerable periods of time.

Hears Voices

Occasionally, in talking with someone who demonstrates feelings of persecution or grandiose ideas, the police officer may note that the person appears easily distracted and is not paying attention to what is going on around him. On further inquiry, he might determine that the person is hearing voices.

Actually, these voices are the person's own thoughts, projected from himself to the outside (auditory hallucinations). Some who hear voices may tell you, however, that they do not know from where they are coming or who they are, while others may tell you they are coming from a radio (which is not on) or from someone who is not there.

Sees Visions, Smells Strange Odors, or Has Peculiar Tastes

Instead of, or in addition to, hearing voices, the person may say he has seen his dead mother standing by his bed before he goes to sleep or that he has seen God or the devil (visual hallucinations). Unlike voices, however, these types of hallucinations are more often related to physical influences or abnormalities, such as the effect of alcohol on the brain or brain tumors.

Similarly, a person may smell strange odors (gas in the apartment) or complain of peculiar tastes (poison in the food). In these instances, physical illness should also be thoroughly investigated.

Thinks People Are Watching or Talking about Him

Sometimes someone will complain that he is being watched or that people are talking about him. Because of his own conflicts, he has become, through the mechanism of projection (chapter 4), supersensitive to other people. He sees two people talking and he is sure they are talking about him. He feels that he is being followed, but when he looks over his shoulder, no one is there. He interprets remarks made within his hearing as pertaining to him even though the person speaking may have no idea that he exists.

At first, he is not sure about these things. He tries to check them out. However, as he becomes more disturbed, he becomes more convinced of the accuracy of his perceptions and resists attempts to convince him that his beliefs are wrong. Finally, these *ideas of reference,* as they are called, become fixed delusions of persecution or grandeur.

Unrealistic Physical Complaints

All people have physical complaints at one time or another. The person who exhibits abnormal behavior or is mentally ill, however, often believes that things are wrong with, or happening to, his body that are not anatomically or medically possible. He may tell you, for example, that his brain is decaying or that half of his body is different from the other half. He will often tell you these terrible things with little or no emotion. If he is convinced that he has an incurable disease, he may try to take his own life. It is important to realize that these symptoms are very real to the person and that he can suffer as much as any individual with a physical ailment.

Extreme Fright

Some people become frozen with fear while others panic. A person may tremble, speak haltingly, glance about in terror or demonstrate a marked startle reaction at the slightest sound. The officer should protect this person from any injury which may result from his efforts to get away from what he fears. He may also attack the officer if the latter attempts to stop him.

Dangerous or Destructive Behavior

As we shall see in a later chapter on psychopathic behavior (chapter 9), some emotionally disturbed people will not show any of the above-mentioned symptoms but will, time after time, do things which are destructive or dangerous to themselves or others. Although they may get hurt or hurt others, they do not seem to learn from the experience or show any emotion about it.

Depression

The officer should be alert for the individual who doesn't respond to his questions and seems very depressed. He may be a potential suicide or a suicidal risk.

How to Handle the Mentally Ill

The police officer must not only be able to recognize abnormal behavior and the mentally ill person but must also be prepared to guard, restrain, or take into custody someone whose behavior suggests the presence of a mental illness. The following are suggestions for handling these difficult situations:

1. *Calls involving known emotionally disturbed individuals should be answered by more than one officer.* If it is not known that the call involves a disturbed person, the officer who arrives first on the scene should immediately ask for backup. Do not try to handle the case alone. Handling it alone does not prove you are a better policeman than if you ask for help.

For many years psychiatric attendants, doctors, and nurses who have been working with very disturbed people, including both the homicidal and suicidal, have suffered very few injuries. Even prior to tranquilizers, mental health professionals have been able to work on a ward housing forty to fifty such patients without difficulty. One reason for this is their ability to use effectively the *show of force* principle. For example, an attendant might approach Mr. Brown and tell him that he had to go to X ray. He would, of course, try to convince Mr. Brown to go. If Mr. Brown showed signs of resistance and refused to go, the attendant would not argue or try to force him to go. Instead, he would withdraw and reappear with three or four more attendants and again tell Mr. Brown that, for his own welfare, the doctor had ordered X rays and that he had to go to X ray. He would be told, without anger or threats, that he could walk down to X ray under his own power or be carried down to X ray by the attendants. He would also be told that more attendants could be called if needed.

Faced with this show of force, most patients usually elect to proceed under their own power. This show of force does two things for the disturbed individual: it gives him a face-saving out if he has been bragging how tough he is or that no one can force him to do anything he does not want; and it shows him that many people are interested in him and that they care enough to insure that his treatment orders are carried out.

This process can work the same way on the street. If the disturbed person has been boasting that no cop is going to take him anywhere, he may feel required to put up a battle against one policeman. With two or three officers present as backup, he has a face-saving out. The officers can also use their numbers to assure him that they are able to offer him protection against any threat. As with the hospital patient, their numbers also give him a sense of importance and show him that somebody does care about him.

2. *Stay with the disturbed person until additional help arrives.* If necessary, ask someone to phone for assistance rather than leaving the person.

3. *Move slowly.* Resist the impulse to act hastily. This may be difficult, since most police training teaches the importance of quick decisions. With the emotionally disturbed, it is better to take time and carefully assess the situation. Immediate action is only necessary when handling an *immediate* danger.

4. *Reassurance is important.* Acutely disturbed individuals are generally very frightened.

5. *As a matter of policy, it is usually a good idea to send uniformed men.* Sirens are not usually helpful since they tend to attract crowds that are not wanted. Keep spectators away if at all possible.

6. *Solicit help from friends, relatives, and others known to the emotionally disturbed person.* The time spent in getting this help may make the task easier and prevent violence and harm from coming to the individual, yourself, or others.

7. *Don't lie to or try to deceive the emotionally disturbed person.* If he is aware of deception, dealing with him will become more difficult. If you lie, you also create a barrier to his willingness to accept future help.

8. *Do not rely on your weapons.* The threat of a gun is quite meaningless to a person who is acutely disturbed. He may grab it and use it, or you may be tempted to use it. A weapon should be used if needed only in the very rare situation when it is necessary to save a life.

9. *Don't be fooled by the individual's size.* For the same reasons that some people are impervious to intense pain during periods of emotional stress, others may have unusual physical strength during these times. Experienced policemen are familiar with this phenomenon and can cite cases where several patrolmen have found it difficult to subdue a 125-pound senior citizen.

10. *Don't meet hostility with hostility.* This is often a natural reaction since a hostile person tends to elicit hostility in others. It is important to maintain a professional attitude. Meet hostility and anger by being calm, objective, and accepting. Ask why he is angry or afraid. If he will tell you, he may begin to calm down.

11. *Don't argue with delusions, but don't agree either.* Rather, try to

steer the person away from whatever subject is exciting him. If he demonstrates by his actions, facial expression, increased agitation, or bizarre behavior that the subject being discussed is making him upset, switch to another subject.

Try to bring him back to reality by asking concrete questions such as: "How long have you lived here?" "Who is in your family?" and "Where do you work?" By maintaining control of the discussion, you will reassure the person. Because he senses that you are in control of the situation it will help him to gain control.

12. *Don't be fooled by a sudden return to reality.* The emotionally disturbed individual can return to his delusions just as quickly. Consider him potentially dangerous because his behavior is unpredictable, and remain alert even if he calms down.

However, you can remove any restraints that have been applied if, in your judgment, his behavior warrants it. However, be ready to reapply them if his behavior makes it necessary. Leather cuffs similar to those used in mental hospitals are best, if they are available. Agitated people have been known to pull tendons and cut wrists while in handcuffs. If handcuffs have to be used, check frequently to see that circulation has not been cut off. When restraints are unavailable, safety devices can be made on the spot using pillows, mattresses, and belts or by reversing an ordinary coat or jacket.

13. *Take all suicidal behavior seriously.* People making threats, gestures, and suicidal attempts should be referred for professional psychiatric help. Do not excuse or gloss over a person's behavior just to reassure anxious relatives.

14. *Make sure the individual is not physically ill or injured.* Diabetic coma, fever delirium, brain tumors, convulsive disorders, and other medical conditions are often mistaken for drunkenness or combativeness. Head injuries often go unnoticed, especially if there is an odor of alcohol on the breath. If any doubts exist, get medical attention.

15. *Keep a record of a person's complaints regarding plots against him.* If the complaints change from a vague "they" to a particular person or small group of people, there may be a threat to the safety of those named. Try to persuade someone who knows the person to take him to his family doctor, a clergyman, or a local psychiatric facility.

16. *Learn what facilities are available in the community.* These exist to help the mentally ill and their families, especially in an emergency.

17. *Remember that most disturbed people are afraid.* They experience extreme fear because they do not understand their feelings and because they are not certain how others will treat them. When an

emotionally disturbed person becomes aggressive, it is almost always because of fear. Therefore, the officer should attempt to handle him in a calm, understanding, and humane way. This will often reassure the person that the officer is there to help him.

18. *Don't make fun of other people's troubles.* It is easy to become callous, especially in dealing with a disturbed person.

19. *Maintain your sense of humor.* This is important, especially in stress situations. Many a day has been saved because someone did.

Summary

This chapter has presented some differences between normal and abnormal behavior and has discussed some of the misconceptions regarding abnormal behavior and mental illness. Certain guidelines have been offered to assist the police officer in deciding whether the behavior he is dealing with at a particular time is abnormal and, if so, to what degree. We have been pointing out that abnormal behavior differs from normal behavior in three general characteristics—appropriateness, flexibility, and impulsivity—and that certain specific signs and symptoms indicate mental illness. Finally, we have offered various suggestions on how to handle individuals manifesting abnormal behavior in order to increase the officer's effectiveness and decrease the chances of injury to himself or to others.

BIBLIOGRAPHY

ALTROCCHI, JOHN. 1980. *Abnormal Behavior.* New York: Harcourt Brace Jovanovich.

GOLDENBERG, HERBERT. 1977. *Abnormal Psychology: A Social/Community Approach.* Monterey, Calif.: Brooks/Cole.

KLEINEBERG, O. 1954. *Social Psychology,* 2nd Edition. New York: Holt, Rinehart and Winston.

MATTHEWS, R. A. 1970. "Observations on Police Policy and Procedures for Emergency Detention of the Mentally Ill." *Journal of Criminal Law, Criminology and Police Science* 61(2):283–295.

MATTHEWS, R. A., and ROWLAND, L. W. 1974. *How to Handle and Recognize Abnormal Behavior.* New York: National Association of Mental Health.

SOKOL, R. J., and REISER, M. 1971. "Training Police Sergeants in Early Warning Signs of Emotional Upset." *Mental Hygiene* 55:303–307.

PART III

Understanding
Mental Illness

Chapter 6

Personality Disorders

IN THE NEXT three chapters, we will discuss the three most commonly encountered categories of mental disorders. We will examine their major characteristics and provide case examples illustrating situations often associated with these conditions.

The diagnostic terminology is consistent with the contents of DSM-III (the recently adopted *Diagnostic and Statistical Manual* of the American Psychiatric Association) except in chapter 7, where the authors have chosen to retain the term *neurotic disorders* because of its familiarity to nonpsychiatrists.

Other categories of mental disorders which will not be discussed in this section include mental retardation, organic mental disorders (caused by or associated with impairment of the brain or its associated functions), psychological factors affecting physical conditions, and specific disorders usually first evident in infancy, childhood, or adolescence (excluding mental retardation).

General Characteristics of Personality Disorders

Patterns of normal and abnormal behavior originate during early development. Personality disorders result from aberrations in this developmental process, influencing patterns of perceiving, relating to, and thinking about the environment and oneself.

The path from normal personality development to personality disorder is *not* analogous to a divided highway where a normal personality becomes a personality disorder as soon as the center divider is crossed. Rather, the path is more analogous to a two-lane highway divided by a dotted line where an individual with certain traits may use them to his advantage at times (for example, stay in the proper lane), but may also use them to his disadvantage (for example, cross over into the opposite flow of traffic).

There are many significant periods in childhood development during which a failure to receive the appropriate care from parents and others can lead the child to develop abnormal behavior patterns. These serve to defend him against increased environmental stress. However, once adopted, they are very difficult to give up, especially if the child is not encouraged to change but is instead rewarded for the maladaptive behavior. For example, if Johnny gets what he wants by having a temper tantrum, he may repeat this behavior because it has been rewarding.

Other negative early experiences may include the unreasonable demands which parents sometimes place upon their children by failing to accept excuses when the child's behavior does not meet their expectations. Faced with this situation, a child may adopt a behavior pattern in which he quickly mobilizes energy to meet each demand, not necessarily with the goal of being successful but simply to avoid punishment if he fails.

Those with personality disorders often lack flexibility in responding to situations. While the normal personality is flexible and responds with appropriate patterns of behavior to different environmental events, the person with a personality disorder cannot significantly alter or change his pattern of behavior to events which require different responses. As a result, he experiences distress and often has trouble in social and occupational situations.

In contrast to neurotic disorders, personality disorders are generally ingrained in the development of a person's life-style over a long period of time; neurotic disorders more often exhibit specific symptoms, such as anxiety or depression, rather than a pattern of behavior. Psychotic disorders are marked by thought disorders—delusional thinking or hallucinatory experiences.

This chapter will describe four types of personality disorders most commonly encountered by law enforcement officers. Other personality disorders include the schizoid (in which the major defect is in the capacity to form social relationships); the narcissistic (in which the major defect is a grandiose sense of self-importance); and the borderline personality disorder (in which there is instability in interpersonal relationships, mood, and self-image). The psychopathic personality disorder will be discussed in chapter 9.

THE PASSIVE-AGGRESSIVE PERSONALITY DISORDER

The passive-aggressive personality disorder is a major cause of failure in jobs, school, and interpersonal relationships. The essential feature is a direct or indirect resistance to demands for adequate performance. Those with this disorder often passively express hidden aggression. Their behavior may be characterized by procrastination, stubbornness, intentional inefficiency, forgetfulness, and delaying tactics. Despite their aggressiveness, these people are often dependent and lack self-confidence. They may express pessimism about the future but at the same time are unable to recognize that their behavior is responsible for the difficulties that they encounter. They frequently blame others. Authority figures are a favorite target for their resistance and resentment. Many of these people also have a magical anticipation that all of their needs will be met regardless of their behavior.

Case Example. Gregory Martinez, who is twenty years old, came to the police's attention one evening when his mother called the emergency number. She said that her son was lying on the bathroom floor and that his arm was bloody. Upon their arrival, the paramedics administered emergency first aid and took Gregory to the hospital, accompanied by his mother.

While the doctor was treating the cut Gregory had inflicted on his arm, the officer obtained the following information: Gregory had just graduated from a vocational rehabilitation program after taking courses in automobile body work. He had entered it after his parole. He had served one year for felonious assault on a boyfriend of a girl whom he had been dating. More recently, his mother said that he had been very upset recently because, even with his diploma, he couldn't find work. In the days before cutting himself, Gregory had been complaining bitterly of the prejudice he felt from others because of his past prison record and his Mexican-American heritage. In reality, however, it was a period of high unemployment in the community, and jobs were scarce all over.

Gregory had been a spoiled only child and had never demonstrated any motivation to help himself until recently. Even his entrance into the rehabilitation program had occurred only after he had been cajoled by his parents, girlfriend, and other friends. Gregory's mother said, "He always seems to want everything to happen for him, and when he doesn't get his way, he strikes out." When asked to explain further, she recalled how, as a teenager, he had many problems in school with both classmates and teachers because he would not accept direction when it was offered. His teachers had told his mother that he couldn't handle criticism, no matter how small, and that his typical response was to become more disruptive. They all felt he could do better, but noted that he was his own worst enemy and always managed one way or the other not to do what he was asked.

THE HISTRIONIC PERSONALITY DISORDER

Those with histrionic personality disorders are easily excitable and overreact to many situations in a dramatic manner. Minor stimuli lead to emotional excitability. This dramatic behavior is always attention-seeking and usually seductive. Furthermore, these people are generally self-centered, immature, and tend to be impressionable. They are easily influenced by others, particularly authority figures.

The police often encounter them as victims of sexual attack, particularly in situations where it is not clear whether they were wholly innocent. In presenting their stories of the attack, they are likely to embellish dramatically the details of the event, missing nothing in describing it to the investigating officer.

Those with this disorder are often incapable of forming mature heterosexual relationships, acting dependent and helpless while constantly seeking reassurance. They are perceived by others as shallow even if they are superficially warm and charming.

Case Example. Hilda Davis is twenty-two years old and twice divorced. She was brought to the emergency room after she had reportedly fainted at home. She had been living with her sister and her sister's husband and children in a small trailer following her most recent divorce. She remembered feeling nervous almost as soon as she had moved into their house.

On further questioning, Hilda revealed that she had had an affair with her brother-in-law several years ago. Although not seeing any connection between this event and the feelings of nervousness she had in their home, Hilda did reveal, perhaps inadvertently, that she felt edgy and dizzy at night when she was alone with her sister and he was working, and got better during the day when he was there and her sister was working.

Hilda was given some tranquilizers and asked to return to the clinic the next day. When she appeared, the doctor immediately noticed a remarkable change in her appearance. Instead of the disheveled young woman he had seen the night before, Hilda was now seductively dressed with somewhat overdone makeup. When invited into his office, she immediately said, "I'm so glad to be here. That medicine you gave me last night made me feel so much better."

More than seeking a sexual relationship, these people seek attention. When this attention was lacking during childhood, they learn to get it by dramatizing their behavior or feelings. If this is not successful, they may try other routes, such as feigning illness.

THE PARANOID PERSONALITY DISORDER

Hypersensitivity, rigidity, unwarranted suspicion, jealousy, and feelings of excessive self-importance, coupled with a tendency to blame others for any failure which they encounter, characterize those with a paranoid personality. They often use projection as a defense mechanism and see the entire world through a very personal set of references. They view their frustrations as further justifying their suspicions about the world.

These people often have an exaggerated sense of importance. They generally see themselves as the focal point of all activities which surround them whether or not this is true. They make mountains out of molehills and are often concerned with hidden motives and special meanings. Usually appearing tense, they are rejected by others because their underlying hostility and lack of humor makes others very uncomfortable.

Case Example. Mary Rutherford is twenty-six years old and single. She is employed as a secretary and is the least liked woman in the office. She is impossible to get along with because of her constant accusations that others are picking on her, giving her too much work, and not treating her properly. This is puzzling because she appears intelligent and ambitious.

63

The woman who used to share a corner of the office with her remembers one encounter she had with Mary which illustrates why she is not well liked.

One day, this woman was called into the office of one of the men for whom she and Mary worked. The two women had been proofreading a manuscript. When Mary's co-worker got up to go into the office, she said, "Be back in a minute." Unfortunately, co-worker's return was delayed because the man had a lengthy task to explain to her.

When the woman finally returned to her desk, Mary was enraged, sarcastic, and jealous. Without provocation, Mary immediately lunged into a tirade accusing her of trying to seduce the boss. Attempts to quiet Mary were unsuccessful, and both the conversation and the accusations ended only when the woman excused herself, went to the powder room, and remained away from Mary the rest of the day.

Paranoid personalities usually grow up in a home filled with parental conflict. One parent is usually domineering and the other submissive. Not only is the child unable to deal with the domineering parent, but he or she also does not receive help from the submissive parent.

As one way of handling this devastating situation, the child adopts a behavior pattern in which he or she reacts defensively to almost any situation in which a threat is felt from the domineering parent. The child becomes constantly vigilant, and fearful of individuals and situations, whether or not fear is justified. Feelings of rejection are exaggerated and further reinforce this vigilant attitude.

THE COMPULSIVE PERSONALITY DISORDER

Excessive concern with rules and conformity, adherence to strong standards of perfectionism, an inability to relax and to tolerate ambiguity, a characteristic rigidity which makes it impossible for them to change their minds after having arrived at decisions, and a failure to express warm emotions characterizes those with a compulsive personality. At work they often initially draw the positive attention of superiors because of an ability to organize thinking and to conduct affairs in an orderly fashion. However, these positive traits quickly become obscured by their stubborness and eventual recognition of their inefficiency.

Case Example. After several years as a patrolman, Mike Morris was promoted to sergeant. While complimented in the past for his attention to detail, his excellent reports, and his seemingly appropriate attention to rules of safety, he was a total failure as a supervisor.

Those who had been his peers and were now his subordinates quickly found it impossible to work for him. With his new responsibility of enforcing rules and regulations rather than following them, he made life miserable for his men. His attention to detail, while admirable as a patrolman, interfered with the ability of his men to perform their work. His demands for more and more reports and his tirades when they did not "go by the book" created a morale problem.

While his excessive attention to orderliness was ignored by his peers when he was at their level and was complimented by his superiors, it now became obstructionistic and antagonistic. Initially, his men tried to please him but soon found that they could not succeed. Finally, they gave up and began to devise ways of getting around him and discrediting him behind his back. The situation deteriorated, and finally the men felt forced to go to Mike's superior and ask for his removal or their transfer.

Mike's compulsive personality disorder nipped a promising career in the bud. However, like most compulsive personality disorders, he never came to psychiatric attention. Many such people can function effectively, provided they are placed in a suitable environment.

This need to maintain rigidity is an outgrowth of early developmental problems involving parental controls. Faced with the necessity of complying with them and overly threatened with the danger of loss of love if he does not, the child will either be overly compliant and compulsive or become rebellious. The latter alternative is often given up quickly because of the demands of the parents and the child's need for love. The child learns quickly that parental approval and love will come if he is compliant. By paying attention to detail, he avoids dangerous feelings of fear and anger directed at the parent for enforcing this standard of behavior. In attempting to gain control of his anger, he pays the price of giving up opportunities to express these emotions. If he encounters a stressful situation in which these emotions are overwhelming, the compulsive behavior pattern can break down and a psychotic reaction with severe depression can occur. Even in this decompensation, he may continue to pay attention to detail. A famous example of this behavior is Lady Macbeth who, while psychotic, focused on a spot of blood and compulsively repeated, "Out, damned spot!"

Helpful Hints to the Law Enforcement Officer

The interpersonal relationships of those with personality disorders present a unique problem for the law enforcement officer. A police officer who is called into a situation involving someone with a personality disorder often finds behavior out of control and violence threatening. The officer should remember that this person has adopted this disorderly behavior pattern to protect himself from life's stresses. When this pattern is threatened, he may become dangerous and apt to act impulsively in a desperate attempt to protect himself.

In handling these situations, law enforcement officers should work in teams. The team approach enables officers to assess the situation quickly and to divide up those responsibilities which will help to bring the situation under control rapidly. When a person is in tense conflict with another person, the officer should remember that it will not be enough to direct all attention toward the individual with the personality disorder even if it is obvious which one he is. Since he is reacting to a stress from another individual, he will be reassured if the officers are also directing their attention to the other person.

It is important to remember that since those with personality disorders may do poorly under an acute stress, they will respond positively to any activity which helps remove that stress. This does not mean that the officer should give in to any magical expectations. Rather, he can help to remove the stress by indicating to the person involved in forceful, clear, and tactful terms that there is no way that his wish can be granted. This direct confrontation with reality, in clear and nonargumentative terms, can have a calming influence because it helps the person to reestablish contact with a reality which has temporarily been lost as emotions have gained control.

Summary

In this chapter, we have described those personality disorders which police most often encounter in their work. An officer can learn to recognize the signs of passive-aggressive, histrionic, paranoid, and compulsive personality disorders in a variety of situations. The officers can act more effectively if he is aware of their characteristics and their influences on behavior.

Although the clinical examples in this chapter tend to focus on non-criminal aspects of law enforcement, those with personality disorders can readily be found in the criminal aspects. This will become clearer when we later examine the subjects of psychopathic behavior, deviant sexual behavior, deliquent behavior, and drug abuse.

BIBLIOGRAPHY

AMERICAN PSYCHIATRIC ASSOCIATION. 1980. *Diagnostic and Statistical Manual of Mental Disorders.* 3d ed. Washington, D.C.: American Psychiatric Association.

CAMERON, N. 1963. *Personality Development and Psychopathology.* Boston: Houghton Mifflin.

DALLY, ANN G. 1978. *The Morbid Streak: Destructive Aspects of the Personality.* London: Wildwood House.

FRIEDMAN, A. M., KAPLAN, H. I., and SADOCK, B. J. 1975. *Comprehensive Textbook of Psychiatry.* 2d ed., Baltimore: Williams and Wilkins.

REDLICH, F. C., and FREEDMAN, D. X. 1966. *The Theory and Practice of Psychiatry.* New York: Basic Books.

WISHNIE, HOWARD. 1977. *The Impulsive Personality: A Manual For Understanding Criminals, Drug Addicts, and Sociopaths.* New York: Plenum Press.

Chapter 7

Neurotic Disorders

HAVING REVIEWED the major personality disorders, we will now focus our attention on the next major category of emotional disturbance —neurotic disorders. Whereas abnormal behavior in personality disorders is characterized by maladaptive behavior patterns which have become a life-style, neurotics constitute a group whose abnormal behavior is usually characterized by the episodic presence of anxiety in one form or another. The neurotic, unlike the psychotic, is not divorced from reality. He lives in the same world as we do. Instead of acting out his conflicts as those with personality disorders do, the neurotic suffers with his conflicts by developing symptoms.

Before we discuss the specific symptoms of each of the major neurotic disorders, it will be helpful to understand some of their general characteristics.

General Considerations

The most important element in the development of symptoms is the presence of an impulse, generally coming from the id, which is likely to create anxiety if allowed into consciousness. If it becomes conscious, symptoms may also occur if the impulse is not dealt with appropriately. Defense mechanisms are used to ward off anxiety, but symptoms may occur if the defenses do not work effectively or work so well that the behavior resulting from them impairs functioning.

This is a simplified description of the process of symptom formation and does not do justice to its complexity. The complexity results in part from childhood experiences. Consequently, a specific impulse which creates anxiety in one person may be warded off by another. Similarly, the way one person wards off anxiety may differ from another person's method.

An illustration will help clarify this point. Suppose that the unacceptable impulses coming into consciousness are sexual. Let us say that this example involves a woman. One woman might handle these impulses through sublimation by choosing a job, such as modeling, which helps her successfully channel her unacceptable sexual impulses. Another might use projection and channel unacceptable sexual impulses into a belief that others are looking at her on the street and thinking about picking her up. Why one chooses sublimation and the other projection to handle the same unacceptable sexual impulse may be a reflection of early development factors, including those defense mechanisms which the child used to handle the positive or negative reactions from parents.

Both women could develop neurotic symptoms if their defenses come under attack. Suppose that the first loses her modeling job or the second is picked up on the street. Both events could generate great anxiety just as emergence of the original impulse would.

While neurotic symptoms may be disturbing, they also can serve a positive purpose. Freud called these advantages *secondary gain,* referring to the benefits obtained from being sick when others may pay more attention and do things that they would not ordinarily do if the person were well. Although secondary gain may not play a major role in the onset of neuroses, it may support their continuation. If its benefits are great, there is less motivation to give up the neurotic symptoms. The pursuit of secondary gain is not conscious. When it is, it is called *malingering.* Sometimes it is difficult for the professional to distinguish between conscious malingering and unconscious secondary gain.

Anxiety Neurosis

An anxiety neurosis (also referred to as a generalized anxiety disorder) is defined in DSM-III as an episode of "generalized, persistent anxiety of at least one month's duration" without the specific symptoms that characterize other mental disorders. It is characterized by apprehensive expectation, physical complaints, and hyperattentiveness, but should be differentiated from normal apprehensiveness or fear.

Historical Background

The concept of the anxiety neurosis has been used by many psychiatrists and psychologists in their attempts to explain the dynamics of personality development, abnormal behavior, and emotional disturbance.

In his early theory, Freud viewed anxiety as resulting from an inability to discharge physical tension. In his later theory, however, he adopted a more psychological orientation and made an important contribution to our understanding by recognizing the protective function of anxiety. In his concept of *signal anxiety,* he described a state in which the individual first perceives danger and then uses signal anxiety to mobilize defense reactions to avoid the danger. If these attempts to avoid danger are not wholly successful, anxiety may increase and become a diffuse state which affects all behavior, thereby contributing to the development of an anxiety neurosis.

Harry Stack Sullivan, a later theoretician, stressed the early mother–child relationship in the origin of anxiety neuroses. In his formulation, he proposed that the original model for adult anxiety could be found in the child's fear of mother's disapproval. This early anxiety is related not only to the child's knowledge that maternal approval is essential to his own comfort, but can also serve as an *alerting mechanism* to the child in situations where maternal disapproval might be forthcoming.

Characteristics

The person with an anxiety neurosis may have a history of chronic anxiety not necessarily related to any specific situation. This anxiety can become more acute in some situations, but there is usually not any particular pattern to the casual observer. Physical complaints can be wide-ranging and involve almost every organ system of the body. Head-aches, nausea and vomiting, shortness of breath, palpitations, menstrual dysfunction, and insomnia are often associated with anxiety neuroses. In addition to these specific physical complaints, general uneasiness may be present, characterized by statements such as "I feel uptight," "I can't sleep," "I don't like to be by myself," or "I'm always worried."

Mild depression symptoms, along with the feeling of anxiety, are common. It is not rare to encounter abuse of alcohol, barbituates, and tranquilizers, especially in those whose anxiety is persistent or where episodes have occurred frequently. The following example will help illustrate further the characteristics of the anxiety neurosis.

Case Example. Hazel Newton is a twenty-one-year-old college junior who was brought to the hospital after the police were called to the campus. Her roommates had found her apparently unconscious with a half empty pill bottle by her bed. After receiving medical attention, she told the following story to the psychiatrist who interviewed her.

Although she had never gone for help, she recognized that she had not been her normal self for at least a year. During the summer be-tween her college freshman and sophomore years, she had broken up with the fellow she had been dating since her sophomore year in high school. Up to that time, he was the only man she had ever dated.

Since then, she said, "I have been uptight all the time." Upon further questioning, she also told the doctor that she had had insomnia for two years. She had made many visits to physicians because of vague physical complaints and had had many tests to find the cause of these symptoms but without success.

Furthermore, her grades, excellent during her first year of college, had gone steadily downhill. When asked about the suicide attempt, she revealed that, several days previously, she had been called into the Dean of Women's office and told that, if she did not pull her grades up, she would not be able to graduate.

Hazel also stated that she no longer felt comfortable with men and that no man she had dated in the past year had asked her out again. She commented, "I just can't seem to relax on dates."

Underlying Factors

Hazel's anxiety is consistent with the definition of an anxiety neurosis, since it is diffuse and not restricted to definite situations or objects. Her case illustrates another common characteristic, the inability to link the onset of the neurotic behavior with any single precipitating factor. In Hazel's case, the breakup with her boyfriend two years previously and the prospect of failure and rejection conveyed to her by the Dean several days before her suicide attempt were critical factors in the original onset and recent worsening of her anxiety neurosis.

As previously suggested, events in early childhood serve as the focus for the development of an anxiety neurosis. In Hazel's case, her mother's long absences from home because of work and illness may have been an important underlying factor. Prior to breaking up with her boyfriend two years ago, Hazel had been able to cope with her fears of abandonment and rejection through a close and clinging relationship. However, after the relationship ended she could no longer handle her fears of abandonment. Her anxiety grew and grew until it culminated with the suicide attempt.

Depressive Neurosis

Depressive neurosis (also referred to as *dysthymic disorder*) is a condition in which there is a chronic disturbance of mood or a loss of interest in almost all usual activities. It differs from a major depressive disorder (chapter 8) in that the person with a depressive neurosis does not experience the severe or lengthy distortion of reality and behavioral disorganization which characterize a psychotic disorder.

Historical Background

Theoreticians during the past seventy years have paid much attention to the differences between the various types of depression, specifically the neurotic and the psychotic. These differences have become more critical since the advent of medication because it appears to have a variable effect on different types of depression. Recent classification of the types of depression have been based, in part, on these differential responses to medication.

Characteristics

A person with symptoms of depressive neurosis feel disturbed, sad, blue, miserable, and depressed. Along with this alteration of mood, the person may show a general loss of interest in his environment including his home, his family, his work, or his schooling; a tendency to be more self-critical without apparent reason or justification; and an increase in physical symptoms, such as a sleep disturbance, loss of appetite, and a marked change in weight. Suicidal thoughts may be present, often associated with a pessimistic attitude toward the future.

Like the anxiety neurosis, this depression is pervasive. In full force, the depressed mood colors all life events. A specific precipitating experience may be identifiable, although it can be absent. The following example will illustrate.

Case Example. Martin Dine, a twenty-six-year-old police officer, had recently been divorced. He took twenty-five Nembutal after drinking beer for several hours and was found by the police whom he had called just prior to passing out. He was taken to the emergency room, and after receiving medical attention he was interviewed.

He had been depressed for some time since his wife had told him that she was involved with another man, did not love him anymore, and wanted a divorce. When she was interviewed later, she said that Martin seemed to take the news very well initially, that he recognized their marriage was on the rocks and that perhaps a divorce was for the best.

However, shortly after the divorce became final and six weeks prior to his suicide attempt, he became very depressed. His fellow officers noticed that he was paying less attention to his work and occasionally taking unnecessary risks. Furthermore, he was obviously losing weight as he was not eating when his squad took a dinner break.

On the day prior to his suicide attempt, he was called into the sergeant's office and told that his poor work was noticeable and that, if it did not improve, he faced disciplinary action and possible termination. Later that day, his former wife called him to say that she could not care adequately for their two children on his alimony payments. Feeling more depressed and seeing his situation as hopeless, Martin decided to kill himself.

Underlying Factors

Those with a depressive neurosis, like those with an anxiety neurosis, have usually encountered difficulties in early childhood which contribute to a personality foundation highly susceptible to the development of a neurosis. These early factors may include a poor self-image, which develops either as a result of a lack of positive parental reinforcement, or the presence of over-critical parents. People with depressive neuroses usually have very strict superegos developed as a result of an identification with the over-critical parent. Thus they become over-critical of themselves.

When faced with failure, as Martin was when his marriage ended and his job was threatened, they perceive these events as a natural consequence of their own inabilities, a point of view consistent with their underlying poor self-image. Prior to the onset of the neurosis, they often attempt to compensate for their poor self-image by being extremely organized or entering a profession with a good image. If they fail, they also experience guilt because they have been unable to live up to not only their own expectations but also those of their parents and their profession.

In a depressive neurosis, one of the principal underlying characteristics is an inability to handle feelings of anger appropriately. The unexpressed hostility Martin felt toward his wife at the time she told him about her extramarital affair and requested a divorce was an important contributing factor to the onset of his depressive neurosis. In treatment, Martin later learned that one of the reasons he was unable to express this hostility was because of the nonacceptance of hostility in his early childhood surroundings. He was forced to hold back these feelings unless he was willing to run the risk of further criticism and rejection from his parents.

Obsessive-Compulsive Neurosis

The obsessive-compulsive neurosis is characterized by ideas, thoughts, or impulses which are repetitive (obsessions) and by actions which are repeated for unexplained reasons in a patterned form of behavior (compulsions). These obsessions and compulsions are usually perceived as unwanted or unacceptable. The person usually recognizes the senselessness of these thoughts and derives no pleasure, other than a relief of tension, from this behavior.

Historical Background

Observations of obsessional thinking patterns and compulsive acts date from medieval times when these people were often viewed as being under the devil's influence. Consequently, many early theories about the origins of obsessive-compulsive neuroses dealt with spiritual forces or witchcraft.

By the nineteenth century, however, theorists began to view obsessive-compulsive neuroses differently. Pierre Janet was the first to assume a more modern view of this emotional disturbance, describing a biological base in which the central disturbance was the result of a lessening of mental energy.

However, it was Freud who recognized the importance of the unconscious and conflict, and devised the modern theory. He viewed obsessive-compulsive symptoms as related to three defense mechanisms— isolation, undoing, and reaction formation.

He saw obsessive thinking as an attempt to remove any associated feelings from consciousness. Only after fully isolating these feelings successfully could the individual allow the previously unconscious and dangerous thought into consciousness.

The amount of energy required to keep the emotional component *isolated* often involves the entire personality in the process. In the preneurotic state, this defense mechanism of isolation begins to break down, and the emotional component of the thought or impulse constantly threatens to break through into consciousness and escape the controls placed upon it.

Other defenses must then be employed to counter this threat. The defense mechanism of *undoing* is a behavioral attempt to handle the obsessional thought which makes the person anxious. This leads to the compulsive act. For example, a mother's compulsion to check the baby's room three times before going to bed might be her way of unconsciously undoing a death wish which she has toward the baby.

Reaction formation is the third defense in which the person tries to handle unwanted thoughts and emotions by channeling them into a pattern of behavior that is the opposite of the behavior associated with the underlying impulse. For example, the overprotective mother may really be a rejecting mother who deals with this unacceptable impulse by becoming over-concerned about her child's welfare.

These formulations will be clearer as we talk about the characteristics of the obsessive-compulsive neurosis and present an example.

Characteristics

As described previously, the characteristics of the obsessional-compulsive neuroses are the presence of obsessional thinking accompanied by a pattern of compulsive and ritualistic behavior. Kleptomania (compulsive stealing) and pyromania (compulsive fire setting) are variants of the compulsive neurosis occasionally encountered by the police officer. These kinds of behavior protect against the release of even more dangerous, usually aggressive, impulses. In later stages of the illness, the person may give into them, no longer having the desire to resist them.

This aggressive content may not be recognized or accepted by the neurotic because it is too threatening, but it is usually obvious to a trained observer. Likewise, the neurotic who is experiencing the compulsive behavior pattern designed to ward off the obsessional thoughts is not able to make the connection between the acts and the thought pattern. The following case is an illustration.

Case Example. Michael Monroe was eighteen years old when he was admitted to the hospital's psychiatric unit because he felt he was going crazy. He told the interviewing psychiatrist that for the past three months he had been constantly preoccupied with thoughts about cleanliness and, more recently, had been spending great amounts of time washing himself and his clothes. His mother confirmed his story and also said that she had also noticed other changes in his behavior, including an increase in nail biting, a willingness to eat only certain foods and a peculiar pattern of leaving notes all over the house to avoid talking with family members.

Several days prior to admission, a new behavior pattern emerged in which Michael, whenever he left the house, would walk out the door three steps and back up four steps into the house. This would be repeated four or five times before he could leave the house.

When questioned, Michael was unable to present any reason for these actions. He could only state that his behavior had completely interfered with his school work and was seriously threatening his expected graduation from high school in June. He also admitted that the reason he had agreed to come to the hospital was that he had begun to have thoughts of violence toward his father.

Underlying Factors

In Freudian theory, an obsessive-compulsive neurosis has its origins in early childhood, particularly during the period of toilet training. In this theory, there is a marked degree of ambivalence and uncertainty during this phase of development. This early ambivalence, of not knowing what to do accompanied by a frequent changing of one's mind, can evolve into a ritualistic pattern of compulsive behavior when stresses are great enough. This ambivalence is exemplified by Michael's inability to make up his mind whether to leave the house. He must first go through a compulsive behavior pattern before he can give himself permission to go.

When obsessive-compulsive patterns begin to fail, regression may become the last defense available as an escape from the ambivalent bind. This regression is illustrated by the observations of Michael's psychiatrist. Although Michael reported being obsessed with cleanliness, he appeared as a dirty, sloppily dressed young man who had not paid attention to his personal hygiene for at least several days.

Michael's mother revealed that, just prior to the onset of this obsessive-compulsive pattern, his father had been seriously injured in an auto accident. Later, in treatment, the therapist was able to identify that this precipitating event had been a magical carrying out of Michael's previous unconscious hostility to his father. A characteristic of the obsessive-compulsive neurotic is an inability to deal with rage, leading to the ambivalence. In this case, the accident had served as the trigger which brought many of these formerly successfully repressed hostile impulses to the surface. The obsessive-compulsive neurosis represented Michael's frantic attempt to prevent these hostile, aggressive impulses and thoughts from breaking through to the surface, which they had finally done in the days immediately prior to admission to the psychiatric unit.

Phobic Neurosis

The phobic neurosis can be distinguished from the preceding three neuroses because its symptomatology is usually limited to a specific *phobic object* or *phobic situation*. A person with a phobia restricts some normal activities. The phobic neurosis often coexists with other neurotic symptoms, such as anxiety and depression.

Historical Background

The term *phobia* did not appear until the nineteenth century. In 1872, Kurt Westphal, a German theoretician, reported on three male patients who had specific fears of open places, a condition which he labeled *agoraphobia*. Today we recognize a variety of phobias which are generally named after a particular fear. Other examples include *claustrophobia,* a fear of closed-in places, and *acrophobia,* a fear of high places.

Characteristics

A phobia must be distinguished from a normal fear. It refers to a *morbid* fear of a particular object or situation—a fear of something which normal persons do not perceive as any great threat or danger.

However, this distinction is not always entirely clear. Some phobic objects or situations may create normal fear. When this occurs, we have to look at the strength of the individual's reaction to the object or situation and judge whether a phobia is present by the degree of fear.

When anxiety about a specific object or situation cannot be handled appropriately, it is displaced in a phobic neurosis onto a previously neutral object or situation which then becomes the phobic object or situation. Phobias are always accompanied by anxiety when the person is in the presence of the phobic object or situation. However, this anxiety is secondary; it is not the original anxiety.

In the phobic neurosis, displacement is used as a defense. The unacceptable feeling or thought is unconsciously transferred from its source to a less threatening substitute. Through displacement, the neurotic combats the original anxiety. If this person avoids the phobic object or situation, he can function effectively.

Occasionally, however, the phobic neurosis becomes more severe because the anxiety generated becomes so great that the person develops a phobia for almost every object or situation. Sometimes one or more of the phobic objects or situations becomes so important to the individual's life-style that it cannot be avoided. An example will help illustrate this point.

Case Example. Judith Rosenberg is a forty-three-year-old woman who was accompanying her husband when he had an auto accident. Mr. Rosenberg told the investigating officer that his wife made him so nervous when he drove that she really caused the accident. In response to the officer's questions, he said that his wife was much less nervous if she drove the car. The officer suggested that Mrs. Rosenberg might seek professional help about her nervousness. She did not do so at first, but when her anxiety became so great that it was almost impossible for them to go anywhere unless she drove, she agreed to professional help.

The psychiatrist learned that Mrs. Rosenberg's aged mother, Mrs.

Schwartz, had died after a twelve-year illness six months ago. During the terminal phase of her illness, Mrs. Schwartz had been in a nursing home. Prior to that, she had lived with the Rosenbergs for close to twelve years. During this time Mrs. Rosenberg had the principal responsibility caring for her mother.

Underlying Factors

Those who are prone to phobic neuroses as adults have a history of observed anxiety, even as a children, in association with certain impulses. Most commonly, the impulses are sexual and aggressive. In normal personality development, the person develops appropriate defense mechanisms which channel these unacceptable impulses.

Prior to devoting all of her energy to her invalid mother, Mrs. Rosenberg had spent much time doing volunteer work for the sick. Consequently, it was natural for her to assume the responsibility of caring for her ill mother. At the outset, before her mother moved into her home, the physician had told Mrs. Rosenberg that he anticipated that Mrs. Schwartz had only a year to live. However, Mrs. Schwartz lived for twelve years, and Mrs. Rosenberg devotedly cared for her every day.

Through this attention, Mrs. Rosenberg could continue through sublimation and reaction formation to channel many of her unacceptable aggressive impulses. She had begun this pattern with her volunteer work and continued it through her care for her mother. Only when her mother became so ill that she was unmanageable at home was she moved to a nursing home. This was done against Mrs. Rosenberg's wishes, but at her husband's insistence. Mrs. Schwartz died several weeks later.

In treatment, it became clear that the onset of Mrs. Rosenberg's phobic neurosis was directly related to her failure to develop adequate mechanisms for handling her unacceptable aggressive impulses. When her mother died, her mechanism for sublimating this aggressive impulse was also lost.

Her choice of the car as the phobic object was related to the corollary phobia of an accident. This latter phobia represented both a displacement and projection of her hostile impulses. She could feel more comfortable if she was in control of these impulses by driving the car but was more anxious when she was not in control and her husband was driving.

Conversion Neurosis

In the conversion neuroses, also referred to as hysterical neuroses or conversion disorder, the person converts the unacceptable impulse threatening him with overwhelming anxiety into a physical symptom, usually associated with the parts of the body under voluntary control. These symptoms lessen anxiety and are often symbolic of the underlying conflict.

The conversion neurosis is both similar to and different from the phobic neurosis. The similarity is in the use of the defense of displacement; the difference is in the displacement to a part of the body rather than to an outside object or situation.

Historical Background

Like obsessive-compulsive neuroses, the unusual symptoms of conversion neuroses contributed to an intense mythology during the Middle Ages, the seventeenth, eighteenth, and early part of the nineteenth centuries. Only in the latter part of the nineteenth and the early part of the twentieth century was a psychological basis for these symptoms recognized and their causative mechanisms worked out by Freud and his predecessors, Jean-Martin Charcot and Hippolyte-Marie Bernheim.

In Freud's theory, the emotions associated with a specific psychological trauma cannot be expressed directly because they would lead to unacceptable impulses and behavior. Consequently, these feelings and impulses are displaced and converted into physical symptoms. Furthermore, they are so well blocked that the person is characteristically indifferent to his physical symptoms. If he is hysterically blind, for example, he will not display the emotional concern of most of us.

Characteristics

The physical symptoms associated with conversion neuroses are either motor or sensory. Motor disturbances usually take two forms—impaired movement and paralysis. In both cases, complete neurological examination will not reveal any organic basis for the symptoms. The symptoms are often inconsistent with known anatomical pathways. In sensory disturbances, the areas affected will also not be consistent with known anatomical pathways (for example, in *stocking anesthesia,* the patient's insensitivity will cover the same area of the leg that a stocking would, an anatomical impossibility). While it is more likely that those with repeating episodes of conversion neuroses will experience the same symptom during each episode, it is also possible that the conversion symptom may vary in site and nature. Usually the symptom appears suddenly in a situation where extreme stress is present.

Case Example. Officer Clarence Kanner had been transferred to Vice from Patrol about six months prior to his admission to a hospital. He complained of blinding headaches and feared a brain tumor. Thorough medical and neurological examinations were negative. A consulting psychiatrist was called in, and he established the following sequence for the development of the symptoms.

The officer had led a rather protected life as a youth and had dated only one woman since high school. Shortly after graduation, they were married. After several short-term jobs which did not interest him, he joined the police department. After he had been in Patrol for about four years, he was transferred to Detectives and assigned to Vice. Here he was thrown into association with many young women who, despite their lack of an acceptable moral code, were physically attractive to him. It was also evident that a number of them also found him attractive.

When he came home from work to his wife and family (he had two small children), the problems of family living contrasted sharply with the night life environment of his job. His own strict moral code and sense of responsibility as husband and father were in conflict with the role he had to play at work. Unable to resolve this emotional conflict, he developed a blinding headache—sometimes on the job (perhaps when temptation was becoming too great for his unconscious desires) and sometimes at home (when family pressures built up). He began to suspect that he had a brain tumor, and this aggravated his symptoms. His emotional conflicts were thus converted into physical symptoms that had no real organic basis.

Underlying Factors

The benefits of a conversion symptom to the neurotic are twofold: the person achieves a primary gain by keeping an internal conflict or need out of conscious awareness; and the person may also achieve a secondary gain by using the conversion symptom to avoid a specific activity that is unacceptable or by obtaining support from important people who would not otherwise provide it.

In contrast to other neuroses which have their origins in conflicts surrounding very early stages of development, the roots of the conversion neurosis are related more directly to the sexual conflicts which the child encounters between ages three and five. As in Officer Kanner's case, conversion neuroses and conversion symptoms occur as a result of the displacement of unacceptable sexual impulses which, if allowed to come into consciousness, would cause overwhelming anxiety.

Dissociative Neuroses

The dissociative neuroses (or dissociative disorders) are especially important to the law enforcement officer. It is in this category that psychogenic amnesia falls. This psychological forgetting is often difficult to distinguish from a true amnesia based on organic injury or disease.

Historical Background

In early theories, dissociative neuroses and conversion neuroses often were included together under the general label of hysteria. However, later theoreticians, including Freud, differentiated between the two on the basis of the physical symptoms present in conversion neuroses. In DSM-III, the distinction is even greater; conversion neuroses are considered part of the class of somatoform disorders, while dissociative neuroses are a separate class altogether.

Characteristics

The dissociative neuroses form a complex group of emotional disturbances because of their many forms. It is important to know whether the temporary alteration of personality integration is in the area of consciousness, identity, or motor function. These forms include hysterical amnesia, the multiple personality, the sleepwalking trance, and, of special interest to law enforcement officers, the phenomenon of *highway hypnosis.*

All are related by the phenomenon of *dissociation,* in which events originally blocked from consciousness because of their unacceptable nature become so overwhelming that the only way to deal with the

82

problem is to dissociate completely from the environment. A case of highway hypnosis will serve as an illustration.

Case Example. It was a clear day when John Vincent, twenty-seven years old, died at 2:14 P.M. in a single car accident on an interstate highway in northwestern Arizona. The investigating officer reported that a thorough perusal of the highway on which John Vincent had been traveling just prior to crashing into a telephone pole did not reveal the characteristic pattern of weaving associated with falling asleep at the wheel or the skid marks commonly noted when the brakes are applied abruptly after the victim awakes. The death of John Vincent was probably a result of highway hypnosis.

Underlying Factors

In highway hypnosis, the victim becomes dissociated from the environment as a whole, losing track entirely of the passage of time and place. Mild cases of highway hypnosis are known to all of us. When we emerge from our dream state, we recognize that we have been driving for seconds or minutes and have passed several familiar landmarks without realizing it.

In serious cases, such as led to John Vincent's death, this trance state leads to complete immobilization at the wheel. Because of it, the driver is often unable to negotiate a curve. Highway hypnosis associated with fatal traffic accidents is most likely to occur on long, straight, monotonous stretches of turnpikes where curves are few and far between, offering little challenge to the motorist to pay attention to the road.

Helpful Hints to the Law Enforcement Officer

In handling someone with overwhelming anxiety, it is important to provide reassurance in order to help that person regain control over panic. It is not helpful for the police officer to attempt to persuade the person that the anxiety or panic is unrealistic or unwarranted.

Even if the officer readily perceives the reasons for the anxiety and considers them ridiculous, he must recognize that they are not ridiculous to the person experiencing the anxiety. Instead of belittling the person's symptoms, he should offer reassurance and try to remove the person to a protective situation. Then he can begin to talk with the person about his anxious feelings.

When the police officer encounters someone who is depressed, he should be alert to the seriousness of this condition. Even though he may not perceive any realistic cause for the depression, he should try to identify with the person's depression by recognizing how painful it must be and by empathizing with his pain. After all, it is not how the officer sees it but how the depressed person sees it that will determine what that person will do.

If the depression appears so great that a suicide attempt is possible, the person should be placed in a hospital immediately and watched very carefully until the depression has lifted. However, a word of caution: Many commit suicide at a time when it looks as if they are improving. It is thought that this false improvement is actually due to the neurotic's having made his final decision to commit suicide. Having done so, he is able to put on a happy face because he knows that all worries will soon be over. This happy face will sometimes fool even the professional, who may decide that the danger has passed.

The officer who has responsibility for prisoners should know that many depressed persons are encountered in jails. The stress of incarceration is likely to precipitate a depressive neurosis. The officer must be alert for depressed inmates so that he can make a judgment regarding suicidal potential. He should always be especially sensitive to the inmate who, several days before, was profoundly depressed but now has undergone a remarkable mood alteration unrelated to any significant external event, such as his imminent release. This person may have also made the decision that life is no longer worth living. The observant officer should then summon appropriate medical help.

If the officer encounters someone with severe obsessional thinking or a ritualistic compulsive behavior pattern, it is important for him to recognize that this person is disturbed and should not be passed off as "crazy." It is easy to assume the latter, since compulsive acts, in particular, are often nonsensical and funny to the casual observer.

The officer as a professional observer of behavior should recognize these obsessive thought patterns and compulsive acts for what they are, symptoms of an emotional disturbance. Knowing this, he will be able to guide the person toward a therapeutic setting. Because of the seeming irrationality of the behavior, and in most instances its apparent harmlessness, it is often easier to ignore it rather than to take the trouble to refer the person to an appropriate facility. However, it can be equally rewarding to suggest or make such a referral because the neurotic person is generally very receptive to the suggestion that he seek help. He is in full contract with reality and recognizes that his obsessional thoughts and compulsive behavior are symptoms of illness. His ambivalence stops him from seeking help on his own, but the influence of the officer will generally help him overcome it.

When the officer encounters someone who is experiencing an unreasonable fear (phobia) in relationship to an actual situation, he can also help by reducing the person's panic through supportive intervention.

Summary

The neuroses include many examples of emotional disturbance which the law enforcement officer is likely to encounter. Awareness of the various types, their characteristics, and some of the underlying factors will enable him to assess their severity, the necessity for immediate intervention and, most importantly, his own response to the one who is experiencing the symptoms. Without this knowledge, the law enforcement officer may respond to neurotic people inappropriately. With it, he is more likely to function as an ally of the medical and nonmedical therapeutic professional by assessing these troubled persons correctly, responding appropriately, and referring them, if necessary, for treatment.

BIBLIOGRAPHY

AMERICAN PSYCHIATRIC ASSOCIATION. 1981. *Diagnostic and Statistical Manual of Mental Disorders,* 3d ed. Washington, D.C.: American Psychiatric Association.
FENICHEL, O. 1945. *The Psychoanalytic Theory of the Neuroses.* New York: Norton.
FRIEDMAN, A. M., KAPLAN, H. I., and SADOCK, B. J. 1975. *Comprehensive Textbook of Psychiatry,* 2d ed. Baltimore: Williams and Wilkins.
FREUD, S. 1961 (originally published in 1936). "Inhibitions, Symptoms and Anxiety." in *Standard Edition,* vol. 20. ed. J. Strachey. London: Hogarth Press. pp. 87–122.
GOSSOP, MICHAEL. 1980. *Theories of Neurosis.* New York: Springer-Verlag.
GRAY, MELVIN. 1978. *Neuroses: A Comprehensive and Critical View.* New York: Van Nostrand Reinhold.
REDLICH, F. C., and FREEDMAN, D. X. 1966. *The Theory and Practice of Psychiatry.* New York: Basic Books.

Chapter 8

Psychotic Disorders

PSYCHOTIC DISORDERS may be functional or organic in origin. If functional, they are believed to derive from developmental and situational factors. If organic, they are usually thought to result from injury to, or involvement of, the central nervous system. But much about the origin of these disorders is still unknown.

This chapter will focus on the two major groups of functional psychoses: schizophrenic disorders and affective disorders. We will discuss their characteristics with illustrations from several case examples and explore theories of their underlying factors. We will then provide helpful hints to the law enforcement officer in handling psychotic behavior.

Common Characteristics

The common characteristic of all psychotic disorders is a *loss of contact with reality.* In addition, there are six other major psychotic symptoms: disturbances in thinking, disturbances in thought content, disturbances in perception, disturbances in judgment, disturbances in mood and emotions, and regression. The diagnosis of a specific psychotic disorder depends on the particular combination of these symptoms.

Disturbances in thinking occur when thought is no longer rational, logical, and goal-directed. Many terms are used to describe these types of disturbed thinking, ranging from the less serious, *circumstantiality,* to the more severe, *loosening of associations.* An officer listening to someone with an emotional disturbance will be better able to judge its seriousness if he understands these terms.

In *circumstantiality,* the person's thinking remains goal-directed, but he reaches the goal only after a series of lengthy digressions. For example, by the time he answers a question the person who asked may have forgotten the question. In *tangential thinking,* the person never reaches the goal, but his thoughts still have logical connections. In contrast to both of these, the person with a *loosening of associations* neither reaches the goal nor connects between his thoughts rationally.

Other forms of disturbed thinking affect the flow of thought rather than the pattern of associations. These include the *flight of ideas,* in which the person goes so rapidly from one connecting thought to another that the listener becomes lost trying to follow. In contrast to this increased flow of thought, *blocking* refers to a slowing down, or complete cessation, of thought expression because of threatened anxiety.

In addition to disturbances in the forms and expression of thinking, another important characteristic of a psychotic disorder may be *disturbances in the content of thought.* The most common form is the delusion, a false belief arising without appropriate external stimulation that is maintained more or less unshakably in the face of all reason. These false beliefs are generally not shared by other members of this person's peer group. Delusions may be either persecutory or grandiose. Their presence may relate to the person's mood. Someone who is depressed is more likely to experience delusions of persecution ("the Mafia has put out a contract on my life"), while the hyperactive person is more likely to experience delusions of grandeur ("my father was Jesus Christ, and my mother was the Virgin Mary").

Closely related to disturbances of thought content are *disturbances in perception.* In many psychotic disorders, delusions are accompanied by disturbances in perception (hallucinations). A hallucination refers to the apparent perception of an external object, such as a voice, when no corresponding real object exists. In most functional psychoses, these hallucinations are auditory ("I hear my mother telling me I'm no good"), but in the organic psychoses, visual, tactile, gustatory (taste), and/or olfactory (smell) hallucinations are more common.

The loss of contact with reality is also commonly associated with *disturbances in judgment.* If judgment is a mental function whose purpose is to insure reality-oriented action, then the psychotic is invariably impaired in this area. The police officer can assess the degree of impairment by posing hypothetical problem-solving situations ("What would you do if you smelled smoke in a theater?") or by simply observing ongoing behavior.

In psychotic disorders, *disturbances in mood and emotions* are usually more severe than in the neuroses and interfere with effective functioning to such an extent that hospitalization is often necessary. These disturbances may include sudden changes in mood without accompanying changes in the person's situation, or the complete absence of mood change despite major changes in the environment which would normally result in the person's change of mood.

Finally, the psychotic may also show *regression,* in which the ego returns to an earlier state of development in an attempt to avoid the present tension and conflict. The result is a deterioration from a previous level of functioning (chapter 4).

The degree to which some of these signs and symptoms are present can assist the police officer in deciding what type of psychosis is present. Disturbances in thinking primarily characterize the schizophrenias, while disturbed emotions are more prominent in the affective disorders. This does not imply, however, that disturbances in emotions do not occur in schizophrenia or, conversely, that disturbances in thinking do not occur in the affective disorders. Other disturbances described in this section are commonly associated with both types of psychoses.

Schizophrenias

Historical Background

Although observers have recognized many symptoms of schizophrenia prior to the time of Christ, it was not described as a disease until the end of the nineteenth century. In 1898, Emil Kraepelin was the first to combine many of these previous observations into a single entity.

In his paper "The Diagnosis and Prognosis of Dementia Praecox," he included many of these symptoms as having in common an apparent lack of external causes, an occurrence in young and previously healthy individuals, and an impact which led to an ultimate deterioration of the personality as the disease progressed.

Although Kraepelin was the first to bring together the signs and symptoms of schizophrenia, it was Eugen Bleuler who, several years later, substituted the term *schizophrenia* for dementia praecox. Bleuler's substitution reflected his disagreement with Kraepelin's concept of the disease's incurability and associated deterioration. He pointed out that only some patients deteriorated, while others recovered.

The current system of classification (DSM-III) identifies five sub-types of schizophrenia which derive from the thinking of Kraepelin and Bleuler but also reflect more recent diagnostic research. These include: the undifferentiated type, the paranoid type, the disorganized type, the catatonic type, and the residual type. We will emphasize the first two types, in either their acute or chronic forms since these will be those most frequently encountered by the police.

Underlying Factors

There have been many theories on the cause of schizophrenia. Various genetic, biochemical, physiological, psychological, and sociocultural factors have been described, but none of them has been shown to be the sole cause. The cure for schizophrenia is still unknown.

Some researchers believe that the origins of schizophrenia lie solely in developmental processes and, specifically, in the early interactions between the child and family. Disturbances in the mother–child relationship are considered crucial. These predispose the child to a weak ego which, in later life, is not able to withstand stress. Consequently, the personality disintegrates, causing symptoms of schizophrenia.

Others believe that physical conditions are responsible for schizophrenia. Endocrine (glandular) problems, brain damage, and toxic poisoning have been offered as causes. More recently, researchers have concentrated on certain biochemical functions—substances in the body fluids which, when present in excessive amounts, might cause schizophrenia. To date, however, these theories are unproven.

Still others suggest a strong genetic (hereditary) factor. Studies completed with identical twins indicate a higher incidence of schizophrenia in monozygotic twins (born from the same egg) compared to dizygotic twins (born from two different eggs). Although these data support the hypothesis that genetic factors may play a role in the development of schizophrenia, the mechanism is unknown. Whether this genetic factor operates through a physiological defect, such as the absence of an enzyme, or through some broader gene mutation is unknown.

Theorists have also stressed the importance of sociocultural variables in the development of schizophrenia. They remark on the greater prevalence of schizophrenia among the lower socioeconomic classes. Whether this finding is related to the cause or the result of schizophrenia (through the drift of people suffering from schizophrenia into the lower socioeconomic brackets because of poor functioning) is not known.

In conclusion, our current knowledge is inadequate to account for the development of schizophrenia. Despite many years of research, sufficient data are not available to determine conclusively the relative importance of the psychological, physical, genetic, and sociocultural factors that may be involved in predisposing a person to schizophrenia.

UNDIFFERENTIATED TYPE

The undifferentiated type is characterized by a gradual deterioration of drive, ambition, and the ability to function. It is reflected in the absence of social relationships, the inability to work effectively at a job, or difficulty in functioning above a marginal level in school, and in generally disorganized behavior. This impairment is usually accompanied by delusions or hallucinations. While disturbed emotions, primarily depression, are characteristic, the major sign is a thought disorder often accompanied by incoherence. An example will illustrate.

Case Example. Floyd Brown is twenty years old, single, and a recent college dropout during his sophomore year. The police were called to his home one evening by his mother following a violent outburst. When they arrived, Floyd's mother told them that her son had recently been very difficult to live with, pacing and yelling in an irrational manner most of the day and night. On the evening she called the police, he had hit her for the first time. The police officers obtained the following information.

Following graduation from high school, Floyd entered the local university and did well the first year. However, during his second year, his functioning began to deteriorate rapidly. Not only did he lose interest in his studies, which led to his dropping out of school, but he also became preoccupied with many bizarre ideas concerning science and the meaning of life. Totally consumed by the quest for "truth," he began to withdraw and spent most of his time at home despite the family's urging to go out. He lost interest in his personal hygiene. The family found it more difficult to cope with him because, as his mother remarked, "We couldn't talk to him, and he didn't make sense."

Within the past two weeks, he had talked about his special powers to control life and had even stated his conviction that his father, who had died the previous summer, had communicated with him and would soon be "returning home." When he was severely agitated, as he had been the evening he had hit his mother, he talked about her as an agent of the devil, implying that she had something to do with his father's death.

The police decided that Floyd was a danger to others. When he was not willing to go to the hospital voluntarily, they contacted the hospital by phone and received permission to take him into protective custody so that he could be transported there for a psychiatric evaluation and possible involuntary admission.

PARANOID TYPE

The paranoid type of schizophrenia is characterized principally by delusions of persecution and/or grandeur. Hallucinations, usually auditory, are often present. Prior to onset, the paranoid schizophrenic often displays a suspicious and guarded attitude toward everyone. This person usually shows less impairment of functioning if he has not acted upon the delusional material. Severely disorganized behavior, as noted in the undifferentiated, catatonic, and disorganized types, is rare. A case example will illustrate.

Case Example. Judy Eden, twenty-eight years old and single, called the police to her home. When the responding officer arrived, Judy told him that she had a problem she wanted to explain. She began by saying that there were bottles of liquid in her home killing her and her dog and that the dog was already very ill. She took a wad of Kleenex from her purse and asked the officer to smell the odor. He did so and found no odor. When he did not confirm her suspicion, she told him that another officer had been to her home before and had told her to throw away the bottles. She said that she had done this but that both the bottles and odors had returned. In addition, she mentioned that her air conditioning was spreading the odors throughout the house.

On further questioning, Judy revealed that lately she had received messages from the television set. She told the officer how most of the people on the television were talking to her and telling her that she was going to die if she did not mend her ways.

The officer also learned that Judy had been widowed a year ago when her Air Force husband was killed in a plane crash while on a test flight. Initially, she had seemed to make a good adjustment to this tragedy, continuing her job as a secretary. However, several months later, her bizarre behavior began. She mentioned that her friends and co-workers had seemed concerned, but she soon realized that it was because "I have a pension and they want my money."

Although Judy did not demonstrate evidence of violence, the officer recognized that Judy's illness had been progressive and that violence to herself or others was an eventual possibility (chapters 13 and 14). Consequently, he asked her if she would accompany him to the hospital and talk to someone else. She refused. The officer left but immediately notified the local mental health center which sent a social worker to see Judy the next day.

RESIDUAL TYPE

This category applies to those who have had at least one prior episode of schizophrenia. While it is true that individuals with other types of schizophrenia may also have recurring episodes, the feature distinguishing the residual type is the recurrence of episodes without prominent psychotic symptoms. For example, while delusions, hallucinations, and grossly disorganized behavior are usually not present—or if present occur in a very muted form—these people generally demonstrate illogical thinking, loosening of associations, emotional blunting, social withdrawal, and eccentric behavior.

By definition, therefore, this is the most chronic of the schizophrenias. People with this disorder usually do not have repeated acute episodes in which severe symptoms of hallucinations, delusions, and disorganized behavior are present, except perhaps at the first episode. A case example will illustrate.

Case Example. Mary Michaels was picked up by the police at 3:00 A.M. on an interstate highway. A patrol car had been notified that several motorists had seen her standing at the side of the street and throwing various items of clothing from a large suitcase into the middle of the road.

When the police officers approached her and asked what she was doing and why, she replied, "I like to travel light, and besides the last guy who gave me a ride didn't like the way I was dressed. He said, 'I looked a mess and put me out of the car.' So there."

Further questioning revealed that Mary not only was unable to explain where she had been and where she was going but also spoke about how she was hoping to find the "end of the rainbow" so she could be young again.

Feeling that she represented a potential danger if left by the side of the road, the officers encouraged her to come with them to the local hospital. She agreed to accompany them.

In the emergency room, the doctor who spoke with her learned that Mary was thirty-eight years old and had been traveling for the past ten years from city to city, staying in one place no more than three months at a time. During this time, she had been hospitalized on at least six different occasions, once for as long as four months in a state hospital. Each time, she was given medication which "helped her think better," but she usually discontinued it shortly after her discharge and headed on her way.

The doctor agreed to admit her for a few days so that she could be put back on her medication. However, he was not optimistic that this would do much more than calm her down enough so that she could continue her travels without being an immediate danger to herself or others.

CATATONIC TYPE

The catatonic type is rare. Its importance to the law enforcement officer lies in the extreme violence which may be associated with one of its forms—catatonic excitement—in which there is excessive motor activity, grimacing, talkativeness, and unpredictable emotional outbursts. When these symptoms are not present, the person is usually in a stupor, a state of total silence and often bizarre posture. The person can remain in this single position for hours, seemingly paying attention to nothing and responsive to no one. This lack of verbal or physical response is accompanied, paradoxically, by an increased awareness of what is going on. This helps to explain why, without warning, the person may fly into the rage of catatonic excitement, becoming extremely dangerous. In either case, careful supervision is required, and hospitalization is indicated.

DISORGANIZED TYPE

The disorganized type is also rare. Knowledge about it, however, is important for the law enforcement officer because of the severe disintegration of the personality.

If an adequate history can be obtained, this clinical picture is usually

93

associated with extreme social impairment, a lengthy history, early onset of the illness, and a chronic course.

Generally, people with this disorder are so disorganized that hospitalization is essential and should be arranged as quickly as possible.

Affective Disorders

In contrast to the schizophrenias, the affective disorders are psychoses in which the primary signs and symptoms are related to *disturbances in emotions* rather than to *disturbances in the form of thinking* (circumstantiality, tangentiality, and loosening of associations). However, disturbances in the flow of thinking, thought content, perception, judgment, and regression are also characteristic.

The affective disorders may be classified into two types: manic-depressive (bipolar) disorder and major depressive disorder. Recent research suggests that although they are grouped together because of the primary disturbance in emotions, there also are major differences between them.

Historical Background

Theories about affective disorders go back to the early writings of Hippocrates, who described the interaction of the four bodily humours (blood, black bile, yellow bile, and water) as closely related to the occurrence of mania (unusual elation) and melancholia (unusual depression). It was not until the passing of the Middle Ages, with its emphasis on demonology, that a modern classification of affective disorders could emerge.

In 1854, Jean Pierre Falaret published a description of an illness which he called "La Folie Circulaire," the first description of the "circular" syndrome associated with the manic-depressive psychosis. Karl Kahlbaum, in 1882, was the first to view mania and melancholia as different stages of the same psychosis rather than as two different illnesses. Emil Kraepelin first proposed the diagnosis of manic-depressive insanity for this entire group of disorders. Although these are now more commonly referred to as affective disorders, the manic-depressive disorder is still recognized as one of the two major types—the other being the major depressive disorder.

Underlying Factors

Current research into the causes of affective disorders is at a similar level to research on the schizophrenias. A genetic (hereditary) factor has been suggested. Affective disorders occur with significant frequency in the children of parents with affective disorders as well as in children of alcoholic parents. However, the presence of one or the other in a family does not necessarily mean that an affective disorder will occur in any or all of its children. Similarly, theorists have noticed many biological changes in those with affective disorders, but whether they are causes or symptoms of the illness has not been clearly demonstrated.

Earlier inquiries into these disorders focused primarily on developmental and psychological factors. For example, Karl Abraham, in the early twentieth century, drew attention to the obsessive-compulsive personality structures of those who were most likely to develop an affective disorder in later life. Freud added to our understanding of this illness by pointing out the similarities and differences between normal mourning after a loss of a loved one and melancholia (depression). He viewed mourning as a period of appropriate grief and melancholia as resulting from an inability to resolve that grief. In melancholia, the loss is no longer confined to the departure of the loved one but is also turned against the self through a loss of self-esteem.

Mania, in contrast to melancholia (depression), is a flight from, and defense against, depression into a state of unrealistic and unusual elation.

MANIC-DEPRESSIVE DISORDER

In manic-depressive psychoses, either severe psychotic depression or an acute manic episode characteristically occurs first when the person is in his late twenties or early thirties.

If the psychotic depressive episode occurs first, it is often difficult to make the diagnosis until it has been followed by a manic episode. Sometimes it is also difficult to distinguish an acute manic episode from an acute schizophrenic episode.

In contrast to schizophrenics, manics are more apt to exhibit a flight of ideas rather than a loosening of associations. In addition, there is usually a marked increase in activity, either social or physical. Individuals in a manic state tend to be more talkative than usual and have a decreased need for sleep. They are usually quite distractable; their attention is easily drawn to unimportant or irrelevant external stimuli. Finally, they have a potential for an excessive involvement in activities which may bring painful consequences that they do not generally recognize, such as buying sprees, sexual indiscretions, poor business investments, and occasionally reckless driving.

While these are some characteristics of a manic state, it is important to recognize that people with the manic-depressive disorder may also first experience a major depressive episode. However, in contrast to individuals with a major depressive disorder, manic-depressives who suffer a major depressive episode eventually develop a manic episode.

Case Example. Alan Farr, twenty-seven years old, came to the police's attention in an unusual manner. He had been under a physician's care for his manic-depressive disorder for several months and had been placed on medication. One evening, he found himself out of medication and planned to return to the hospital the next day to get more. However, he postponed his visit for several days because he did not have transportation and, as time elapsed, became increasingly manic. As he recognized the impending recurrence of his illness, he began to panic.

One evening, he left the house and began walking. He passed a police officer on patrol and accosted him, demanding to be taken to the hospital so that he could get his prescription. When the police officer refused, indicating that this was not within his line of duty, Alan who at the time was standing in a gas station, took a book of matches out of his pocket. He lit one and dropped it into a small puddle of gasoline on the ground. It immediately ignited and Alan was placed under arrest for arson. He was taken to jail where, without his medication, he became increasingly manic and was eventually transferred to the hospital. Prior to his transfer from jail, the detention officers noted in their log the following comments about his behavior: "Won't stop talking, constantly making jokes, seems on the verge of losing control, doesn't sleep."

In the hospital, he was placed back on medication and his manic behavior subsided after a week. For a period of several weeks, he appeared normal. Then he gradually became depressed, increasingly withdrawn, and slow of thought. His condition gradually worsened until he was no longer responsive to the staff's questions. He spent most of his time in bed, had a poor appetite, lost weight, and began to have suicidal thoughts.

MAJOR DEPRESSIVE DISORDER

In contrast to the manic-depressive disorder, where the manic episodes are usually the most prominent feature of the illness, the person with a major depressive disorder displays a marked loss of interest and pleasure in all usual activities. This may occur only once in a person's life, or often, in similar episodes. The onset may occur at any time.

Physical and psychological symptoms feature marked agitation, restlessness, and depression. The person's appetite is either poor or absent, and sleep is disturbed. Many physical complaints may also be present.

Disturbances in thought content include delusions of sin, guilt, and unworthiness. Suicidal and paranoid thoughts are common. Delusions may also develop around somatic complaints (for example, the person may show an unrealistic concern over cancer). Hallucinations are less common. When they occur, they are usually auditory and have a condemning quality consistent with the delusions of sin, guilt, and unworthiness. An example will illustrate.

Case Example. On a Friday morning, police were called to the residence of Karen Bragen, age twenty-four, by neighbors who heard gunshots. They found Karen sitting quietly in the living room with her face buried in her hands. In the bedroom, they found the dead body of her three-month-old son, who had been shot twice in the head.

From their interrogation of Karen, her husband, and family the police obtained the following information. She had an uneventful pregnancy and, in fact, her husband commented how much happier she had seemed when pregnant. However, shortly after the baby's birth, she began to be depressed. Initially, both she and her husband attributed this depression to postpartum blues, typically seen within several days after a baby's birth.

However, her blues did not go away after a week or two, as is common in postpartum cases. Instead, she began to have bizarre thoughts, which initially occurred in the late afternoon or early evening, particularly when she was alone. These thoughts consisted of fleeting mental images in which she saw herself with a gun, killing her baby and husband.

She tried to get them out of her mind by keeping busy. When this failed, she began a compulsive pattern in which she sat with a book reading for several hours in the late afternoon and early evening while

97

the baby was left in the bedroom. When this did not stop her violent thoughts, she began to lock the bedroom door so that she could not reach the baby.

This was also unsuccessful. One week before the murder, Karen began to hear the voice of her mother with whom she had always had a poor relationship. The voice condemned Karen, saying that she was a poor mother and accusing her of not taking care of the baby. She began to hear her mother's voice coming from the television set.

Her husband told police that, during the two weeks prior to the infant's death, Karen became increasingly withdrawn and was constantly finding fault with herself as a mother. He tried to reassure her, but to no avail. She never told him her violent thoughts.

On the day of the murder, she heard a voice telling her to kill the baby. The voice said that then her problems would be solved because she would no longer have to be a mother. To Karen, in her psychotic state, this seemed to be a perfect solution. In response to the voice's continued urging, she took her husband's gun from the closet, walked into the bedroom, and fired two bullets into the sleeping baby.

This case underlines the serious homicidal and/or suicidal potential associated with this mental illness. If the possibility of a major depressive disorder exists, an officer should always try to get the person to a hospital or a doctor.

Helpful Hints to the Law Enforcement Officer

Because of the confusion, the bizarre behavior, and the capacity for violence of the psychotic, the police officer is often the first one called to the scene when a mentally disturbed person, displaying signs of psychosis, is involved. The officer's ability to handle the psychotic person appropriately is not only important for his own safety and the safety of others (chapters 13–15), but it is also important to the psychotic person, who is probably experiencing tremendous fear. In addition, the ability of the officer to form a trusting relationship with this person may be very important in determining the outcome of further efforts at treatment.

The mental confusion, distortions of thought content, and disturbances of perception increase the possibility that the psychotic will distrust anyone, even those attempting to help. This person may then react with violence.

It is important for the officer to remember to approach the psychotic in the most nonthreatening manner possible. He should avoid any display of force, including guns and restraints, unless the officer suspects that his own safety or the safety of others is threatened.

In the psychotic, sensory awareness is heightened. Consequently, it is important for the officer to reduce sensory input in order to reduce the psychotic's fear. This might include removing all nonessential people from the person's environment, the use of a slow, soft voice by the officer, and the reduction of other sensory stimuli such as police radios, bull horns, and other equipment. By reducing sensory stimuli, the officer helps the psychotic gain control of himself, making him more approachable.

The person suffering from depression is frequently in an ambivalent mental state, unable to make decisions, vacillating between pros and cons. Consequently, this person may argue the opposite of whatever the officer suggests. For example, should the officer suggest hospitalization, the psychotically depressed person may immediately resist the suggestion, saying that he doesn't need to be in the hospital and offering all sorts of reasons to the officer why he can't go. The officer should stick firmly to his decision, regardless of the person's pleading.

It is, therefore, important for the officer to make up his own mind as to what must be done before revealing his decision to the person concerned. Once he has stated the decision, he must act as if there is no other alternative. Surprisingly, officers will find that their firmness is reassuring and that the person, in response, may stop debating and arguing and instead follow the dictates of the officer.

The officer's approach to the person who demonstrates delusional thinking is also important. He should neither argue with the delusions nor agree with them. Rather, he should listen and hear out the person's concerns. He can then suggest that there are others who would like to talk with the person about his concerns and who can do more to help him. Mention of going to a hospital or a clinic may disturb some people, but they are more likely to go with the officer who handles the situation in a tactful and firm manner.

Summary

The police officer frequently comes in contact with psychotic behavior because the psychotic is acting in a strange or violent manner. Consequently, the officer should be aware of the strategies he can use to minimize the danger to others, the psychotic, and himself. He also should be cognizant of the signs of these disorders so he can distinguish them from less serious illnesses, such as personality disorders and neuroses.

Chapters 6–8 have presented descriptions of each of the major classifications of mental illness. Since one of the law enforcement officer's primary responsibilities is to assess and manage deviant behavior, the next seven chapters (9–15) will take a closer look at the most common forms of deviant behavior that the officer is likely to encounter.

BIBLIOGRAPHY

AMERICAN PSYCHIATRIC ASSOCIATION. 1980. *Diagnostic and Statistical Manual of Mental Disorders*. 3d ed., Washington, D.C.: American Psychiatric Association.

BLEULER, E. 1950. *Dementia Praecox or the Group of Schizophrenias*. New York: International Universities Press.

EYSENCK, HANS JURGEN. 1976. *Psychoticism as a Dimension of Personality*. London: Hodder and Stoughton.

FREEMAN, THOMAS. 1976. *Childhood Psychopathology and Adult Psychoses*. New York: International Universities Press.

FREUD, S. 1955. "Mourning and Melancholia." In *Standard Edition*. Vol. 14. ed. J. Strachey. London: Hogarth Press.

FRIEDMAN, A. M., KAPLAN, H. I., and SADOCK, B. J. 1975. *Comprehensive Textbook of Psychiatry*. 2d ed., Baltimore: Williams and Wilkins.

KISKER, G. W. 1972. *The Disorganized Personality*. New York: McGraw-Hill.

KRAEPELIN, E. 1918. *Dementia Praecox*. London: E. and S. Livingstone. REDLICH F. C., and FREEDMAN, D. X. 1966. *The Theory and Practice of Psychiatry*. New York: Basic Books.

PART IV

Assessing and Managing
Abnormal Behavior
in the Field

Chapter 9

Psychopathic Behavior

PSYCHOPATHIC BEHAVIOR is of particular importance to the police officer. A Dallas, Texas, police department study states that although psychopaths comprise only 40 percent of the criminal population, they are responsible for 80–90 percent of all crime (Dallas Police Department 1973).

Alan Harrington, a specialist in this area of abnormal behavior, claims that there are about ten million psychopaths in our country (Harrington 1972). They include unprincipled businessmen, crooked lawyers, high-pressure salesmen, unethical physicians, imposters, and a great assortment of criminals. The terms *sociopath* and *antisocial personality* are sometimes used to describe these persons.

The cases that follow represent a wide variety of abnormalities associated with psychopathic behavior. (The sexual psychopath, a variant of psychopathic behavior, will be explored in more detail in the next chapter.) These cases will serve to focus discussion on the psychopath's characteristics and the underlying factors behind this behavior. The discussion will provide helpful hints to the law enforcement officer in handling this behavior.

Historical Background

Psychopathic behavior was originally described by an English psychiatrist James Prichard, in the nineteenth century. He called those with an unimpaired intellect who had lost their power of self-control *morally insane.* After he introduced this concept, it was first thought that these people might have an organic disease of the central nervous system which caused this morally insane behavior. The term *constitutional psychopathic inferiority* was used to indicate this organic component, which some observers still believe exists.

Studies have shown that there are common characteristics shared by those who manifest different types of psychopathic behavior as well as a developmental history which sets them apart from the norm. We will discuss these characteristics after presenting several case histories.

Case Histories

Case Example. After being persuaded to give up his precarious position on the window ledge of a hotel high above Louisville, Kentucky, Michael Crawford sobbed to sympathetic listeners a tale of despair. Newspaper reporters called to the scene gave considerable attention to his story.

John Flynn, a local policeman read his morning newspaper the next day and recalled a similar incident which had taken place in Boston several weeks earlier. Details of the events were so similar that, out of curiosity, he decided to check further. To his surprise, Michael Crawford and the man rescued from the hotel window ledge in Boston were the same person. With heightened interest, he checked further and discovered that Michael was AWOL from an army hospital, where he had been taken after his first suicide attempt in Boston.

The Louisville police quickly returned him to military control and he was admitted to a nearby army hospital, for evaluation and treatment. After several days on a closed ward, he was transferred to an open ward and allowed to roam the hospital.

He soon found his way to the Red Cross building, where he offered his services to the overworked staff. Very shortly he was their "right hand", showing movies, setting up chairs, serving refreshments, and being helpful in every possible way. Volunteers quickly began to comment how charming, earnest, and hardworking he was. They began to talk at coffee about the patient, the heroic combat record he described (which was not true), and his desire to leave the army and return to college (he had never finished high school). The impression that he made was so great that they began to discuss ways in which they might assist him in achieving his goals after his discharge.

These early discussions of possibly assisting him became even more positive following a fire in one of the hospital buildings. During the fire, Michael led other patients to safety, helped drag equipment out of the building, and performed heroically.

However, the impressed, appreciative volunteers lost their enthusiasm several days later when they discovered that Michael had set the fire. Following his arrest, he was taken to the stockade to await a court-martial. While there, his behavior became so unmanageable that he had to be sent back to the hospital and admitted to the closed ward. Following his return, he made numerous dramatic suicidal gestures, organized a small patient rebellion, and finally escaped from the facility, never to be heard from again.

Case Example. Some citizens in Crescent City and in Hollywood would like to talk to Billy Dalton about a grand hoax on local business-men involving the filming of a television show. A small man in his late thirties dressed in western-style clothing, Billy arrived in Crescent City on Sunday and was gone by Tuesday. In these forty-eight hours, he left a trail of actions still being talked about.

He came to town with a briefcase marked "Paramount" and represented himself as an advance agent for a currently popular television series. He checked into a local motel and told the manager that he needed accommodations for 210 cast and crew members who would be arriving within several days to film a segment for the show. However, he immediately booked seven rooms for the next night to be used by some production company members who would be coming early.

He then contacted the new owner of the local theater, Mr. Chapman, and gave him the same story. He obtained the use of the theater as well as a promise to help him put together a Monday night dinner party for the star of the show. He also secured the local fairgrounds building as a mess hall for the arriving cast and crew.

As Mr. Chapman later recalled, "He struck me at precisely the right moment." The prospect of having a well-known actor help publicize his theater interested Mr. Chapman. Consequently, he not only accompanied Billy to a local bakery and ordered refreshments for the party but also gave him close to $300 to go out and buy the rest of the food for the party.

At 3:30 P.M., on the day of the party, Billy told the hotel manager that he was going to meet the star at the theater. Shortly thereafter, the manager received a call from a man, who identified himself as the star and asked him to tell Billy that he would be a little late.

When the dinner began, with no sign of the production company members but with others invited by Mr. Chapman present, Mr. Chapman received a phone call from an unidentified person who told him that the star had been delayed in another city, but would arrive later.

He never appeared. Mr. Chapman picked up the entire tab and began to become suspicious. The next day, he called Paramount Studios and was informed that they had never heard of Billy Dalton and that there were certainly no plans to film anything in Crescent City. At approximately the same time, Billy was leaving the motel, telling the manager that he was going to a local laundromat to wash some clothing. No one in Crescent City has seen Billy Dalton since.

Several months later in another state, Billy Dalton was arrested and charged with obtaining property by false pretenses. His rap sheet showed fifteen arrests since 1968 for bogus checks, grand theft, drawing checks on insufficient funds, theft by fraud, and other similar offenses. The pre-sentence evaluation included the following excerpt from the report of the court psychologist:

> Mr. Dalton presents himself as a mousy, insecure, extremely nervous little man who is overwhelmed by society's callous disregard for his obvious virtue. This attitude is difficult to understand in view of his record of collisions with the law. His history illustrates his incapacity to learn from experience and his inevitable failures. He does not appear to be conscience-stricken for any of his acts and avoids accepting blame for them.

Case Example. Larry Lindgren graduated 229th out of 240 students in his high school class and started to work in an auto plant where his father had worked for many years. Although he was soon offered an opportunity to become a sponsored trainee, which would eventually mean a better paying and more responsible position, he decided that this job was too dull.

Although he had never been interested in college, he told his father after quitting his job that he was going to a nearby university to look things over. However, he was refused admission because he did not have credits in certain subjects which he had failed in high school. Instead of returning to another regular job, he continued to wander about the campus and to attend classes without formally enrolling. After a while, he became quite comfortable with his masquerade and began to fake report cards to send home to his parents, telling them that he had won a scholarship.

In his biology class, he became interested in the human body. He went out and bought a second-hand stethoscope and a record which played the sounds of normal and abnormal heartbeats. After he had listened diligently to this record and compared the sounds to those of his own heart, he began to walk through the corridors of the university hospital wearing an intern's white coat and carrying the stethoscope protruding conspicuously from the pocket. Because of his large size, he looked older than his age and, consequently, no one questioned his masquerade. He later recounted, "I knew what I was doing; I was the perfect image of the young doctor." Larry spent three years in this environment, observing everything as he walked around the hospital, becoming friendly with the staff, but always being very careful not to overact.

He became enamored of this way of life. One day the idea occurred to him that, if he could keep it up, he might eventually be able to become a doctor. For the next three years, while holding down a job, he continued to go to the hospital and mingle with the students. He became fast friends with many of them, telling them that he worked elsewhere in the hospital.

Finally, he felt ready and "his" class graduated. He even attended graduation, standing in the back as the Dean conferred the degree of Doctor of Medicine on the students. Shortly after his "graduation," Larry had a fake diploma made and moved to another town, where he hung up his shingle and waited for patients to come.

His co-tenant in the building was a dentist who complained to Larry about feeling tired most of the time. From what he had learned and his powers of astute observation, Larry diagnosed his condition as anemia and discovered a bleeding ulcer, which he treated. The dentist was very grateful and became one of Larry's strongest boosters. Soon, patients and money began to roll in. One patient later recalled, "He made us feel so cheerful and healthy because he was young. Children loved him."

Within seven months after opening his practice, Larry was seeing an average of two hundred patients a week. His practice grew and, at the time he was exposed, he was netting many thousands of dollars a year. He had married several years earlier, but his wife was not aware of his masquerade. They enjoyed their new-found affluence by joining a country club, building a new home, and owning two cars.

After several years of practice, Larry began to notice that he was stumbling, becoming awkward with his instruments, and tiring quickly. Privately, he consulted a doctor in another community without revealing his profession or his identity. The doctor told him that he had multiple sclerosis.

Larry's immediate concern was for his family. Knowing that his disease might eventually be fatal, he asked his local insurance agent, without revealing that he had multiple sclerosis, to double his policy. This insurance application was his undoing. A routine credit check revealed that no doctor by that name was licensed in the state. At first, he tried to lie his way out by claiming that he had been licensed in a different state and simply had not had the time to take out a new license. However, when he was asked to produce evidence, he realized his scheme had been uncovered and confessed the entire hoax.

Patients and friends immediately came to his defense. Many wanted to give him money for his defense while others wrote or phoned the prosecutor urging him to drop the charges. At Larry's church, one of the ministers reminded the congregation of the biblical injunction to "judge not, lest ye be judged" and suggested that its members pray for the young doctor, their friend, who was "in a little trouble." One member of the congregation even wrote to the President of the United States, asking for special dispensation for Larry.

Larry was charged with practicing medicine without a license and illegal possession of barbiturates and narcotics. He was sentenced to one year in prison. At his sentencing, the judge stated, "Maybe you helped people. I am not sure. But it is also possible you might have hurt people." The pre-sentence evaluation of the probation officer stated that Larry had shown no remorse and had freely admitted, "I'd do it all over again."

Characteristics

Manipulation of People

The psychopath manipulates people like objects to gain his own ends. Billy Dalton used people to get what he wanted and, when their usefulness was ended, left them stranded. In this way, and through similar behavior, the psychopath not only ends up with no friends but also does not seem to want any.

The psychopath is generally self-centered, with little or no regard for the welfare of others, even though he may be a good con artist and inspire confidence and faith. Like Billy Dalton, he can bring people with whom he comes in contact to do things that they might not do, under normal circumstances, for anyone else. Unfortunately, much of the faith and confidence he inspires only ends in grief and misery.

This ability to manipulate people can also lead the psychopath to remarkable success in almost whatever role he assumes. Larry Lindgren, without a formal education, was able to manipulate people and inspire confidence in himself, becoming remarkably successful in his masquerade as a physician.

Unexplained Failure

Although many psychopaths are above average in intelligence and have periods during their life when they succeed at almost whatever they choose, sooner or later they usually fail. Alan Harrington remarks, "We have one near certainty; sooner or later, when the classic psychopath comes on stage, things will go wrong . . . patterns of temporary success or at least stability are followed by strangely brutal and irresponsible behavior with accompanying stupid and unnecessary falls from grace for which there can be no rational explanation" (Harrington 1971, p. 201).

Single, unexplained failures are often not enough to unmask the psychopath. Only after many failures will people begin to realize that something is indeed wrong. Prior to this, they are more apt to look for shortcomings or mistakes in themselves rather than see the situation for what it is—shrewd manipulation by a psychopath.

Absence of Anxiety

The psychopath is rarely plagued by anxieties, phobias, or psychosomatic symptoms. Like Larry Lindgren, he is most often at ease and poised in situations where a normal person would be tense and upset. How many normal individuals could successfully carry off a masquerade for almost six years and eventually achieve the success of "graduation" from medical school?

However, it is equally important to recognize that, if the psychopathic personality is deprived of the opportunity to act out his abnormal behavior, *situational anxiety* may occur. When Michael Crawford was taken to the stockade to await a court-martial for setting the fire, he became so unmanageable that he had to be transferred to a hospital and admitted to a closed ward. Furthermore, after admission to the closed ward, where his opportunities to act out were more limited, he made numerous and dramatic suicidal gestures as a further consequence of his situational anxiety. In contrast to the neurotic whose anxieties are often unrelenting, the psychopath loses his anxiety when the pressure is relieved—thus the term *situational.*

Absence of Psychosis

The well-integrated and functioning psychopath is not psychotic. His behavior is neither divorced from reality nor does he have delusions or hallucinations. However, like Michael Crawford, he can act crazy to escape an unpleasant situation. The ability to act crazy can present a difficult diagnostic problem to anyone who is called upon to evaluate the psychopath. However, like situational anxiety, the apparent psychosis will tend to disappear when the stress is removed.

Persistence of Self-Defeating Antisocial Behavior

Although a psychopath is capable of plotting and executing very clever crimes to attain a material goal (such as money), he may also follow a pattern of criminal activity that is self-defeating to all personal goals he claims are important. Even after he had the support of the Red Cross volunteers to go to college, Michael Crawford set fire to a portion of the hospital, losing the support that they had previously offered.

Inability to Distinguish Truth from Falsehood

Cleckley, in his book *The Mask of Sanity,* comments on the psychopath's remarkable capacity for disregarding the truth (Cleckley 1955). Like the "physician," Larry Lindgren, the psychopath can appear confident and wholly at ease in situations where the average person would feel embarrassed. It is not enough to realize that the psychopath may lie. It is equally important to know that these lies are not trivial and that the psychopath has a remarkable capacity to live with them as if they were true.

Inability to Accept Blame

When Larry Lindgren was interviewed during his pre-sentence evaluation, he demonstrated no remorse for his activities during his masquerade. Similarly, after Billy Dalton, was caught, he did not appear conscience stricken to the psychologist who evaluated him prior to sentencing. It is characteristic of the psychopath not to accept blame.

Incapacity for Love and Closeness

Although the psychopath may possess an astonishing ability to engender and receive devotion from many people, this person has no real capacity for love. He is unable to form mature relationships with others and finds it difficult to tolerate closeness. If a friendship is developing, he will generally take steps to alienate that person to avoid closeness.

Lack of Insight

Because of his intelligence, it often appears to the casual observer that the psychopath has a remarkable capacity for insight. This is strengthened by the impression that he is always ready to reassess his position, identify his misbehavior, and plan for change. However, his subsequent actions demonstrate not true insight but, rather, as Cleckley has called it, a "mimicry of insight" (Cleckley 1955). He resolves to do better without any real understanding of the behavior which led to his particular situation.

Shallow and Impersonal Responses to Sexual Life

As a corollary to his incapacity for love and closeness, the psychopath is also unable to achieve any deep response in a sexual relationship. This is true despite the notorious promiscuity of many psychopaths of both sexes. On close examination, it is apparent that these sexual activities are shallow, impersonal, and very self-centered.

Callousness and Sadism

Although we will devote greater attention to these topics in the next chapter on aberrant sexual behavior, it is important to note that callousness and sadism are often important characteristics of psychopathic behavior (Blackburn 1975).

Suicide Rarely Carried Out

Michael Crawford's suicidal behavior is typical of the psychopath, who frequently threatens suicide or even makes sham suicidal attempts with a high degree of dramatic content. These gestures, designed to gain attention, are often staged with stunning authenticity. On one of the many occasions when Michael attempted suicide, he staggered dramatically down the hospital corridor, dripping blood from the "slashes" in his chest. In reality, these were only superficial cuts which he had made with a small piece of glass or a razor blade. He had very carefully cut nothing but small capillaries on the skin's surface. However, before this could be discovered, Michael had created quite a stir by collapsing in a moaning heap at the feet of the nurse whose sympathy he was trying to get.

When the rare suicide occurs in the psychopath, it is common for him to die with a surprised look on his face, probably a result of poor judgment in overstepping the bounds of "safe" suicidal behavior.

Periods of Marked Creativity

Because of the psychopath's pattern of self-defeat, repeated failures, criminal activity, and even hospitalization, it is easy to overlook periods of extensive creativity, industriousness, and effectiveness. One of the problems in helping the psychopath is how to convert brief periods of creativity into a stable pattern of behavior, thus avoiding the pattern of self-defeat.

Underlying Factors

The factors underlying psychopathic behavior are not specifically known. However, the difficulties that the psychopath encounters in all forms of interpersonal relationships suggest the importance of a careful examination of early childhood development.

O'Neal and her co-workers, in their study of families of those who eventually developed psychopathic behavior, determined from their data that parental rejection in early childhood, a high frequency of broken homes, alcoholism, and low socioeconomic status were important underlying factors. They also found that those who developed psychopathic behavior have usually encountered a specific form of parental rejection, characterized by either the complete absence of parental discipline or its presence in a very inconsistent or lenient form (O'Neal et al. 1960).

From this, it may be hypothesized that the absence or inconsistency of parental discipline deprives the child of an important mechanism for obtaining feedback about his behavior. This mechanism helps the child to develop his own internalized system (the superego) for controlling his behavior during adult life. Furthermore, not having experienced early parental relationships based on positive interactions, he does not develop any capacity for engaging in compatible adult relationships.

This view presents psychopathic behavior as an acting out against society which, in adulthood, represents the early rejecting parents. Furthermore, the psychopath's absence of anxiety about this behavior, is another reflection of the absence or inconsistency of parental discipline during childhood. Without it, the child has not been able to assess what behavior or situation should make him anxious.

As we mentioned earlier in this chapter, many have thought that psychopathic behavior may have some underlying organic factors. Some studies have tried to demonstrate that the psychopath is constitutionally inferior. Recent research, especially, has looked for evidence of either brain injury or brain damage. However, despite many studies which show high rates of abnormality in the brain wave patterns of adult criminals, there has been no positive proof that this abnormality is a precondition to the development of psychopathic behavior.

Helpful Hints to the Law Enforcement Officer

There are several important signs which help the police officer recognize the possibility that he is dealing with a psychopath.

1. Review the arrest record. The psychopath's rap sheet will reflect a variety of crimes. Because of his immature need for immediate gratification, this person's crimes are extremely unpredictable. Unlike other criminals who tend to develop a specialty and stick with it, the psycho-

path may commit a variety of crimes that range from sodomy to armed robbery and murder. Further, when he commits a crime he may not hesitate to kill his nonresisting victims or witnesses just to experience the sensation of killing.

2. The police officer must develop the ability to recognize the con-man's glib style of conversation. When this is coupled with the psychopath's inability to follow through or engage in any behavior that is not self-seeking, it should tip off the officer as to the kind of person with whom he is dealing.

3. If the police officer is interviewing a suspect whom he finds himself liking or hating too much, that person might be a psychopath. From training and experience, most professionals will develop a professional attitude toward those with whom they come in contact. Generally, there are those whom they like, those whom they do not like, and even some to whom they are indifferent. However, a person who gets them so irritated that they tend to lose their professionalism or who motivates them to want to enter into some type of rescue on his behalf is possibly a psychopath.

4. The police officer should very carefully consider as a possible psychopath the criminal who is able to involve many people in his behavior, his crimes, and his rescue. Many cases in this chapter did not involve the psychopath alone.

5. The well-integrated and functioning psychopath can usually beat a lie detector (polygraph) or at least produce an inconclusive result. The polygraph measures certain physiological corollates of anxiety and guilt, such as skin response, blood pressure, pulse, and respiration; it is an "emotional detective." If the test subject feels guilty or anxious about certain questions, there will be disturbances in the polygraphic pattern. However, since the psychopath is often immune to feelings of guilt and anxiety unless placed under severe stress, these physiological disturbances are not likely to appear even when he is responding to questions which might make the normal person feel guilt or anxiety.

6. Speech is often used to conceal thoughts. This is certainly true of the psychopath. He is completely capable of responding to vague questions with vague answers and to concrete questions with concrete answers. In this way, he is often able to persuade himself that he is telling the truth. For example, if an officer asks a suspect who is a psychopath a vague question such as "What did you do after leaving Los Angeles?" he may reply that he took a plane to Denver. He conveniently omits his stop over in Las Vegas, where he participated in three armed robberies, or in Tucson, where he committed two rapes.

As another example, if the officer asks him if he has ever been in jail before, he may answer "No!" since he can assume that the person is talking about this particular jail. He may, however, have been in several others or in a state penitentiary. Unless specifically asked, he will conclude, with proper justification to himself, that he has not lied in response to the question.

Consequently, it is easy to become discouraged when interviewing the psychopath. It may often be necessary to repeat the question several times and to formulate it in different ways. Only persistent and careful questioning will bring out the necessary information. However, if this procedure is done with hostility, the psychopath is likely to clam up and not respond to further questioning.

7. It is important not to bluff a psychopath. He is a master of bluffing and is certainly better than most officers. The best way to interview him is to prepare yourself by knowing every detail of the case.

8. It is important to be firm and clear with the person who is suspected of being a psychopath. The police officer should say exactly what he means and set appropriate limits on his actions. These tactics are critical to handling the psychopath appropriately. Although the psychopath can be very charming, he can also make an officer very angry and may maneuver an officer into a situation in which he violates the psychopath's rights. This is obviously to be avoided.

Differences Between the Lawbreaker and the Psychopath

While it is true that many criminals show some evidence of psychopathic behavior, there are important differences between the ordinary lawbreaker and the psychopath.

1. The ordinary lawbreaker is most often motivated by what his crime will net him, whether it is $25,000 from a bank robbery or another profitable venture. The psychopath, on the other hand, often steals things for which he has no particular use. He may forge a check for a small amount when he has more than that in his own pocket.

2. The ordinary lawbreaker seeks to avoid detection and apprehension. The psychopath does likewise for a period of time, but if he goes undetected for too long, he commits foolish crimes, leaves telltale clues behind which tend to ensure his apprehension.

3. The ordinary lawbreaker will avoid the police and not volunteer to help them solve crimes. The psychopath, on the other hand, often sees his criminal activities as a game between himself and the police and is often detected in this way.

4. The ordinary lawbreaker generally maintains some creed of loyalty to friends, his family, or even to his opposition to society. The psychopath, however, is an uncommitted, with loyalty to no one and no sincerely held attitudes for or against anything.

Summary

Because of his persistent involvement in antisocial behavior, the psychopath is very likely to come in contact with law enforcement officers. Because of his unique features, he presents specific problems in detection, handling, and care following his arrest. The psychopath is potentially a very dangerous person because he doesn't need a reason to kill anyone, including a police officer.

BIBLIOGRAPHY

AUSUBEL, DAVID PAUL. 1977. *Ego Psychology and Mental Disorder: A Developmental Approach to Psychopathology*, New York: Grune & Stratton.

BLACKBURN, R. 1975. "An Empirical Classification of Psychopathic Personality." *British Journal of Psychiatry* 127: 456–460.

CLECKLEY, H. M. 1955. *The Mask of Sanity.* St. Louis: Mosby.

DALLAS POLICE DEPARTMENT, PLANNING & RESEARCH SECTION. *The Dallas Repeat Offender Study.* January 1973. Dallas: Dallas Police Department.

FRANKS, D. M. 1956. "Recidivism, Psychopath and Personality." *British Journal of Delinquency* 6: 192–201.

GRANT, V. 1977. *The Menancing Stranger.* Oceanside, New York: Dabor Science Publication.

HARRINGTON, A. (December 1971). "Coming of Age of the Psychopath." *Playboy* pp. 201–203.

HARRINGTON, A. 1972. *Psychopaths.* New York: Simon & Schuster.

McCORD, W., and McCORD, J. 1964. *The Psychopath: An Essay on the Criminal Mind.* New York: Van Nostrand.

NATHAN, PETER E. 1980. *Psychopathology and Society.* New York: McGraw-Hill.

O'NEAL, P., BERGMAN, J., SCHAFER, J., and ROBINS, L. 1960. "The Relation of Childhood Behavior Problems to Adult Psychiatric Status." In *Scientific Papers and Discussions.* ed. J. Gottlieb and G. Tourney. Washington, D.C.: American Psychiatric Association.

PRICHARD, J. C. 1837. *A Treatise on Insanity and Other Disorders Affecting the Mind.* Philadelphia: Haswell, Barrington, and Haswell.

Chapter 10

Aberrant Sexual Behavior

ABERRANT sexual behavior represents an important category of abnormal behavior with which the police officer frequently comes in contact. The officer who encounters sex crimes, such as rape, child molesting, and exhibitionism, or crimes which often have an underlying sexual component such as arson, shoplifting, and homicide, will be able to carry out his work more effectively if he has a basic understanding of the psychological concepts associated with these crimes.

The community, because of the threats to its welfare posed by those who engage in aberrant sexual behavior, often places great pressure on law enforcement, challenging its competency if apprehension of the criminal is delayed. The public often does not realize the many obstacles which frequently impede investigation of sexual crimes, such as scanty evidence, lack of witnesses, and the reluctance of victims to file complaints.

Sexually aberrant behavior can arouse feelings of disgust and indignation in the average person, and the police officer is no exception. This personal reaction may decrease the effectiveness of the officer in the performance of his duties. A better understanding of the psychology of sexually aberrant behavior may help the officer handle his personal reactions more effectively, thereby allowing him to deal with this behavior from a broader and more professional frame of reference.

General Definitions and Concepts

Before examining specific types of sexually aberrant behavior, it is important to understand some general concepts relating to normal and abnormal sexual behavior. In this discussion, we have relied heavily on the recent work of Stoller (1975) which, we believe, has particular relevance for the police officer.

Sexuality

Sexuality may be defined as all behavior associated with relations between the sexes and reproductive functions. In the theories of Sigmund Freud, discussed in chapter 3, normal sexuality depends on the successful completion of a sequence of early childhood events between birth and age five. During this time, the person's involvement with and reactions to the various reproductive, receptive, and eliminative organs primarily determine the direction of personality growth. Relations with parents and peers further serve to shape individual identity and personality.

Normal development leads to a mature, adjusted person who is capable, during adulthood or sooner, of entering into relationships with a member of the opposite sex which are both physically and emotionally stable and satisfying. Adult sexual relations are goal directed and designed to achieve satisfaction without excessive fear or guilt.

Although these relations may not be free from conflict, they are generally based on a core of emotional stability which allows for a resolution of any conflicts which may occur. Consequently, those who have attained normal sexual behavior patterns possess an awareness of their own physical and emotional needs and have the judgment necessary to fulfill them realistically within their environment.

Aberration

Just as it is difficult to define *normalcy,* it is equally hard to define *aberration.* Statistical methods are commonly used to distinguish between what is normal and what is aberrant. Generally, aberration is behavior set apart from common behavior by its infrequent occurrence. In our society, "aberration means an erotic technique that one uses for completion of the sexual act and that differs from the culture's traditional definition of normality, in our case gratification by heterosexual, genital intercourse" (Stoller 1975, p. 3).

Stoller divides aberrations into two types: deviations and perversions. Deviations are aberrations that are not primarily a result of forbidden fantasies, especially fantasies of harming others. Included in this category is sexual experimentation, which is carried out primarily as a result of curiosity and is not exciting enough to repeat.

In contrast, perversions, which will be the major subject of this chapter, are "erotic forms of hatred" (Stoller 1975, p. 4). Through them, a person acts out fantasies in a habitual manner to achieve complete sexual satisfaction. The core of hostility in perversions is the fantasy of revenge. This is hidden in the actions that constitute the perversion and usually serves to convert a childhood trauma to a situation of adult triumph. The perversion also contains a strong element of risk-taking, which enhances excitement.

Perverse sexual behavior usually reflects the past history of the person's sexual development, especially the dynamics of the early family setting. Through the perversion, the person turns the earlier childhood trauma into a victory. The need to repeat it is derived not only from the inability to get completely rid of the earlier trauma, but also to gain the revenge against the object that the person perceives as the cause of the trauma.

Aberrant Sexual Behavior and Criminality

Just as all aberrant sexual behavior does not indicate mental illness, all sexually deviant behavior should not be considered criminal. While the mental health professional is interested in sexually aberrant behavior to determine if it is a sign of mental illness, the police officer is interested in it to determine its legality or illegality.

Unfortunately, the laws of our society which determine the legality or illegality of behavior are not always clear or rational. An example is offered by the crimes of *statutory rape* and *assaultive rape*. In the first, a person is liable for criminal action even though sexual intercourse took place between a consenting couple, and the behavior was not sexually aberrant. In the second, assaultive rape involves an unwilling victim and is clearly an example of criminally related aberrant sexual behavior.

In other sex crimes it is often unclear what actions the police should take. Some are *victimless crimes,* either because the partners are consenting (as in a homosexual act) or one person's sexually aberrant behavior is not directed against another person (as in transvestitism).

It is not our purpose to resolve these complex legal issues, but simply to point out to the police officer that the confusion surrounding many laws in this area allows him some flexibility of judgment in determining his course of action. Since he has this opportunity for discretion, it becomes even more important that he understand the underlying psychological principles associated with the varieties of sexually aberrant behavior. This will help him to choose a course of action consistent with individual needs and with the laws of our society.

The Varieties of Aberrant Sexual Behavior

In describing the aberrant forms of sexual behavior, we will focus on their basic characteristics, the underlying factors in their development, and the problems which they present to law enforcement.

Homosexuality

With the recent trends toward liberalization of sexual mores and attitudes, the labeling of homosexuality as a form of aberrant sexual behavior has aroused great controversy. Many groups have consistently attacked this labeling, suggesting that the choice of a partner of the same sex is as normal as a choice of a partner of the opposite sex. Although statistics do not support this claim, the argument is valuable since it helps point out that much homosexual behavior is not criminal.

Many have theorized that there are latent homosexual tendencies in everyone, including those who prefer and engage exclusively in heterosexual relationships. This is evident in the many varieties of exclusively male or female associations which are considered normal, socially acceptable outlets for these latent homosexual tendencies. These can include men's clubs, women's clubs, sporting groups, civic organizations, and others.

Although a continued pattern of homosexual behavior is uncommon, the occurrence of occasional overt homosexual activity in the lives of many individuals is more frequent. Many of these can be classified as childhood experimentation or as a one-time experience during early or middle adulthood growing out of a period of pressure or crisis. It is important to recognize that, for these people, homosexuality is not the dominant sexual outlet and that they invariably return to a normal heterosexual pattern of behavior.

However, for others, early homosexual experiences tend to be repeated and may become the exclusive form of sexual relations. If the behavior is a repetitious acting out of a fantasy, converting early childhood trauma to triumph and containing a core element of hostility directed toward the homosexual love object, it may be a perversion. If this is not the case, the homosexual behavior is deviant but not perverted.

In some people, a homosexual behavior pattern may emerge in early adolescence and continue unabated into and through adulthood. In others, this pattern may first be adopted in later life as the person encounters some great stress, such as marriage and its responsibilities.

Those who experience anxiety about their homosexual behavior are often excellent candidates for treatment, since their anxiety is a motivation toward a therapeutic relationship. Recovery of a normal heterosexual pattern depends not only on motivation but also on the length of time the homosexual behavior has been practiced. The people who began this pattern during early adolescence and have continued it exclusively through adulthood are more difficult to convert to a heterosexual pattern than those who began homosexual relations later in life and have practiced them concurrently with heterosexual behavior.

Homosexual behavior which contains elements of perversion is of particular concern to the law enforcement officer because of its frequent association with other illegal forms of perversion. Furthermore, because perversion, by definition, contains elements of hostility, it is possible that this behavior will be violently directed toward others, thus bringing the problem to the attention of the law enforcement officer.

Fetishism

The fetishist achieves sexual excitement and gratification by substituting an inanimate object or a part of the body for the human love object. The range of fetishistic behavior is great and can include many activities, some of which are normal and others which are highly abnormal. For example, nearly everyone is engaging in fetishistic behavior when they preserve mementos from a loved friend or relative. Similarly, it is also a form of fetishistic behavior when people choose sexual partners on the basis of their conformity to certain preferences of hair color, body shape, or other physical features.

However, the fetishistic behavior which usually comes to the police's attention is associated with an inability to achieve sexual satisfaction through contact with the whole person and the displacement of the potential sexual response to an object or anatomical part which more safely represents the person. In benign forms of fetishism, the revenge and risk-taking associated with this behavior are minimal. However, in other cases, it is not possible for the fetishist to control the hostile impulses, and the object must be truly, not symbolically, harmed or even destroyed. In these instances fetishistic behavior may be dangerous.

Transvestitism

The transvestite achieves sexual excitement and gratification from wearing the clothes and at times enacting the role of the opposite sex. (This is in contrast to the transsexual, who completely assumes the identity of the opposite sex either through behavior or a sex change operation.)

Homosexual transvestites primarily seek out someone of their own sex as a partner for the gratification of sexual desire. To make themselves more attractive for this homosexual relationship, they dress and affect the mannerisms of the opposite sex, becoming male or female impersonators. Other transvestites engage in this behavior less frequently and between periods of normal heterosexual activity. In these cases, sexual aberration is less pronounced.

Since parental attitudes are key factors in the child's development of a proper sexual identity, it is not surprising that confusion of sexual identity in early childhood can be an underlying factor in the later development of transvestite behavior. For example, if the male child is subjected to behavior which attacks his masculinity, one possible refuge from this attack is to deny masculinity through *cross-dressing*, which is commonly associated with transvestites. Alternatively, many transvestites have an early childhood history which includes being forced into an unmasculine role by being cross-dressed. At these times, the child feels extremely threatened and, in such instances, may resort to fantasy as a way of controlling the threat. It is the fantasy which converts the trauma of the experience into a triumph. As the child grows older and becomes sexually active, this fantasy can become associated with sexual satisfaction, and traumatic aspects of cross-dressing can be converted into a pleasurable experience. However, the underlying hostility associated with the earlier traumatic event does not disappear. If not properly controlled through the triumphant fantasy, this hostility can lead to perverse behavior which may come to the attention of the law enforcement officer.

Sadism and Masochism

When someone with a perversion cannot control hostility, sadism and masochism often result. The sadist obtains sexual gratification by inflicting pain upon others, while the masochist achieves the same level of sexual gratification by enduring pain inflicted upon himself. The sadist may achieve this sexual satisfaction by engaging in serious criminal acts, such as torture, rape, and homicide. In other instances, such as arson, the underlying sadistic sexual impulses may not be clearly evident to the police; but the officer who is familiar with the underlying sexual aspect of this behavior should keep this in mind as he conducts his investigation.

While the masochist may not pose as great a danger to the community as the sadist because his impulses lead to activities in which he himself is the victim, it is important to recognize that his behavior may still involve others. For example, in *bondage,* the masochist places himself under the power of a person of the opposite sex, or if a homosexual, under a person of the same sex. He then encourages this person to tie, chain, or beat him in order to achieve sexual excitement. Fantasy both during and after the bondage is an important component for achieving sexual satisfaction and to stimulating continuation of the behavior.

Both sadism and masochism can also represent an acting out of subconscious or unconscious feelings of guilt derived from the repeated fantasy. Associated with these guilt feelings is a need for punishment, which the sadist directs against others and a masochist takes upon himself. A variation of sadistic behavior is its association with psychopathic behavior (chapter 9). This may seem paradoxical since the psychopath operates with a lack of guilt while the sadist is usually motivated by excessive guilt. However, it is important to remember that the psychopath's absence of guilt is in realty a severe repression of guilt dating back to the developmental years. Sadistic behavior, which directs aggressive feelings toward others, also helps keep guilty feelings repressed.

This combination can lead to highly dangerous behavior and is associated with some of the most severe crimes noted. Homicides accompanied by extreme sadistic behavior are commonly the work of sexual psychopaths, who combine within their personality the extremes of sadistic and psychopathic behavior. The following case example is an illustration.

Case Example. In the case of the Boston Strangler, the police photographer's description of Mary Sullivan's body indicated the probability that the offender was a psychopath. Mary Sullivan, killed shortly after Christmas, was described as a cheerful, friendly person who worked as a nurse's aid in a Cape Cod hospital.

She had moved into a third floor apartment with two other women her age. On a Saturday, the two women came home from work, opened the door, and found Mary murdered. The following police photographer's report described the body:

... on the bed in propped position, buttocks on pillow, back against headboard, head on right shoulder, knees up, eyes closed, vitreous liquid, probably semen, dripping from mouth to right breast. Breasts and lower extremities exposed, broomstick handle inserted in the vagina, steak knife on bed, seminal stains on blanket. Knotted about her neck was a charcoal colored stocking, over that a pink silk scarf tied with a huge bow under the chin, and over that, tied loosely, almost rakishly so that one could admit one's hand between it and her neck, a bright, pink and white flowered scarf. A gaily colored New Year's card reading "Happy New Year" had been placed against the toes of her left foot.

Only a psychopath could have been so callously sadistic and still have added that last touch of macabre humor (Frank 1971).

Rape

Some police officers assume that all rapists are sadists, but this oversimplifies a complex subject and deserves separate attention.

Groth (1979) has distinguished between three types of rape: anger rape, power rape, and sadistic rape. In each, it is important to assess the nature of the aggression, the type of assault, the offender's mood, the patterns of offenses, the use of language, the underlying dynamics, the nature of the assault, and the impact on the victim. These differ in each of the three types.

In anger rape, the aggression is more physical than necessary, and the victim is often battered. The assault is usually impulsive and spontaneous, and the offender is generally angry and depressed. Offenses are more often episodic and are accompanied by the use of abusive language. The underlying dynamics concern retribution for perceived wrongs or injustices, or a put down experienced by the offender from a specific victim. The assault is generally of short duration and the victim usually suffers physical trauma to all areas of the body.

In power rape, the rapist generally uses only the amount of force or threat necessary to gain control of the victim and overcome the resistance. In these situations, the assault is generally premediated and preceded by persistent rape fantasies. The offender's mood state is one of anxiety, in contrast to anger and depression. The offenses generally tend to be repetitive and may show an increase in aggression over time. The language of the rapist is more often instructional and inquisitive, frequently giving orders, asking personal questions, and inquiring of the victim's responses. In this instance, the underlying dynamics involve compensation for deep-seated insecurities and feelings of inadequacy. The assault may be carried out over an extended duration of time, with the victim held captive throughout. The victim may be released otherwise physically unharmed. Bodily injury is generally inadvertent rather than intentional.

In contrast to the above two patterns of rape, sadistic rape generally involves an erotic use of physical force. The assault is calculated and preplanned, and the offender's mood is generally one of intense excitement. The pattern of the offenses is often ritualistic, involving bondage, torture, and bizarre acts. The use of language by the offender is commanding and degrading. The actions are characteristic of perversion, as they feature symbolic destruction and elimination. The assault may be extended, and the victim may often be kidnapped and occasionally killed. The victim suffers extreme physical trauma to the sexual areas of the body and in some cases may be mutilated or murdered.

Many myths surround the rapist. To describe this person as oversexed is not only inaccurate but oversimplified. Rape is not an expression of sexual desire as much as it is an expression of other nonsexual needs. Rape is never simply the result of sexual arousal that has no other opportunity for gratification. In fact, a significant percentage of rape offenders are married and sexually active at the time of their assaults.

Rape is always a symptom of some type of psychological dysfunction, either temporary and transient or chronic and repetitive. It is usually a desperate act which results from an emotionally weak and insecure person's inability to handle the stresses and demands of life.

Although rape may cut across all diagnostic categories of psychiatric disorders, the majority of offenders are neither insane nor simply healthy and aggressive. The most prominent defect of the rapist is the absence of any close emotionally intimate relationships with other persons, male or female. The rapist has little innate capacity for warmth, compassion, or empathy.

Although the rapist's judgment under stress may be poor, there is generally no problem with intellectual functioning. The rapist commits this irrational act often as a desperate attempt to deal with stresses which he is unable otherwise to contain and which he believes will destroy him.

In summary, the behavior of the rapist can only be understood by careful study of the offense, the psychological characteristics of the offender, and the events which lead up to the sexual assault.

Exhibitionism

The exhibitionist triumphs over an early childhood trauma by the impulsive exposure of his own genital organs or his entire body. To the police, this usually harmless form of sexual aberration often presents problems because of the reaction of the community rather than the reality of any actual harmful threat posed. Exhibitionism therefore, provides a good example of the confused situation which can arise from legal restrictions that vary from locality to locality—because of the different standards and mores of the community—rather than from the behavior itself.

In our own society, although exhibitionism of the genitals is prohibited by law, many acceptable forms and forums for exhibitionism have been sanctioned, including beauty contests, movies, and magazines.

The exhibitionist is not oversexed; the opposite is true. Most exhibitionists lack overt aggressiveness and self-confidence and feel markedly inferior to others. Furthermore, the exhibitionist often shows an indifferent attitude toward the opposite sex. What power exhibitionists possess is achieved through their behavior.

This is an important consideration in understanding why exhibitionists always act as if they wish to be caught. As Stoller (1975, p. 130) points out, most exhibitionistic behavior of men occurs following a humiliation, sometimes at work, or from a woman, often the exhibitionist's wife. The exhibitionist then takes to the street, searching out a woman to whom he can exhibit himself. Overwhelmed by tension, the exhibitionist carries out his compulsive behavior unaware of why he needs to, but clearly preoccupied with the desire to experience the risk rather than a concern about being caught.

In fact, most police officers note that exhibitionists are often easily caught because they are reluctant to get away. To a normal person, this behavior is often incomprehensible. Furthermore, an officer is often put off by the exhibitionist's behavior after he is caught, which appears peaceful and pleasant.

Stoller's theory of perversion (1975, p. 131) helps us to understand the male exhibitionist's unusual behavior. At the conclusion of the exhibitionistic behavior, the risk has been run and surmounted; the trauma has been converted to triumph. The police are not the risk, nor is being caught the risk which the exhibitionist is attempting to overcome. Rather, the police become the agents of the triumph. The real risk for the exhibitionist arises from the humiliation which occurred earlier in the day, usually a repeat of some earlier childhood humiliation that left him feeling impotent and less masculine. The real risk for the exhibitionist is therefore not that he will be caught but that the humiliation will persist. Displaying himself is a demonstration that he has not been humiliated or defeated by women. The woman who is the victim of this behavior and who becomes shocked, angry, and frightened and calls the police proves to the exhibitionist that he has reversed the childhood situation. He is now complying with a necessary part of his fantasy in that she becomes the attacked one and he is the attacker. When he is arrested, he is content because the arrest proves, however briefly, that he is potent—potent enough to create a disturbance that involves not only a victim, but also the official agency of society, the police. Thus, his exhibitionism clearly reverses the feeling of humiliation associated with the original childhood trauma and turns this trauma into revenge and triumph.

Voyeurism

The voyeur achieves sexual gratification by watching a nude woman or man in some form of the sexual act. The "Peeping Tom," as he is popularly known, is usually, but not always, harmless and more of a nuisance than a serious threat to others in the community. He is less frequently apprehended than others because the triumph over trauma contained in his fantasy is associated with the secretiveness of the behavior.

Voyeurism may be associated with a wide range of deviant sexual behavior. While some may only look, others may employ voyeurism as a prelude to further sexual activity which may be aggressive and violent.

The simple voyeur engages in immature sexual behavior, more appropriate to a very early stage of development. Normally, this curiosity about anatomical differences and the manner in which sexual organs function reaches a peak between ages three and five. During this time, there is considerable peeping and displaying behavior by children. Parents often make many demands in their attempts to divert this curiosity into more acceptable forms of behavior while, at the same time, allowing their children to satisfy their desire to know more about sex.

A too prudish attitude may instill in children a morbid curiosity which may later result in an irresistible desire to peep. Likewise, very strict prohibitions and overly severe punishment may make children fearful of normal sexual activity.

Incest

Incest is the practice of sexual intercourse between closely related persons whose marriage is prohibited by law. Prohibition against incestuous relations is practically universal, but the laws against it and the proscribed punishments vary considerably.

Incest is not a sexual aberration in the same sense as homosexuality, fetishism, and exhibitionism because it does not involve difficulty with normal heterosexual intercourse. However, it is considered a form of sexual aberration because it violates normal societal values and may be perversely associated with a recurrent fantasy containing elements of erotic hatred.

The young son or daughter who is forced or enticed into incest by either mother or father will be thrown into a severe conflict. Resulting guilt and anxiety may lead to profound regression and mental illness.

Sociologically, incest is viewed as a threat to the basic fabric of society and its principal unit, the family. However, the prohibition against incest does not prevent the development of strong erotic interests between family members. Consequently, many family activities are designed to divert these erotic interests into normal and acceptable behavior. Failure in this process may often be an underlying factor in family disputes and should be taken into account by the police officer when intervention becomes necessary.

Pedophilia

Like the person who commits incest, the pedophile, or child molester, chooses an inappropriate love object. A pedophile whose sexual object is a child of the opposite sex is a heterosexual pedophile; one who is attracted to a child of the same sex is a homosexual pedophile.

The overwhelming majority of pedophiles may also be assessed in relation to their ability to interact with women and children. One type of pedophile is unable to interact socially with women because of anxiety, but can be sexually aroused by them. These people experience less sexual anxiety with children. Another type of pedophile may interact socially with adult women, but is unable to become sexually aroused by them. This type is sexually aroused only by children. Finally, the last category can neither interact socially with women nor be sexually aroused by them. They are sexually aroused only by children.

Groth has described two types of pedophilia pathology—the *fixated* pedophile and the *regressed* pedophile. In the fixated pedophile, the primary sexual orientation is to children. This interest usually begins in adolescence without an identifiable precipitating stress or feeling of distress. The behavior is more persistent and compulsive, and the offenses are usually preplanned. In this group, male victims tend to be the primary targets (homosexual). The offender generally has little contact with women of his age and is usually single. Alcohol and drug abuse are usually not associated with the offense.

In contrast, the regressed pedophile's primary sexual orientation is to women his own age. His pedophilic interests emerge in adulthood and are generally identified with a precipitating stress. The pedophilic involvements tend to be episodic, and the initial offense may be impulsive rather than premeditated. In contrast to the fixated pedophile, the offender usually replaces a conflictual adult relationship by involvement with a child; the child is therefore a pseudo-adult substitute. Female victims are most often the target of this pedophilic behavior. The regressed pedophile is usually able to have sexual contact with adult women. In many instances, his offense may be alcohol related and is clearly an attempt, although maladaptive, to cope with specific stresses in life.

It is important to note that violent behavior toward children may occur in either category and depends upon the nature of the fantasy associated with pedophilic behavior. Therefore, the police officer should always be alert to the underlying importance of fantasy and should endeavor, sometimes with professional assistance, to determine what the fantasy is as a way of determining whether the pedophile is likely to commit actual physical violence.

Helpful Hints to the Law Enforcement Officer

Because some sexual deviations are against the law and because crimes are committed in association with or as a result of these deviant sexual motivations, it is important for the law enforcement officer to acquire professionalism in dealing with the sexual offender.

The police officer should examine his own attitudes toward sexual aberrations and recognize that these offenses result from motives and impulses which are often not understood or controllable, rather than from moral perversity. This does not lessen the seriousness of crimes associated with sexual aberrations but should increase the officer's ability to act professionally and responsibly.

This professionalism should also carry over into contacts with the victims. If they are not treated respectfully and courteously, they may be unwilling to divulge information which could be helpful in identifying and apprehending the offender.

Homosexuality

The officer who encounters homosexual behavior must have an attitude which will allow him to objectively examine whether any criminal element has been associated with it. Failure to do this may often not only result in an inappropriate arrest but could also lead to a citizen's complaint against the officer(s) involved and the possibility of legal action against the department or the city.

Consequently, the officer should approach each incident involving homosexual behavior with tact, indicating respect for the individual's choice of behavior while, at the same time, pursuing his concern that a criminal act may have been committed. The empathetic officer who acts in this manner will avoid placing the homosexual on the defensive, decreasing his anxiety about the situation, thereby perhaps eliciting his cooperation.

But the officer should not automatically assume that all homosexual behavior is between consenting adults. The pressure of an active partner in a homosexual relationship can often make the passive partner willing to consent while feeling an underlying resistance.

Finally, the officer should also take into consideration the environment in which the homosexual behavior has taken place. For example, if it occurs in a public place in association with pick-ups or solicitation, it may be criminal, in contrast to its occurrence in the privacy of the home. This criminality will vary, however, in different jurisdictions.

Fetishism

It is rare for fetishistic behavior to come to an officer's attention since the fetish is usually inanimate or a part of the body. Because fetishism does not usually involve another person, it may not be associated with criminal behavior.

However, some episodes of shoplifting are associated with fetishistic behavior. The objects sought have significant value through the sexual feelings which they arouse. In these cases, shoplifting becomes a fetishistic experience and exemplifies how aberrant sexual behavior can indirectly lead to crime. If it is not suspected, it may be missed as an underlying factor in the crime.

Finally, fetishism occasionally results in violent behavior if the person is aggressively pursuing a particular part of another's body or an object belonging to someone else unwilling to give it up.

Transvestitism

Like fetishism, transvestitism does not usually involve the police, since most transvestites are clever about concealing their true sexual identity and do not call attention to themselves.

However, some are more overt and can present a problem to the officer when their behavior is called to his attention by outraged members of the community. It is important for the officer not to overreact to these pleas. There is usually little he can do, except to encourage the transvestite to be more considerate.

Exhibitionism

In most cases, the law enforcement officer should not consider exhibitionists as dangerous criminals. These people usually lack the ability to demonstrate normal levels of aggression and are more passive than the average. Also, exhibitionists do not usually demonstrate a tendency to progress to more serious or violent crimes unless these are associated with sadism or masochism. However, the police officer should be aware that arrests for nuisance offenses such as exhibitionism and voyeurism are commonly found in the case histories of convicted rapists and lust murderers.

From this discussion, it is apparent that law enforcement officers who handle sex crimes must know enough about sexual aberrations to be able to make appropriate judgments about each sexual criminal as an individual. This is true not only for the specialist in sex crimes, who is usually trained and experienced, but also for beat patrolmen, especially those in small departments that do not have specialized personnel readily available.

Common misconceptions about sexual criminals include the beliefs that there is a high correlation between brain damage and sexual deviancy and that sexual offenders are usually suffering from severe mental illness. Furthermore, while hard drugs are rarely a factor in sexual crimes, there appears to be a strong connection between the use of alcohol and deviant sexual behavior since excess alcohol leads to the release of inhibitions.

Although overt aggression is relatively infrequently associated with sexual aberration, hostile fantasies are common. For this reason, police officers should *always* be alert to the potential for dangerous behavior. In questioning those with sexual aberrations, the officer should go beyond the actual behavior and try to find out more about the person's fantasies to determine if perversions and erotic hatred are present. By doing so, the officer can better determine this person's potential dangerousness.

Summary

This chapter has outlined several varieties of aberrant sexual behavior, their characteristics, and their importance to the police officer.

The criminality of aberrant sexual behavior can vary considerably. Not all forms of it are criminal, nor are all sexual aberrants criminals. Only by understanding the characteristics of the individual sexual aberrant will the officer be able to maintain a professional attitude. This attitude should include a recognition that while the sexual criminal is not necessarily a monster, he is also not simply an unfortunate person. This person should neither be treated inhumanely nor be allowed to involve others in his aberration to the detriment of others' welfare and freedom of choice.

BIBLIOGRAPHY

BIEBER, I. 1962. *Homosexuality.* New York: Basic Books.

EYSENCK, H. J. November 1973. "Personality and Attitudes to Sex in Criminals." *The Journal of Sex Research* 9:295.

FRANK, G. 1971. *The Boston Strangler.* New York: New American Libraries.

GAGNON, J. H., and SIMON, W. 1970. *Sexual Encounters Between Adults and Children.* SIECUS Study Guide, no. 11. New York: SIECUS.

GROTH, A. N. 1975. *A Typology of Pedophilia.* Connecticut Sex Offender Program. Hartford: State of Connecticut.

GROTH, A. N. 1979. *Men Who Rape: The Psychology of the Offender.* New York: Plenum Press.

HOWELLS, K. 1978. "Sexual Attitudes of Aggressive Sexual Offenders." *British Journal of Criminology* 18:170–174.

KAIPMAN, B. 1954. *The Sexual Offender and His Offenses.* New York: Julian Press.

McDONALD, J. 1973. *Exhibitionism.* Springfield, Ill.: Charles C Thomas.

MEISELMAN, KARIN CARLSON. 1978. *Incest: A Psychological Study of Causes and Effects With Treatment Recommendations.* San Francisco: Jossey-Bass.

STOLLER, R. J. 1975. *Perversion: The Erotic Form of Hatred.* New York: Pantheon Books.

Chapter 11

Delinquent Behavior

UP TO THIS POINT, our discussion of abnormal behavior has focused on the adult. However, the abnormal behavior of the juvenile offender also poses significant problems for the law enforcement officer.

General Considerations

Most police officers come in contact with juveniles only when they have indulged or are indulging in antisocial behavior. Because of his limited range of contacts with juveniles, an officer may perceive most children as either delinquent or potentially delinquent. Although common sense tells us that this is not true, it is sometimes easy for the police officer to develop negative attitudes towards those juveniles he must encounter.

The line between *delinquent behavior* and *delinquent criminal behavior* is not always clear. For example, many offenses for which a juvenile may be arrested and, therefore, labeled a criminal are not those for which an adult would be detained. Running away from home, violation of curfew, and possession of alcohol are not offenses for which an adult would be detained. This is not to suggest that an officer should ignore or condone these actions; rather, a referral to another community agency might be more helpful to the child than a referral to juvenile court.

The officer's flexibility in decision making when dealing with juveniles makes it even more important for him to understand delinquent behavior. The appropriate use of this flexibility may not only prevent a child from acquiring the stigma associated with a juvenile criminal record but may also help prevent the progression of delinquent behavior to a point where it becomes a fixed life-style, continuing into adulthood and leading to an adult criminal record.

Before presenting some helpful hints to the law enforcement officer for handling delinquent behavior, it is important to discuss more specifically some of the underlying factors involved in the onset of antisocial, or delinquent, behavior.

Underlying Factors

Broken homes, neglect, poverty, low intelligence, brain damage, mental illness, and other factors have been proposed at one time or another as the "causes" of delinquency. However, none, in isolation, has stood the test of time or scientific scrutiny. Rather, juvenile delinquency is a series of complex behavior patterns involving many factors which have complex relationships with each other.

In today's society, it is often tempting to look for simple answers to complex problems. Oversimplifications, such as "Delinquency is caused by parents being too easy on their kids," or "All delinquents are suffering from emotional confusion and an identity crisis," should be avoided.

To know more about the factors which underlie delinquent behavior, it is important to be aware of important stresses during childhood and adolescence. The stress situations to be presented are not exhaustive but are intended only as examples of those situations that can lead to delinquent behavior.

Childhood

When a child experiences rejection, it is not unusual for him to disappear. Feeling that no one wants him, he may indicate his anger by running away. Through this retaliation, the child is saying "I don't want you" in response to the rejection. Alternatively, the child may decide to test his parents as a way of finding out if they really care. These tests may include accidental arson, in which the child lights a match to see what might happen (for example, a lot of attention).

The death of a loved one, particularly a parent, may also lead to a child's antisocial behavior. Instead of expressing feelings of depression and grief, the child may demonstrate hostility against society for having taken the parent away.

Sometimes a child may be labeled as a troublemaker by teachers, playmates, and parents with little basis in fact. However, once labeled, the child may begin to act as others see him. For example, if you are going to be blamed every time something is missing, then you might as well take it and enjoy it; or if you are going to be blamed for starting a fight no matter what happens, then probably the best way to handle things is to hit the other guy first and at least get an advantage.

Antisocial behavior may also result from conflicts with parents. Some parents are overprotective and overindulgent while others are too strict. Some may set standards of conduct and/or achievement which no child can possibly attain, while others do not set any goals for their children. Many parents are so busy trying to maintain their own marginal adjustment that they are unable to help their child handle his problems. These parents, through their behavior, may indirectly encourage the child to act out as a way of placing the blame for their own failures on the child.

Adolescence

Adolescents can be affected by the same stresses of childhood which have been described, but they are also subject to other stresses unique to this period of life. For example, as a child grows older, he may begin to face stresses with regard to a choice of schooling, particularly whether to go to college. Difficulties with parents may increase because, as the child grows older, he is able to be more independent; or he may want to remain a child and not grow up. This difficult choice between independence and dependence may lead to conflict with the parents, who also have mixed feelings about watching their child grow up.

As the teenager searches for an identity, he may have trouble with his self-image and worry about his popularity. A girl may have difficulty finding an acceptable moral code; a boy may feel uncertain as he begins to relate to girls socially. Anxiety and other feelings may lead to antisocial behavior—an inadequate way of resolving them.

Finally, if the teenager finds as he grows up that adolescence does not meet his expectations, he may become depressed and isolated. He may conclude that he is a failure because others have goals that they are striving toward, but he does not. Faced with loneliness and isolation, he may engage in acting-out behavior to enhance his self-image.

An adolescent's ability to handle these stresses will be dependent on the strengths which he has developed while growing up. If his self-image is adequate, he will be better able to withstand these stresses, and the likelihood of his resorting to delinquent behavior as a means of dealing with these situations is less.

If he is unable to handle these stresses, except by developing a pattern of delinquent behavior, he is likely to come in contact with the police. Through his actions, the officer inadvertently may support the continuation of acting-out behavior or he may be able to offer help before more serious trouble occurs. Consequently, it is important for an officer to recognize what he shouldn't do and what he should do when confronted with juveniles' aggressions.

Helpful Hints to the Law Enforcement Officer

In the opinion of many juveniles, the police officer has two strikes against him even before contact occurs. First, to some, he is a symbol of all bad experiences with other authority figures, including fathers, mothers, teachers, and older siblings. As a result, the officer may become a victim of displacement, as angry feelings the juvenile has for other authority figures are put upon the officer.

In addition, the norms of the juvenile's peer group may dictate that the police should be viewed as enemies and that toughness is demonstrated by "not letting the cops shove you around" or by "clamming up" whenever an officer asks questions. It is, therefore, important for an officer to recognize that any relationship he forms with a juvenile will be dependent upon the manner in which he approaches this person, the methods he uses, and his ability to communicate.

Negative Approaches

Regardless of what abusive language may be used by a juvenile, the officer should never respond in kind. He must remain professional at all times and treat the youth with courtesy and respect, at least until the juvenile's conduct clearly shows that he does not merit this treatment.

An officer should never make fun of juveniles or their predicament. A deputy recently stopped two boys riding their motorcycles along the side of a country dirt road. While he was writing out a citation for this illegal activity, another deputy, who had arrived on the scene, sat in his car and smiled. What he was actually smiling about was never determined, but the boys interpreted it as being directed at them. Later, they told others that the sheriff's department "stunk" and that deputies had nothing better to do but drive around and hassle teenagers who were riding bikes too close to the road. This incident certainly did not improve the officers' image.

Police officers should avoid using excessive authority. Although an officer should be firm, he should not be overbearing. Juveniles will not respond positively to an approach which implies, "I'm a cop and you kids have to do what I say." The officer who is afraid that he will lose control of a situation unless he adopts an overbearing attitude is in trouble from the beginning. Children are very sensitive to the insecurities of adults, and the officer who is overbearing will be tuned out.

While nothing will make the average officer angrier than an awareness that the person to whom he is speaking is not listening, police often do this themselves, especially with juveniles. A local judge reported that this is a frequent complaint of those brought to the Juvenile Court Center. For example, if an officer has found a juvenile out after curfew, he should listen to him and learn the circumstances. This will let the juvenile see that the officer is interested in what he is saying.

Although traffic laws should be enforced, many juveniles complain that the officer doesn't give them a second chance on questionable offenses. Too rigid enforcement of minor traffic laws against juveniles may be related to an officer's unwillingness to listen to reasons a juvenile gives for his actions. For example, a juvenile may not interpret certain traffic control procedures in the same way as an adult. An adult who gets a speeding ticket is more likely to dismiss it as bad luck or concede, after reflection, that he deserved it. However, because a juvenile is usually more insecure, he is more likely to feel that the officer was unfair because someone down the street "speeds all over the neighborhood and never gets caught."

In these minor offenses, justice may be better served if an officer is somewhat lenient. A warning, administered firmly but with respect for the juvenile as a person, may give him a good feeling about his interaction with the officer. Giving a citation, even though it is technically justified, may turn the juvenile off and leave him with the impression that the police's main goal in life is to harass kids.

Some officers refuse to help juveniles in situations where they would normally offer assistance to adults. When this occurs, the juvenile feels discriminated against.

Officers should not talk about a juvenile or his actions as if he were not present. Reciting a person's offenses, especially in a way which will cause embarrassment or shame, is not advisable. Officers should avoid lecturing or sermonizing and confine their communications either to advice or clear admonishment.

Finally, it is important for an officer never to lie to a juvenile. If an officer gives a juvenile the impression that certain actions will or will not be taken and then does not follow through, the juvenile will feel betrayed and angry. Deception and a failure to keep promises are doubtful policies with anyone; with juveniles, they are never advisable. If this person develops an early mistrust of law enforcement, it is unlikely that trust will ever be regained.

Positive Approaches

Officer should respect juveniles as they would adults. Even if a juvenile is wrong, the officer should be patient. He should remember that children test limits, not only with parents and teachers but also with the police.

The officer should be firm but not grim. Humor and a relaxed manner can reduce tension, dispel hostility, and help ease a situation. This approach will help a juvenile to see that police officers are human and compassionate and that they can understand how a person feels.

An officer should explain his actions and answer a juvenile's questions. He should recognize that explanation is different from justification. Justification may not be necessary, but an explanation is always useful.

While it may be appropriate for an officer in some situations to criticize a juvenile's behavior, an officer should never attack his personality or character. In treating a child, a therapist tries to help a child understand that it is certain aspects of his behavior which are not acceptable, rather than his entire personality. This principle also applies to the interactions between police and juveniles. The focus should always be on the offending behavior and should not attack the juvenile's worth as a person ("that behavior was stupid" rather than "you are stupid").

An officer should become familiar with those agencies in the community concerned with the welfare of children and adolescents. He should be acquainted with their programs as well as their eligibility and referral policies. In larger communities, there is usually a book available listing those resources offering programs for juveniles. All officers should be familiar with this reference, and those assigned to juvenile work should have a copy readily available.

Finally, it is important for law enforcement officers to be involved with the community's youth through activities which may include police department tours, athletic and other school programs, university courses, and visits to juvenile court centers and detention homes.

Summary

In this chapter, we have presented some of the more important issues for law enforcement officers who work with juveniles. The officer should recognize that juveniles are people and that a knowledge and understanding of child and adolescent behavior will enhance his ability to rehabilitate children who stray. The effective officer may also be able to avoid placing many of them in the criminal justice system through the juvenile court.

We have suggested that there is no single cause or cure for the juvenile's complex behavior but that stress situations in childhood and adolescence are important indicators. Finally, we have presented some kinds of police behavior which turn juveniles off and have also suggested more desirable approaches that will help improve communication.

By following these prescriptions, the professional officer cannot only carry out his law enforcement responsibilities but may also perform a responsible community service through helping to guide and direct the growth of young people.

BIBLIOGRAPHY

AICHORN, A. 1935. *Wayward Youth.* New York: Viking Press.

FERDINAND, T. N., and LUCHTERHAND, E. G. 1970. "Inner-City Youth, the Police, the Juvenile Court and Justice." *Social Problems* 17:510–527.

HAGAN, J. L. 1972. "The Labelling Perspective, the Delinquent, and the Police: A Review of the Literature." *Canadian Journal of Criminology & Corrections* 14:150–165.

McCORD, W. 1956. *Psychopathy and Delinquency.* New York: Grune & Stratton.

MALMQUIST, CARL P. 1978. *Handbook of Adolescence: Psychopathology, Antisocial Development, Psychotherapy.* New York: J. Aronson.

PURSUIT, D. 1972. *Police Programs for Preventing Crime and Delinquency.* Springfield, Ill.: Charles C Thomas.

RUSINKO, W. T., JOHNSON, K. W., and HORNUNG, C. A. 1978. "The Importance of Police Contact in the Formulation of Youths' Attitude Toward Police." *Journal of Criminal Justice* 6:53–67.

Chapter 12

Drug Dependent Behavior

DRUG DEPENDENT behavior usually occurs along with more basic patterns of maladaptive behavior. It appears not only in people with personality disorders but also in those with neuroses and psychoses. Before proceeding to a more detailed discussion of specific forms of drug dependent behavior, its underlying factors, and behavioral manifestations, we will present some general considerations to assist the law enforcement officer in developing a comprehensive perspective on this critical police problem.

General Considerations

A drug may be defined as a chemical substance which, when introduced into the body, produces changes in the body's functioning. For example, if a person has a fever, he uses aspirin to lower it.

Some drugs also affect psychological functioning. For example, a small quantity of PCP (Phencyclidine) will cause a disturbance in psychological balance through hallucinations, both visual and auditory, derived from false perceptions of the environment.

Because of the impact of drugs on their behavior, drug abusers often come to police attention. Approximately half of all incidents the police encounter are related to the use or abuse of alcohol and other drugs. These may include a traffic accident involving a drunken driver, a heroin overdose brought to the emergency room, or a homicide occurring during a drug rip-off.

Because the police officer most frequently sees the most sordid effects of drug abuse, he should beware of the tendency to classify all abusers as drunks, junkies, acid freaks, and pot heads with all the moral condemnation that these terms imply. By becoming thoroughly familiar with the behavioral aspects of drug use and abuse, the officer can approach this aspect of his job in a professional and nonjudgmental manner.

The point at which drug use is transformed into abuse is largely determined by point of view. *Medically,* the doctor considers the use of aspirin to relieve headache and reduce fever as legitimate. However, he would consider it a case of aspirin abuse if a patient had swallowed dozens of aspirin tablets in a suicide attempt, arriving at the hospital unconscious. Likewise, the physician may legitimately prescribe morphine, an opiate, to ease the suffering of a terminal cancer patient. This use of an opiate is appropriate when nothing else will alleviate the severe pain. From these examples, it is clear that a physician considers a drug abused if it does not contribute to the person's ultimate health and well-being.

Drug use and abuse can also be viewed *behaviorally.* For example, LSD was originally synthesized to be used under carefully controlled experimental conditions in the treatment of certain personality disorders. However, when abused through indiscriminate use without expert supervision, it produces abnormal behavior which may be dangerous to the user and to others.

Drug use and abuse can also be defined *legally.* For instance, while it is legal to sell and use alcohol, it is illegal to drive an automobile while intoxicated, a condition defined in most states as a blood alcohol concentration of greater than .10. Even though a person may not have actually reached this level of blood alcohol, he may still be abusing alcohol if he stops at his favorite bar on the way home from work to have several highballs, knowing full well that he must drive after drinking. However, other drugs, regardless of their impact on behavior, are considered as having been abused simply because their possession is illegal.

From these examples, it is apparent that the precise understanding of drug abuse depends upon the circumstances of the user and the viewpoint of the observer.

Definitions

To understand behavioral aspects of drug abuse, it is important to be acquainted with the proper definitions of those terms that commonly describe individual reactions to drugs. These terms describe behavioral responses associated with continued use or sudden cessation of drugs. We will categorize these drugs according to their impact on the user.

Intoxication

Intoxication is the state or condition induced through excessive use of any drug, although it most commonly refers to alcohol. In defining intoxication, the critical issue is not how much of the drug has been taken into the body, but rather how much of it is there at any one time and for how long. For example, it is not the quantity of alcohol a person consumes that governs the impact, but how much is in the bloodstream at a specific time.

However, since most officers do not have immediate access to blood, we generally conclude that a person is *intoxicated* when his behavior changes. Common indices are loud or slurred speech, uncoordinated movements, and/or overaggressive behavior.

Addiction

The addict is a person who cannot abstain from the use of a drug *without suffering severe physical symptoms.* This *withdrawal syndrome* is a combination of painful and debilitating physical reactions that occur after an addicting drug is withdrawn.

If the heroin addict appears hurried, preoccupied, and impatient to get his next fix, it is often to prevent withdrawal symptoms. In fact, many addicts continue taking addicting drugs not to seek a new high but to avoid the discomfort of withdrawal.

Tolerance

All drugs that are addicting,—capable of producing the withdrawal syndrome—also produce tolerance. This term refers to the inability of the individual to experience the same effects from a drug over a period of time from the same dose. If the effect is to remain the same, the user must constantly increase the dose. It is important to recognize that not all drugs which produce tolerance are addicting because they do not all produce a withdrawal syndrome.

Habituation

In contrast to addiction and tolerance, which are physiological terms associated with drug abuse, *habituation* refers to a psychological aspect of drug abuse. All drugs which affect behavior are, to some extent, habit forming. The degree to which they are habit forming is a combination of their capacity to produce tolerance, the behavioral changes they produce, and the personality characteristics of the user.

In addiction, psychological dependence is a factor, but physical dependence is primary. In habituation, it is the psychological dependence which is important because there is no physical dependence.

Drug Dependence

Drug dependence is a general term describing the compulsive use of a drug for whatever reason. The specific type of dependence is indicated by the name of the drug, for example, heroin dependence, alcohol dependence, and so on.

Using these terms, we can categorize drugs which influence behavior as follows:

1. *Heroin* produces addiction, tolerance, and habituation.
2. *Alcohol* produces addiction, tolerance, and habituation.
3. *Barbiturates* produce addiction, tolerance, and habituation.
4. *Amphetamines* produce tolerance and habituation but not addiction.
5. *Cocaine* produces extreme habituation but does not produce addiction or tolerance.
6. Minor tranquilizers, such as *Valium* and *Librium,* do not produce addiction but can produce tolerance and habituation.
7. *Marijuana, PCP,* and *LSD* do not produce addiction or tolerance and in most people have only a mild habituating effect.

Although these categories describe essential differences in the physical and psychological effects of these commonly abused drugs, it is also important to recognize that the kinds of behavior associated with them have many features in common. The following discussion will explore the characteristics of drug related behavior that the police officer is most likely to encounter during his duties.

Alcohol

The frequency with which the police officer finds behavior influenced by alcohol indicates alcohol's role as the most commonly abused substance in the United States. If an officer makes an arrest, it may be one of the more than 50 percent of arrests related to alcohol. If he is on the road investigating a fatal accident, there is a very good chance the accident involves a drunken driver. It is, therefore, important for the police to be aware of alcohol and the behavior it engenders.

Characteristics of Alcohol Abuse

Many theories have been developed to explain the causes of excessive drinking. Some theories hold that people drink because they are depressed; others point out that excessive alcohol use is often associated with feelings of guilt. Feelings of inadequacy, failure, and low self-esteem, as well as poor interpersonal relationships, are also factors underlying excessive alcohol intake.

Chafetz describes two types of people who drink to excess, the reactive and the addicted (Chafetz 1959). The reactive, or episodic, drinker usually demonstrates a reasonable adjustment in family, education, work, and social areas as well as an ability on most occasions to move toward realistic goals. However, he tends to use alcohol to excess when he is *temporarily* overwhelmed by a stressful situation and has no other means at his disposal to handle the stress.

The addicted alcoholic's behavior is in contrast. (In using the term *addiction,* Chafetz is not adhering to the strict definition given previously.) His life-style reveals a marked disturbance in adjustments at home, school, and work. In contrast to the reactive pattern, there is no marked stress prior to alcohol abuse. Rather, the addictive alcoholic's entire life appears as a single stress. The pattern of excessive drinking is repetitive, contributing to a marked decrease in the effectiveness of the person's behavior.

Other characteristics of the alcohol abuser of which the police officer should be aware include an extremely low frustration point toward any wish, request, desire, or demand made of him. If any demands which he makes are not granted, he may react with anger or even violence.

The police officer should also be alert to the possible presence of deep depression and suicidal behavior in the alcohol abuser's personality.

146

The loss of self-esteem, which is both an underlying factor in the abuse as well as a consequence of it, is often so intense that it becomes the basis for violent behavior directed against the self. The alcoholic who has recently lost a spouse, family, or job may be a high suicide risk.

Another important characteristic is the almost simultaneous occurrence of feelings of inferiority and superiority. After drinking excessively, the alcohol abuser may feel that he is no good at the same time that he makes demands on others that indicate he considers himself someone special.

The police officer should also know that most alcoholics are fearful. This can have important consequences for handling them when they are intoxicated. If the intoxicated person is approached in a way which increases his fears, he may overreact with an attempt at false bravery, thus making it more difficult for the officer to handle him.

Finally, after a binge, the alcohol abuser can act dependent and clinging. This behavior can arouse angry feelings in others (including police officers) and may lead to an inappropriate ignoring of the person's needs. Such neglect could be dangerous because serious physical problems, often masked by alcohol abuse, may be overlooked.

Helpful Hints to the Law Enforcement Officer

The signs of acute alcohol intoxication can include varying degrees of exhilaration and excitement, loss of inhibition and restraint, bizarre behavior, slurred speech, and lack of coordination. When encountering someone who is intoxicated, the officer might remember the last time he was in a similar state. Remembering his own feelings, including the sense of power and the glibness of his tongue, will help him to relate better to the alcohol abuser. The officer should be patient, but firm. He should remember that the person involved is not his normal self and probably won't remember how obnoxious he was. If he is belligerent, the officer should ignore this as much as possible unless he is in danger of hurting himself or others. If the police can keep him talking while they are working, their job will be easier.

When alcohol intoxication has been especially severe, drowsiness, stupor, and possibly unconsciousness may occur. It is important for the officer to recognize that unconsciousness may mask other physical disorders which have either resulted from acute alcohol intake or are coincidental with it. The former category may include head injuries, pneumonia, fractures, and bleeding from the stomach, while the latter may include such important factors as diabetic coma and the stupor following an epileptic seizure.

In a few cases, even small amounts of alcohol can result in markedly abnormal behavior. This is called *pathological intoxication* and refers to cases in which an extremely small amount of alcohol, which in most individuals would have only minimal effects, can cause an outburst of markedly irrational, combative, and destructive behavior.

The officer may also encounter the alcoholic who has stopped drinking either because of illness or lack of access to alcohol. The alcoholic may then exhibit a number of symptoms of which the officer should be aware so that he can bring the alcoholic to proper medical attention. (These symptoms are not likely to occur in the person who is a reactive user of alcohol.) They may not occur until after the person has been arrested and jailed, since confinement automatically bars access to alcohol.

The most common sign of alcohol withdrawal in the chronic alcohol abuser is tremulousness (shakes or jitters). Most often visible in the hand, it is usually associated with irritability, nausea, and vomiting. All of these symptoms will occur relatively quickly and, in jail, they are often seen the morning after arrest.

When they stop drinking, most chronic abusers will experience nothing more than severe shakes. Some, however, may demonstrate more serious conditions, such as *alcoholic hallucinosis* or *delirium tremens.* In the former, the abuser hears accusatory and threatening voices. These may occur even if the victim otherwise looks all right and knows where he is and what time it is. The treatment is hospitalization, appropriate medication, adequate diet, and good nursing care.

In delirium tremens, seeing and feeling objects that are not present is more common than hearing voices (auditory hallucinations). The person may perceive bugs are crawling on him or see huge insects. In contrast to alcoholic hallucinosis, delirium tremens is associated with a loss of orientation to time and place. Delirium tremens may also be associated with epileptic seizures, which can be life-threatening. Treatment requires prompt medical attention in a hospital with appropriate medication, adequate diet, and good nursing care.

An important part of the police's past difficulties in handling alcohol abusers has been the neglect of other agencies, such as hospitals and clinics. More recently, however, the attitudes of society toward alcohol abusers have been changing. Many states have passed legislation removing public intoxication from the criminal code and defining it as a medicosocial responsibility. More hospitals and clinics are creating comprehensive alcohol treatment programs, including detoxification centers.

With the development of these treatment programs, the police officer can now bring the acutely intoxicated person to an appropriate facility rather than ignoring him or placing him in the "drunk tank."

The need for the police officer to involve himself in these treatment programs as both a referral source and care giver is emphasized by data which indicate the high costs to the criminal justice system of handling the alcoholic abuser without the support of these programs.

The law enforcement officer should work closely with community groups, both medical and nonmedical, in developing programs and methods for getting people who need help to use them. There is no question that police cooperation in this community effort will free the officer to attend to more serious crimes than public intoxication and chronic inebriation.

Other Forms of Drug Abuse

While alcohol is the most commonly abused drug, it is not the only one. There are numerous others to which individuals become addicted, tolerant, or habituated. Since they affect human behavior, and since their nonmedical sale or possession in many instances is legally prohibited, they are also of concern to the police officer. Consequently, he should also be familiar with their characteristics and behavioral effects.

In the following discussion, we have grouped these drugs into several general categories. As the officer encounters specific drugs other than those mentioned, he can determine their category and deduce their general characteristics and effects.

Narcotic Drugs (Opiates)

Narcotics are derivatives of opium and include both natural forms (morphine, heroin, and codeine) as well as synthetics (demerol, methadone, and numorphan). Tolerance and habituation occur rapidly. Abstinence results in a withdrawal syndrome, characteristic of addictive drugs.

Narcotics may be taken either intravenously *(mainlining)*, by subcutaneous injection *(skin popping)*, or by nasal inhalation *(snorting)*. This last use is effective only with a very high-grade opiate, such as was found in Vietnam by our servicemen.

Studies which have attempted to demonstrate personality differences between opiate and alcohol addicts have not yielded conclusive results. The choice of the addicting drug appears to be determined by social and cultural characteristics. Currently many young users are common abusers of both opiates and alcohol, either at the same time or in rapid succession.

Hallucinogens

Hallucinogens, otherwise known as psychedelics, have been used for many years in their natural state as a part of the religious rites of many ancient civilizations. They have only recently been abused in both their natural and synthetic states. Common among the natural hallucinogens is mescaline, derived from the peyote (cactus) plant; common among the synthetics is lysergic acid diethylamide (LSD), first synthesized in 1938. More recently, PCP (Phencyclidine) has become popular.

The acute toxic reactions of hallucinogens include disorganized thinking and an altered state of perception of the environment. These reactions are greatly influenced by the social setting and by the person's expectations prior to taking the drug. These altered perceptions can lead to heightened experiences in each of the five senses (hearing, seeing, smelling, touching, and tasting). In contrast to alcohol and the opiates, hallucinogens are neither addictive nor tolerance producing. For some people, depending on personality, they may be habituating.

Marijuana

While classified by some as a psychedelic, marijuana *(pot)* is probably best considered by itself not only because of its frequent and widespread use, but also because, in its milder forms, it does not produce hallucinogenic experiences approaching those associated with psychedelic drugs. In its strongest form (hashish), however, it can produce symptoms similar to those of psychedelic substances.

Like psychedelics, but unlike alcohol and opiates, marijuana use does not lead to addiction or tolerance. Habituation and dependence can occur in some users, depending on the person's previous psychological state and underlying pattern of behavior. However, many are able to use marijuana without becoming psychologically dependent or habituated.

Cocaine

Cocaine is derived from the leaves of the coca shrub, which is found in portions of South America and Southeast Asia. Like natural psychedelic substances, it has a long history of use, primarily by the Indians of the Andes. It was first isolated for medicinal purposes in 1855 and can be taken by sniffing or injection.

Because of the intense *high* which its marked exhilerating effect produces, it is often used with other drugs. For example, barbiturate abusers may use it to counteract the *down* of sedatives. Unlike alcohol and opiates, cocaine is not addicting nor tolerance producing. The advantage over amphetamines, which also produce a high, is its lack of tolerance effects. However, of all those drugs which do not produce tolerance or addiction, cocaine has the highest degree of psychological dependence. Physically, a person can stop using cocaine rather easily because there is no withdrawal syndrome; however, the psychological effects make withdrawal difficult.

Amphetamines

In contrast to psychedelics, marijuana, cocaine, and many of the narcotic opiates, amphetamines *(speed)* are drugs used formerly by physicians especially to assist patients in weight reduction. Recently, however, the legitimate use of amphetamines has been restricted, primarily because of the high incidence of abuse. Like cocaine, amphetamine abuse is undertaken principally to obtain a high.

Most abusers take speed in the form of pills *(pep pills* or *goof balls)*, but some use it intravenously in a synthetic form (methadrine) to obtain a better high. This *mainlining* of speed is very dangerous because it can lead to a severe paranoid psychosis.

In contrast to cocaine, marijuana, and the psychedelics, amphetamines, while not addicting, build up a high level of tolerance. Increasing amounts are required to produce the same effect over time. As with other drugs, psychological dependence or habituation results.

Barbiturates

Because they are legally available through prescription, barbiturates are probably the most frequently abused drugs except for alcohol. Their abuse is particularly dangerous because they produce habituation, tolerance, and addiction. Furthermore, they can increase the effects of other drugs (principally alcohol) when taken with them. This type of combination abuse accounts for a high number of accidental deaths.

Mild Tranquilizers

Mild tranquilizers, such as Valium and Librium, have an effect similar to the barbiturates. This is not surprising, since many "tranquilizers" are misnamed and actually sedate more than tranquilize. Although they do not produce an actual withdrawal syndrome, like the barbiturates, withdrawal in the tranquilizer abuser may present similar problems and should be done in a hospital.

Because there is a cross-tolerance between many tranquilizers and barbiturates, the abuser may increase the impact of these drugs by taking several kinds.

Helpful Hints to the Law Enforcement Officer

A person who has overdosed should be treated as a medical emergency, and the police officer must be able to recognize the symptoms. Acute opiate overdose is characterized by a marked unresponsiveness in the presence of very slow or labored breathing. Needle marks and/or *tracks* will be noted. The pupils are pinpoints, and both pulse and heartbeat are extremely slow. If the overdose has been very severe and the individual is still alive, body temperature will have fallen. When breathing is poor, it is important immediately to create an air passage and to supply artificial respiration while in transit to the hospital emergency room.

In contrast to an acute overdose, neither chronic intoxication from opiates nor withdrawal are generally medical emergencies. Because of their tolerance-producing effects, the addict will require rapidly increasing amounts of the drug to obtain the same result. However, this process is self-limiting. Once the addict's habit has reached a certain level, his primary motivation for continuing to use the drug is to avoid withdrawal rather than to reach a new high.

Addicts dread withdrawal because it is extremely uncomfortable. Runny nose, excessive tearing, sweating, as well as severe nausea and vomiting occur within eight to sixteen hours after the last dose if no further opiate is taken. Later effects include severe muscle cramps and spasms, marked sleeplessness, and an increase in nausea and vomiting. If untreated, the addict is in a state of *cold turkey,* and the withdrawal syndrome will reach its peak within forty-eight and seventy-two hours. Most addicts are not able to go cold turkey unless they are in jail, where access to opiates is unavailable. Otherwise, the temptation to relieve the withdrawal symptoms by another fix is too great to resist.

Heroin addicts who cannot get into a treatment program will sometimes approach a police officer and ask to be booked for some offense which will draw ten days in jail if they are convicted. The addicts plead guilty in order to withdraw cold turkey in jail because their tolerance level has reached the point where they can no longer steal enough to support their habit. At this point, they arrange to go to jail, not to quit drugs but to lower the amount they need (Talbert 1974).

The difficulties associated with withdrawal and the history of readdiction in many addicts, even after successful withdrawal, have led to the use of a synthetic opiate, methadone, for both withdrawal and maintenance. Methadone is useful in withdrawal because its administration can be more carefully controlled than heroin, since it is long-acting and can be taken orally. It is useful in maintenance of chronic heroin addicts, even though it substitutes one addiction for another, since it appears to enable the addict to function more successfully than on heroin, although he remains addicted.

The criminal aspects of narcotic drug addiction have been well publicized and are related primarily to the addict's need to obtain finances to support the high cost of his addiction. However, some addicts have exhibited criminal behavior before their addiction, and heroin increases their need to engage in that behavior.

The serious problems associated with hallucinogen abuse are secondary not only to the acute psychotic symptoms of a toxic reaction but also to the possible acting out of violent impulses directed either against others or the addict himself. The chronic user may have uncontrolled and overwhelming panic reactions in association with *flashbacks,* in which the effects of hallucinogens are reproduced, although none have been taken. These episodes are extremely frightening and can create severe panic which may make the addict a potential danger to himself or others.

Because of the acute panic often associated with a bad reaction to hallucinogens, emergency measures should include efforts to prevent the user from hurting himself or others. These precautions can include restricting his movement, either by placing him in a closed room or by using restraints. Other efforts to reduce the input of external stimuli coming to him may include placing him in a quiet, non-stimulating environment. Police who come in contact with a person under the effects of a hallucinogen should lower their voices and talk calmly to him (the *talk-down cure*). This also helps to reduce external stimuli.

The acute paranoid psychosis which may result from amphetamines is often difficult to differentiate from the functional paranoid psychosis. However, anyone encountered by the police in an acute paranoid psychosis requires emergency treatment and should be brought to a medical facility. The paranoid psychotic should be approached with extreme caution, since he can be potentially dangerous (chapter 14). He is also frightened, and the officer should not do anything which will increase his fear because increased fear is likely to lead to a greater potential for violence.

The police officer can often identify a chronic barbiturate abuser if he notes a degree of mental confusion, some impairment of intellectual ability, and a staggering gait. Individuals suspected of chronic barbiturate intoxication should also be taken to the emergency room for medical evaluation.

In contrast to the narcotic addict, who is likely to overestimate the amount which he has been taking, the barbiturate abuser may grossly underestimate the amount he is taking because he is reluctant to reveal the cause of his physical symptoms. This becomes extremely serious because an underestimation can lead the doctor to place the abuser on an inadequate amount of the drug prior to beginning withdrawal.

Summary

In this chapter, we have discussed alcoholism and other forms of drug abuse, including their characteristics, underlying factors, and physical and psychological effects. The abuse of these drugs results in abnormal behavior and, therefore, the police officer frequently becomes involved.

The officer's role in handling problems associated with drug abuse is a difficult one at best, but in dealing with drug abusers, he must maintain a professional attitude toward those against whom most of society prefers to turn its back. He must have sufficient knowledge of the characteristics of commonly abused drugs and their effects so that he can give first aid to people who are suffering severe symptoms from their use, insure that they receive necessary emergency medical care, and, if necessary, act as a liaison between them and appropriate long-term treatment facilities.

BIBLIOGRAPHY

ADAMS, J. WINSTEAD. 1978. *Psychoanalysis of Drug Dependence: The Understanding and Treatment of a Particular Form of Pathological Narcissism.* New York: Grune & Stratton.

BAKER, F., and ISAACS, C. D. 1973. "Attitudes of Community Caregivers toward Drug Users." *International Journal of the Addictions* 8:243–252.

CHAFETZ, M. E. 1959. "Practical and Theoretical Considerations in the Psychotherapy of Alcoholism." *Quarterly Journal of Studies on Alcohol* 20:281–294.

FINK, L., and HYATT, M. P. 1978. "Drug Use and Criminal Behavior." *Journal of Drug Education* 8:139–149.

GLATT, M. M., ed. 1977. *Drug Dependence: Current Problems and Issues.* Baltimore: University Park Press.

LOURIA, D. 1968. *The Drug Scene.* New York: McGraw-Hill.

McGLOTHLIN, W. H., ANGLIN, M. D., and WILSON, B. D. 1978. "Narcotic Addiction and Crime." *Criminology* 16:293–315.

PETERSEN, D. M., SCHWIRIAN, K. P., and BLEDA, S. E. 1978. "The Drug Arrest: Empirical Observations on the Age, Sex, and Race of Drug Law Offenders in a Midwestern City." *Drug Forum* 6:371–385.

TALBERT, MARION (San Antonio police department inspector). 1974. Personal communication.

WILLIAMS, J. D. 1968. *Narcotics and Hallucinogens.* New York: Gwinn.

Chapter 13

Paranoid Behavior

The Spectrum of Paranoid Behavior

PARANOID behavior is always associated with a high level of anxiety. Suspiciousness and distrust are the core elements of the paranoid's relationships with others and society. He finds it difficult to confide in others and, if he does, he expects to be betrayed. If he has any close relationships, they are likely to be limited to a very few people and have difficulty surviving any stress. Usually, the paranoid person has a lifelong tendency toward secretiveness, seclusiveness, and solitary rumination, although these may be concealed behind a facade of superficial give and take.

Three categories of paranoid behavior—the paranoid personality, the paranoid state, and the paranoid schizophrenic—may be differentiated as the following table illustrates:

	PARANOID PERSONALITY	PARANOID STATE	PARANOID SCHIZOPHRENIA
Thinking disturbance	No	No	Yes
Delusions	No	Yes	Yes
Regression	No	No	Yes

The paranoid person perceives the world in which he lives as dangerous and believes he must always be on guard against the possibility of attack from others. Consequently, he lives with an endless series of tensions arising from many misunderstandings and misinterpretations.

The Progression of Paranoid Behavior

Paranoid behavior becomes more severe when the generalized suspiciousness and distrust begins to merge with the person's increasing withdrawal. As he isolates himself from others, he becomes more preoccupied with his inner world and experiences strange feelings of alienation from the outside world. The resulting anxiety increases his vigilance and uneasiness. He begins to scrutinize his surroundings with even more suspicion and searches for hidden meanings in all events that go on around him.

While some people may remain in this stage throughout their life, others deteriorate. This hypervigilant person may begin to watch the little things people do and note with increasing wariness their posture, gestures, glances, and movements. He demonstrates a readiness to react to any situation as potentially threatening, whether or not an actual threat is present. This is the first sign of the defective reality testing of the paranoid person.

In this preoccupied state, he begins to believe that everything is somehow related to him although he may not know why. As this process continues, his anxiety increases and his defensive use of projection begins. For example, he may feel that his desk has become disarranged. First he may feel only annoyance, but later he may begin to wonder about it. If he cannot find something in his desk drawer or notices that other things have been disturbed, he grows more anxious. He begins to examine other personal possessions and is concerned that these have also been disarranged. In the street, when people jostle him or crowd him, he begins to feel very angry. He hears remarks and immediately assumes they are about him. If there is laughter, he feels it is directed at him (Cameron 1959).

This use of projection is intended to place many of the paranoid's own unconscious wishes and feelings onto others. For example, he is able to avoid looking at his own hostile feelings by perceiving them instead, through projection, as the hostile attacks of others. He also uses denial to avoid any reality that would argue against his beliefs. Denial also protects him from the stresses he would feel if he faced his own weaknesses and failures. Instead of perceiving them as his own shortcomings, they become the fantasied shortcomings, evil intentions, and/or misdeeds of others. The more he can defensively belittle others, the further he removes himself from looking at his own weaknesses. The more he points out others' mistakes and sins, the less attention he must pay to his own.

All of these events increase his anxiety. Consequently, he must reduce it, so he forms endless hypotheses about what is happening. However, since his ability to test reality is defective, these hypotheses are likely to contain distortions of reality.

To this point in the process, his projections have no specific focus. If he has spoken openly of persecution, he has only referred to "they" or "people" who are doing or planning things, without being able to specify who "they" are or what the exact plan is. This situation, however, cannot endure because its vagueness is too anxiety producing.

To reduce his anxiety, the paranoid person begins to conceptualize these dangerous "others" into a specific group or the plan into a specific plot of which he is the intended victim. He may conceive of this group as an organized gang of criminals, a group of international spies, a secret police force, or a racial or religious group. Some of their members may be identified as people he knows and to whom he attaches an important role in this organization that is against him. His thinking crystallizes around a specific plot which this group is formulating and of which he is the center. When this focusing of his delusions occurs, his anxiety is reduced.

However, he soon discovers that he has a new problem. He must now defend himself against this attack or plot. As he mobilizes his own aggression to defend himself, his tactics alienate others and may lead to counter aggression. Once he has experienced this counteraggression, he can complain that people are "really" against him—that he is being interfered with, discriminated against, or persecuted. He can now point to real events in the world which justify his original unreal and delusional complaints.

In chronic cases, some paranoids may appear to have no more than a nonspecific resentful or aggressively hostile attitude toward the world, behind which their delusions are more or less successfully concealed. In others, these people's beliefs are not so well hidden; they may show outbursts of hostility towards others or make unfounded accusations against them. Their outbursts cause people to avoid close contact with them, pushing them further into social isolation.

Some paranoids, a minority, are driven to even more aggressive action. They abandon the role of passive observer and begin to plan actively against their "enemies." These actions may include an attempt to escape by sudden flight, often with elaborate precautions to cover up their trail. Others, instead of fleeing, may attack to catch the "enemy" unaware and take revenge for what they have suffered or forestall what they fear may happen.

The following case illustrates the important characteristics of paranoid behavior which we have discussed.

Case Example. [This case was adapted and revised from a lengthy case presentation (Cameron 1959).]

Joe Dodge is an unmarried thirty-two-year-old man who was brought to the hospital by police after a suicide attempt. Although he gave the impression of being friendly, polite, and cooperative during their initial interview, it was also apparent that he was very frightened and that, behind his friendly politeness, he was on his guard. Upon further questioning, he told this story without any recognition of its delusional character.

For several years, he had been living alone in a cheap hotel on a modest but steady income from investments. Despite his youth and good health, he lived as though he were an elderly retired businessman. Occasionally, he would look into new business prospects, but he never found anything that attracted him. He preferred to sit around the hotel lobby and think. When asked what he thought about, he would not say. He stated that he conversed with other men, played cards with them, read newspapers, and, following the custom of the hotel, placed a dozen small bets with bookies on racehorses each day.

His first acute paranoid attack came a day after he had been in a violent quarrel with his bookies over a bet. He had placed a number of bets, and one of his horses had come in first and paid good odds. He went for his money only to be told that he had not bet on the winning horse in that race. He was enraged, but did not say anything initially and, instead, went to a nearby bar where he had a few drinks. As he thought more about it, he realized that he had been deliberately cheated. His anger increased, and he returned to the bookies and demanded his payoff.

When they refused to give it to him, he began to shout insults at them and threatened to call the police. They threw him out. For a while, he paced up and down the sidewalk until he cooled off a little and returned to his hotel. Although still furious, he was able to sit down and think about the situation. It suddenly occurred to him that, since bookies were notorious for having gangster protection, he might be in danger because he had threatened them. The more he thought about it, the more in danger he began to feel. He fantasized about the gangsters who would come and kill him.

The next morning, when he came down to the lobby, he noticed some rough looking strangers hanging around. He thought they were watching him closely and waving signals to each other. At one time, during the morning, when an automobile filled with men stopped in front of the hotel entrance, he was immediately convinced that they were gangsters who had come to kidnap and kill him.

Although this did not happen, his vigilance grew and with it so did the evidence that he was in deadly peril. He began to see strangers everywhere, all of whom seemed to be watching and shadowing him wherever he went and whatever he did. He felt there was no escape and was convinced that he was now marked for execution. After several days, he retreated in near panic to his hotel room where he barricaded himself against the coming attack. From his room, he telephoned a relative and told him the whole story.

This relative, who was aware of Joe's intelligence and business skills, accepted everything that he told as truth and agreed that Joe must somehow escape. This relative, who had unwittingly entered into Joe's delusional system, made a plan with him to leave secretly the next day.

During a sleepless night, in anticipation of his escape the next morning, Joe realized that the gangsters had probably tapped the telephone and heard the entire plan. In a panic, he packed his bag, slipped out of the hotel, and drove off alone without daring to notify his relative who was coming to help him in the morning.

In his automobile, he began to head west toward the home of another relative one thousand miles away. As he fled across the country, it became more obvious to him that escape was impossible. When he stopped for gas, casual comments by strangers helped him believe that he was caught in a great net slowly closing around him. In one city, he came out of a restaurant to find a policeman looking at his auto license. To Joe, this meant without question that the police were in league with the gangsters and keeping them informed of his movements. In another town, where he stopped to eat, the counterman eyed him as he worked. He immediately felt panic.

As he became more certain that death was inevitable, he took precautions against having to live through the horrible torture which he anticipated they had in store for him. He stopped to purchase razor blades which he hid in his suit and to forge a prescription for a lethal dose of a sedative which he carefully took out of the capsules and placed in a chewing-gum wrapper. At night, he avoided motels and slept in his locked automobile, hiding under his coat.

Eventually, he reached the home of his relative. However, by this time his anxiety and terror were overwhelming. Consequently, he wrote a suicide note, describing his terror. He then swallowed the sedative from the chewing gum wrapper and lay down. Fortunately, the suicide note which he had left was discovered in time and the police were called. They took him to the hospital where his stomach was pumped out.

This acute paranoid reaction was the first which Joe had experienced. Unfortunately, it was not the last. His delusions continued to persist and eventually he became a chronic paranoid schizophrenic.

Helpful Hints to the Law Enforcement Officer

As indicated previously, basic distrust is the core characteristic of paranoid behavior. Recognition of this is critical to the police officer who must respond to it. Because the paranoid considers significant people in his life to have been undependable or rejecting, he is apt to view any authority figure, including an officer, as undependable and hostile. Consequently, the officer should expect that the paranoid will be suspicious of anything he says and will regard him with dislike and resentment when approached. How, then, does the officer counter this basic distrust?

First, what the paranoid needs most is understanding without condescension. When he has delusions, he requires someone who will listen with courtesy to the delusional material and neither indicate that he believes it (which he certainly does not), argue with the paranoid about it, or convey the impression that the person is crazy. The assumption of a friendly but distant neutrality is usually the safest approach to the paranoid person.

Second, the officer must remember that the paranoid is usually extremely anxious. Consequently, he must approach him in a way which does not heighten further these anxieties. If the paranoid's anxiety increases, his vigilance will also increase, as will the possibility of a violent reaction.

Third, the police officer should remember that paranoids misinterpret reality and, therefore, may misinterpret his intentions. The officer should proceed slowly and with caution, constantly reassuring the paranoid that he is there to assist and protect him.

In situations where an officer has continuous contact with a paranoid, it is important to be alert to any changes in the person's thinking which indicate an increasing severity of his condition and a possible eruption of violence. The officer should look for a focusing of delusional content. For example, if a paranoid who regularly makes complaints to the police begins to change his statements from vague "theys" to specific individuals or groups, this is a danger sign that he may feel forced to take action to protect himself.

If it is necessary to take the paranoid into custody, the officer should not order the paranoid around. He must not frighten him with mace or other weapons. The paranoid may panic and react violently.

However, while attempting to gain the paranoid's trust, the officer must never let down his guard. He must remain alert while guarding against the communication of his suspiciousness to the paranoid. He must remember also that the paranoid can be suicidal as well as homicidal (chapters 14 and 15).

Summary

In this chapter we have reviewed several diagnostic classifications in which paranoid behavior is a core element. We have described the spectrum of paranoid behavior and the methods by which the officer can best approach the paranoid person. In the next chapter, we will discuss violent behavior and the methods by which it can be handled best by the police officer.

BIBLIOGRAPHY

CAMERON, N. 1959. "Paranoid Conditions and Paranoia." In *The American Handbook of Psychiatry*. vol. 1, ed. S. Arieti. New York: Basic Books. pp. 508–539.

CHALUS, G. A. 1976. "Relationship Between Paranoid Tendencies and Projective Behavior." *Psychological Reports* 39:1175–1181.

KRAEPELIN, EMIL. 1976. *Manic-Depressive Insanity and Paranoia.* New York: Aeno Press.

MEISSNER, WILLIAM W. 1978. *The Paranoid Process.* New York: J. Aronson.

TYNHURST, J. S. 1957. "Paranoid Patterns." In *Explorations in Social Psychiatry.* ed. A. H. Leighton, J. A. Clausen, and R. N. Wilson. New York: Basic Books. pp. 31–76.

Chapter 14

Violent Behavior

BECAUSE of the implied and actual danger of violent behavior, a thorough understanding of its causes, characteristics, and management is extremely critical to the law enforcement officer.

Definitions and Concepts

Violence is defined in *Webster's New World Dictionary* as "the exertion of physical force so as to injure or abuse" or "intense, furious, often destructive action." This association of destructive action with the intent to abuse or injure implies that feelings of aggression or hostility are present at some level in connection with almost all violent acts. However, the reverse is not always true, since aggressive and hostile feelings are not necessarily accompanied by violent behavior. Later in this chapter, we shall describe some critical factors which may contribute to the transformation of aggressive behavior into violent behavior.

Violent behavior may be categorized into three broad areas: (1) *individual violent behavior,* in which psychological factors predominate; (2) *social violent behavior,* in which violence is a direct outgrowth of group behavior and the actions of the society itself; and (3) *"mixed" violent behavior,* in which both individual psychological factors and group social factors operate.

Individual Violence

In individual violence, the violent behavior evolves principally from psychological forces within each person. This violent behavior may be normal and socially approved or may be labeled as abnormal and socially condemned. There is a certain amount of violent behavior or the potential for it present in all of us. However, as long as it is controlled or expressed in socially approved forms, the person does not get into trouble. For example, a boxer may inflict mayhem on his opponent and be rewarded by cheers and the victor's share of the purse; the matador will be cheered in the ring as he spears the bull; or the soldier is taught in basic training that the spirit of the bayonet is to kill. In each case, society approves and the person does not suffer a penalty.

Other types of individual violent behavior are not approved by society and, in most instances, are labeled criminal. If the perpetrator is discovered, he must answer to society through its courts and prison system. However, society may make exceptions. For example, if violent behavior is associated with mental illness, the person may be held responsible to a lesser degree or not at all.

Later in this chapter, we will discuss those attempts which have been made to predict the potential for individual violent behavior based on an understanding of some of those factors which may influence its presence. However, at this time, we should point out other important aspects of individual violent behavior. For example, studies have indicated that the consumption of alcohol increases the proneness to aggressive acts such as rape, homicide, and assault. In a Chicago study, districts with the highest alcoholic consumption produced three and one-half times as many violent crimes compared to those with the lowest consumption rates (Horstman 1973). These studies indicate a relationship between alcohol and violence, even though it can be argued that they do not necessarily indicate a direct one-to-one relationship.

We are also beginning to recognize the correlation between self-destructive acts of violence, such as suicide (chapter 15), and destructive acts against others. Both authors have had many experiences with those who were depressed and wanted to kill themselves, but didn't have the guts to do it. Unable to carry out these wishes actively, they began to consider acts which might lead to their being killed, including being shot while holding up a bank or killing someone and then confessing to get the chair. Case histories of mass murderers such as Charles Whitman, Richard Speck, and Albert De Salvo demonstrate the presence of either suicidal ideation or previous suicide attempts prior to the occurrence of their infamous acts of violence.

Recent studies have suggested that some people who are violent may have an associated brain disturbance and that this condition may be partially or wholly responsible for their behavior. Out of 130 violent patients self-referred to the Emergency Room of the Massachusetts General Hospital, one-third had abnormal brain wave patterns, a rate fifty times that of the general population. Other striking behavioral findings associated with violent thinking or behavior included that one-half of the population had a history of bed-wetting after the age of seven; one-quarter had set fires as children; one-quarter had a history of cruelty to animals; and more than half admitted that they drove cars dangerously to vent feelings of aggression. Furthermore, nearly 60 percent of them had been arrested at least once for a violent crime (Mark 1970).

Social Violence

Just as society allows some forms of individual violence, such as boxing, so it does not necessarily disapprove of all social violence. For example, in sports, it is difficult to think of a more violent group activity than hockey or lacrosse. Also, society may not necessarily disapprove of a riot or civil disturbance before it first has made the judgment as to which side it ethically or morally supports. Furthermore, a society may be divided in its approval or condemnation of some type of social violence. For instance, in contrast to the feelings of many others, a significant number of Irish-Americans agree with the goals of the IRA and have lent that organization both direct and indirect support.

However, public support may also be a double-edged sword. While initially encouraging some to take more aggressive or violent steps, it may also determine the limits within which demonstrators must remain if they are not to completely alienate themselves from the support which they have received initially from society. Again, in the case of the IRA, recent terrorist activities have led to the loss of support from many Irish-Americans who earlier approved of their goals. (Some destructive forms of social or collective violence will be considered in more detail in chapters 16 and 17 when we talk about disasters and riots.)

Mixed Violence

This is a category of violent or aggressive behavior in which both individual psychological factors and social factors play a role. Examples are as diverse as prison riots, civil disturbances by minority groups, or college panty raids. In these situations, a particular population or sub-group, such as the inmates of a jail or prison, combined with a social situation, such as bad food, cramped quarters, or alleged discriminatory practices, may lead to aggressive or violent behavior. However, every person who is a member of the subgroup may not become involved, since the person's psychological predisposition will also be a determining factor.

The Prediction of Dangerousness

Definitions and concepts of violent behavior are limited in value unless they also increase the ability to predict the potential for violent behavior in a specific individual. History is filled with many examples of those who committed infamous violent acts which were not prevented because no one could make an accurate prediction of dangerous behavior even though the person, in many cases, had had prior contact with a mental health professional.

Unfortunately, the mental health profession has not yet achieved sufficient understanding of human behavior to allow it to predict with any significant certainty what person will be dangerous and under what circumstances (Cohen et al. 1978). Some mental health professionals have approached this problem by describing signs of dangerous behavior taken from case histories. However, these case histories reveal that many nondangerous patients show many or all of the symptoms which some people consider signs of dangerousness. For example, all of the following symptoms and signs have been named by one authority or another as possible precursors of violent behavior: past history of aggressive acts; enforced repression of normal aggression; parental rejection; the need to protest against dependence upon one or both parents; detachment; introversion; sadism toward children or animals; overemphasis on daydreaming or ritualistic behavior; absence of mood changes; and an increased interest in violent acts on the part of others. However, it is clear that many people demonstrate some of these signs yet do not commit any dangerous acts, even when observed over a period of years.

Despite this negative picture, research into the predictability of dangerousness continues. Hodges studied 447 dangerous offenders at the Pautuxent Center in Maryland and found that 81 percent of those recommended by the clinical staff for incarceration who were not held committed another crime in contrast to only 37 percent of those who were released after being fully treated (Hodges 1971).

Based upon a similar study carried out at Bridgewater State Hospital in Massachusetts, Kozol and his associates stated:

We see the dangerous person as one who has actually inflicted or attempted to inflict serious physical injury on another person; harbors anger, hostility, and resentment; enjoys witnessing or inflicting suffering; lacks altruistic and compassionate concern for others; sees himself as a victim rather than an aggressor; resents or rejects authority; is primarily concerned with his own satisfaction; lacks control of his own impulses; has immature attitudes towards social responsibilities; lacks insight into his own psychological structure and distorts his perceptions of reality in accordance with his own wishes and needs. (Kozol et al. 1972)

To the alert reader, this description closely parallels that of the psychopath (chapter 9). Indeed, Kozol concludes, "Our concept of the dangerous person is nearly identical with the classical stereotype of the criminal antisocial psychopath."

However, it should also be pointed out that studies, such as those by Kozol and others, which allege that dangerousness can be predicted, have been subject to significant criticism. For example, Evenson and Altman (1975) reanalyzed the data provided by Kozol and found that it would have been possible to obtain 89 percent accuracy in the prediction of dangerousness with this group of patients simply by stating that all of the patients were not dangerous. In fact, most of the predictive accuracy of the study came from correctly identifying the large number of patients who were not dangerous. Nearly two-thirds of those patients released contrary to predictions of dangerousness by Kozol's group were not subsequently dangerous. These findings buttress the contention of many that the prediction of dangerousness is not scientifically feasible and that most studies which argue for an ability to predict dangerousness, in fact, contain a serious overprediction of dangerousness. Therefore, it is important to recognize that any criteria for the prediction of dangerousness should not be viewed absolutely, but rather on a continuum from "extremely dangerous" at one end to "absolutely nondangerous" at the other. An interplay of many factors determines where an individual will be on the continuum at any given time and how dangerous the person actually is at a specific moment.

Finally, it is important to point out that those studies which indicate an ability to predict dangerousness have generally been based upon long-term evaluation of the specific person. Professionals will continue to have problems predicting dangerousness on the basis of brief contact, a situation which actually exists most of the time. This difficulty is reflected in recent legislation, which often requires commitment to mental hospitals for dangerous behavior to be based on the actual commission of a violent act rather than on an implied or threatened act alone.

Predicting Front Page Violence

With regard to front page violence, a topic of special interest to law enforcement, Hans Toch, a noted criminologist, commented:

Among men who engage in violence, there are monsters who fill the public mind with special dread and revulsion. These men stir the imagination, displace headlines, disrupt peace and tranquility, and inspire massive official action. And these men are not those who account for the bulk of violence damage, nor are they those who engage in repeated acts of destruction. They are, rather, the unexpected authors of violence that is irrational and senseless—the progenitors of acts that are blood-curdling and bizarre. (Toch 1969)

More recently, Lee and his colleagues have observed:

What terrifies us most about such brutal incidents is their unpredictability and senselessness. How can you defend yourself against aggression that is masked by passivity, against crimes of violence by fine young men of exemplary character? And their lethal reaction is usually inappropriate to whatever instigated it. The crime exceeds the cause: a person is battered to death for taking another driver's intended parking space; an employer is murdered for refusing to give an undeserved promotion; a man is killed for unknowingly taking someone else's seat at the bar. (Lee et al. 1977, pp. 69ff)

On this same subject, Megargee has pointed out some of the chief characteristics of these people, including their lack of previous aggression and violence. They are often not aggressive in situations where the normal person would be. Typically, the males are described as "quiet boys, model young men, slow to anger . . . wouldn't hurt a fly . . . sort of a loner . . . didn't really get to know him" (Megargee 1966). One only needs to recall the recent reports regarding the past history of John

169

Hinckley, who attempted to assassinate President Reagan, to confirm the validity of Magargee's statement.

This extreme passivity is abnormal. It suggests that there are underlying currents of anger and hostility so strong that they cannot emerge into consciousness, even for a moment. The major defense mechanism seems to be reaction formation, in which these people adopt a life-style opposite to what they feel. They become gentle, mild, passive creatures who often have a compulsive need to be perfect. They avoid their rage and destructive impulses at all costs. However, eventually the pressure of these feelings becomes unbearable and then they lash out, seemingly at random, even destroying people they don't know. The prediction of this headline-getting behavior is most difficult because of the absence of any previous history of violence.

The key to prevention may be, as Toch suggests, in focusing attention upon those incidents where violence might have been expected but did not appear. Therefore, school counselors, family physicians, clergymen, and parents should be alert for possible danger signs when a child seems unable to express even normal amounts of hostility and aggression. The child who is silent and unresponsive in situations that would make other children angry should be watched closely. A marked pattern of nonviolent behavior should merit just as much concern and attention from professionals as a pattern of excessive violent behavior.

This discussion has been presented to alert the police officer to the inadequacies of our current tools for predicting dangerousness. This difficulty is, however, only one facet of the police officer's problems in handling aggressive and violent behavior. In many situations, prediction is not an issue if the violent act has recently occurred or is taking place. How the officer reacts will be critical to his effective handling of the person and to his own safety.

The Police Officer's Perception of Danger

James W. Sterling, former Assistant Director of the Professional Standards Division of the International Association of Chiefs of Police, has pointed out one resemblance between police work and military duty. The police officer may be viewed as someone who daily faces the possibility of combat, especially in the inner city with its turmoil and high crime rates. The anxiety and fear an officer experiences will influence how he carries out his duties.

In his study, Sterling attempts to define more clearly those factors which influence the officer's perception of danger. Using interviews as well as an assessment of police reaction to radio calls, Sterling described the following characteristics. Physically, the officer may note an acceleration of his heartbeat and an increase in both the depth and intensity of breathing. Digestive activity is also slowed, with a subsequent release of sugar from the liver providing increased energy.

Perceptually, under stressful conditions, lights appear to be brighter, and sounds seem louder. Because threatening objects look larger than they actually are, the officer may see a source of danger nearer at hand than it really is. Inaccuracies in judging time and speed may also occur.

Finally, as Sterling points out, the officer who has gained experience begins to ascribe more importance to the potential dangerousness of those calls which, as a recruit, he perceived as less dangerous, such as indecent exposure, family disturbance, or suspicious person. At the same time, calls regarding a committed murder or an assault with a deadly weapon which, as a recruit, he perceived as highly dangerous are now seen as less dangerous. The officer learns that it is the unknown and the unpredictable which has the greatest potential for danger rather than the known and the predictable (Sterling 1972).

Assaults on Police Officers

A problem of immediate concern to everyone who carries a badge and everyone who depends on an officer's help is assaults on police. Police are interested not only because their own safety is involved but also because in every department across the country there are police officers who seem to generate an abnormal number of citizen's complaints in their daily contacts with the public. These officers are an administrative nightmare to the brass, while the officer's facility for collecting complaints threatens his own career and self-image. It seems logical to assume that studies of police officers who are assaulted more frequently than their peers and of those who assault them might yield information providing some guidance in dealing not only with the problem of assault but also with the corollary problem of police–citizen contacts which end in citizen complaints.

In a unique study, Toch (1969) conceptualized violent behavior as a "clue, a symptom, a calling card which, if properly read, could expose the central motives and concerns of violent men." Contrary to the popular belief that most violent behavior is senseless, Toch found that it is usually purposive and that its occurrence is often based on the presence of hidden meanings.

Toch's subjects were thirty-two Oakland Police Department officers who had been assaulted at least once; nineteen men who had assaulted police officers (in many instances the officers they had assaulted were part of the officer study group); forty-four inmates in the California Medical Facility at Vacaville; twenty-nine prisoners at San Quentin; and thirty-three parolees with violent behavior records. To test the validity of their findings, the researchers also secured permission to analyze 344 incidents of assaultive behavior on San Francisco police officers.

From their data, Toch and his colleagues classified the following motives for police assaults. They found that the two motives most frequently encountered were: (1) reactions against perceived tampering with the person, either verbally or physically, by the officer; and (2) the desire to rescue or defend a person who is receiving an officer's attention. In over half the sample, the sequence of events leading to the assault on an officer starts with a person's negative reaction to an officer's verbal approach. Typically, the officer approaches a civilian with a request, a question, or an order. No serious crime has been committed, and the contact could be considered as preventive police work or coping with a nuisance. Violence may occur immediately, but most often does not happen until after the civilian has first expressed his displeasure at the officer's words. Then, after the officer has made additional moves, the civilian attacks.

Binder and Scharf (1980) have elucidated the process which often leads to violent police–citizen encounters by delineating four phases. The first is the phase of anticipation, in which the police officer reacts emotionally and intellectually on the basis of a dispatch by radio, direct observation, or information from another person who requests assistance. The response to a radio call stating that a child is having difficulty retrieving a cat from the top of a telephone pole would be expected to be different from the initial reaction to a call asking a police officer to go to a location where there is alleged to be an insane, violent man with a knife. In addition to the actual content of the initial information received, the manner in which it is communicated can also affect the emotional and intellectual response of the officer and his preliminary consideration of alternative actions.

After the phase of anticipation, the officer enters the phase of entry.

When the officer actually arrives at the physical scene of the encounter, he must immediately determine the extent of any danger, establish his authority, clarify his expectation for the citizen, and gather information to supplement his general knowledge and the clues he received by radio or from an initiating person. The potential for physical force may increase or decrease according to decisions the officer makes early in the encounter. (The illustration which follows this discussion will clarify the situation.)

Following the phase of entry, there is the phase of information exchange, which may range from a few seconds, during which the officer may shout, "Police. Don't move," to a longer period of information exchange. Clearly, the longer the period, the less likelihood the incident will lead to a violent police–citizen encounter.

The last phase is the phase of final decision, in which the officer must make the ultimate decision as to whether to use physical force. In this phase, those emotions most commonly associated with a violent police–citizen encounter are fear, extreme frustration, outrage, panic, and humiliation. The greater the presence of these overpowering emotions, the more likely it is that the officer will make a decision to use deadly force.

An illustration may be helpful. Two detectives from Burglary were patrolling late one night in an unmarked car when they encountered, in an isolated, poorly lit shopping center, one white male, age about forty, standing beside a pay phone booth (darkened) and a white-paneled pickup truck (phase of anticipation). Since the shopping center had recently been hit by a number of burglaries, the detectives left their car, showed their badges, and asked the man for identification (phase of entry). He refused to give any identification, stating that "anyone could buy a badge in a dime store, anyone could carry a gun, and besides, people other than policemen have police radios in their car" (phase of information exchange).

Even at this early point, this situation had the potential for escalating into violence. However, the next action of the officers successfully defused the situation. Rather than engaging in further confrontation, they chose another approach. They asked him if he would show identification to a marked patrol unit and he replied that he would do so (phase of final decision). Within five minutes a marked unit arrived, identification was made, and the citizen who turned out to be a reputable telephone company employee, wrote a letter to the police department complimenting the detectives for treating him "like a man" rather than trying to "strong-arm" him around.

In contrast to this situation, Toch discovered others in which the phases are collapsed through "one step games," and the policeman has little chance of avoiding violence. In these cases, the suspect has often been drinking, and the mere approach of an officer is sufficient to trigger violence. There is a high association of alcoholic intake with assaults on police officers.

Toch also reports another group of sequences which frequently lead to assaults. In these situations, violence exists prior to the officer's arrival. Family disturbances are typical examples. The officer's intervention is seen as a source of annoyance or frustration, a possible ally of the opposition, an intrusion, or simply a new problem to be dealt with. The violence, a coping device for frustration, is already in force when the officer arrives, and simply continues with the additional participant—the officer—being assigned one of the above roles.

Toch also offers a useful classification of those approaches to a violence-prone person (citizen or officer) that tend to promote the occurrence of violent behavior:

1. *Defending.* A category comprising persons who are allocated by public recognition a role that includes the exercise of aggressive behavior. (The "Godfather" would be an example of this type of person.)

2. *Norm enforcing.* A self-assigned mission involving the use of violence on behalf of norms that a violent person sees as desirable and universal rules of conduct. In some officers, this role emerges in the form of "Super Cop." This officer sees himself as the only individual standing between a helpless society and the criminal element of the population. He may often violate legal and department regulations in his zeal to stamp out "evils" such as drug addiction, prostitution, and other "low" forms of crime.

3. *Self-Image Compensating.* A relationship between low self-esteem and violence in which violence becomes a form of retribution against people who the person feels have cast aspersions on his self-image. The violence becomes a demonstration of self-worth by those who place an emphasis on their toughness.

4. *Self-Defending.* A tendency to perceive other persons as sources of physical danger requiring immediate neutralization as compensation for feelings of low self-esteem.

5. *Pressure-Removing.* A predisposition to explode in situations that one is unable to handle.

Toch also describes characteristics, such as bullying, exploitation, self-indulgence and catharting, which an officer may observe early in his interactions with a violence-prone person. In *bullying,* the officer observes pleasure being obtained from the exercise of violence and terror against susceptible individuals. *Exploitation* involves a persistent effort by the violence-prone person to manipulate others into becoming unwilling tools for his pleasure and convenience. Violent behavior may emerge when others do not react or respond. When a person is *self-indulging,* he operates under the assumption that others exist to satisfy his needs. Violence often becomes the penalty for noncompliance. Finally, in *catharting,* the person discharges accumulated internal pressure or feelings through violent behavior.

Horstman (1973) points out how the personality and the actions of the officer often contribute to assault. He describes situations in which the officer's overbearing attitude apparently goaded a suspect into attacking him. Although unable to identify a single precipitating event for the onset of violent behavior, Horstman did describe a "process of escalation, building on each experience between officer and suspect until the 'hair trigger' is honed and pulled by the execution of a critical event such as grabbing a suspect's arm to consummate an arrest."

Other dangerous situations with a high degree of associated violent behavior include the arrest of someone in a group and conducting a search. The humiliation of these acts, particularly when they take place in front of friends, may lead the violence-prone person to strike out in frustration. If possible, the officer should get the suspect out of sight of friends and onlookers before patting him down. These potential dangers associated with the arrest procedure suggest several attitudes and kinds of behavior which the officer should keep in mind when making an arrest.

He should indirectly motivate those whom he is placing under arrest into the wagon or car by "talking them in" rather than by grabbing their arm and escorting them. He should carry this out with a calm voice and manner. Once a person's last name is known, it should be used together with his or her correct title. Using other forms of address, such as first or last names only or nicknames, should be avoided unless the suspect is personally known to the officer and willingly accepts this. The officer should be careful not to convey dislike for the person he is arresting and should not treat the situation as a personal matter.

When he encounters a suspect who refuses to comply with his directions, he should clearly indicate that he is acting only as required by law. He might further mention that resistance to arrest only makes the situation more difficult and may result in additional charges. Finally, he may point out that the question of guilt or innocence is up to the court.

In arresting an intoxicated person, it is important for the officer to remember that the person may not fully comprehend the situation. Influenced by alcohol and in an unclear state of mind, he is more likely to resist the arrest. Therefore, it becomes even more important for the officer to avoid provocative and antagonizing comments and actions.

When the officer confronts an extremely excited person, he should realize that many people require an opportunity to yell, scream, or threaten for a period of time before quieting down. The officer who employs discretionary patience will find that the person will often rapidly calm down without the risk of physical injury to himself or the officer.

Horstman describes an interesting complication of the old Mutt and Jeff routine. In this, one cop plays Mr. Good Guy and his partner, Mr. Bastard. The bad cop gives the suspect a rough time and is then interrupted by the good cop, who openly disagrees with the techniques and philosophy of his partner and attempts to convince the subject that he (the good cop) will protect him and help him if only he will trust him and tell him the truth. Horstman found a high incidence of Mutt and Jeff routines in assault cases, in which the bad cop carried his actions too far and violence resulted. Supervisors should watch for this so that those who need additional training in how to handle people can acquire it.

Helpful Hints to the Law Enforcement Officer

Observations, such as those described above, show how and why new officers may pick up violent methods from old-timers. The new officer, just out of the academy and new to the streets, is faced with problems of human behavior that defy solution, make him anxious, frightened, and sometimes in fear of his life. Under such conditions, violence-prone solutions given with confidence ("That's how it really is out here on the streets, kid") by the seasoned officer are often very much listened to by the young trooper. Whether he becomes involved in violence will depend on his own personality, his own sense of right and wrong, and his own disposition toward violence or nonviolence. It will also depend upon the officer's knowledge and understanding of violent behavior. The principles described regarding his ability to enter interpersonal situations in a nonthreatening way will increase his ability to act effectively. These may be summarized in the following code of behavior:

1. When you approach a situation, try to analyze what is going on.

Before you become involved, a few seconds of reflection will enable you to size up the situation more adequately and reduce the possibility of precipitating violence.

2. Do not play "games" with a violence-prone person. Because of his experience, he will be a better game player. The result of game playing is more likely to be the onset rather than the prevention of violent behavior.

3. Learn to listen, not only to what the person is saying but also to the feelings with which he is expressing himself.

4. A display of personal involvement will escalate a situation and increase the potential for violent behavior.

5. The excited person should be given time to cool down. Many loud-mouthed people will calm down after a while, especially if they are not given any further reason by an officer to put on a show.

6. Remember that the person who resorts to violent behavior is often suffering from either a long-term or short-term loss of self-esteem. Therefore, do everything possible to preserve the person's self-esteem and avoid any actions which contribute to its further loss. Leave him a way out so his self-esteem is not further destroyed.

7. Never threaten. Any proposed action which you verbalize should be carried out. On the other hand, if you verbalize something you are not prepared to carry out, you may talk yourself into a corner and end up taking an action which you did not really intend.

8. Treat each individual you encounter with respect, patience, and tact, unless the immediate dangerousness of the situation merits other action.

9. Although you should not become personally involved, do not act like an automoton. Relax, use humor, if appropriate, and recognize that your authority will not vanish if you smile.

10. If you are not sure of department policies, such as those regarding the use of reasonable force, you should ask your supervisor. You should not rely on your peers because their policy interpretations may have been wrong for years.

Summary

In this chapter, we have discussed a subject of great importance to the law enforcement officer—violent behavior and the handling of the violent person. We have presented definitions, concepts, and characteristics of violent behavior. While the ability to predict a person's dangerousness is at best variable, there are many immediate behavioral clues which will enable an officer to heighten his perception of the dangerousness of a person in a specific situation. In this context we have emphasized officer–citizen relations and how, if mishandled, they can lead to an escalation process in which violent behavior results. Finally, we have described a behavioral code for the law enforcement officer to help reduce the possibility of friction and subsequent violent behavior in contacts with criminals and citizens.

BIBLIOGRAPHY

BINDER, A., and SCHARF, P. 1980. "The Violent Police–Citizen Encounter." *Annals of the American Academy of Police Science* 452:111–121.

COHEN, M. L., GROTH, A. N., and SIEGEL, R. 1978. "The Clinical Prediction of Dangerousness." *Crime and Delinquency* 24:28–39.

EVENSON, R. C., and ALTMAN, H. 1975. "A Re-Evaluation of the Diagnosis and Treatment of Dangerousness." Unpublished paper, St. Louis, Mo.: Missouri Institute of Psychiatry.

HODGES, E. 1971. "Crime Prevention by the Indeterminate Sentence Law." *American Journal of Psychiatry* 128:291–295.

HORSTMAN, P. L. December 1973. "Assaults on Police Officers." *The Police Chief.*

KAHAN, F. J. 1973. "Schizophrenia, Mass Murder, and the Law." *Orthomolecular Psychiatry* 2:127–146.

KOZOL, H. L., BOUCHER, R. S., and GAROFALO, R. F. 1972. "The Diagnosis and Treatment of Dangerousness." *Journal of Crime and Delinquency.* 18:373–392.

LEE, M., ZIMBARDO, P. E., and BERTHOLF, M. November 1977. "Shy Murderers." *Psychology Today* 69ff.

LESTER, D. 1978. "Assaults on Police Officers in American Cities." *Psychological Reports* 42:946.

MARK, V. H. 1970. *Violence in the Brain.* New York: Harper & Row.

MEGARGEE, C. I. 1966. *"Undercontrolled and Overcontrolled Personality Types in Extreme Anti-Social Aggression."* Psychological Monographs 80.

MONAHAN, J. 1973. "Dangerous Offenders: A Critique of Kozol, et al." *Crime and Delinquency* 19:418–420.

MONAHAN, J. 1981. *The Clinical Prediction of Violent Behavior.* Washington, D.C.: National Institute of Mental Health.

STERLING, J. W. 1972. *Changes in Role Concepts of Police Officers.* Gaithersburg, Md.: International Association of Chiefs of Police.

TOCH, H. 1969. *Violent Man.* Chicago: Aldine.

Chapter 15

Suicidal Behavior

CONTACT with suicidal behavior is a common occurrence in the work of a police officer. Not only will he be called after a suicide occurs, but he may also be the first to discover the body while on patrol. If suicide is threatened, he is often asked to come to the rescue.

In recent years, suicidal behavior has become recognized as a major public health and mental health problem. At least 25,000 successful suicides take place in the United States each year, and the number of attempts is much higher. Estimates in various studies range from eight to fifty unsuccessful attempts for every successful one.

If we also consider that an officer may encounter many suicide attempts disguised as homicidal behavior (chapter 14) or hidden in auto accidents, it becomes clear why it is important for the officer to know more about and to understand suicidal behavior. In this chapter, after reviewing the historical background of the field of suicidology, we will examine the suicidal person, the clues about the suicidal intentions that he presents, and some helpful hints to the officer for handling suicidal behavior when he encounters it.

Historical Background

Although recently attaining more visibility and popularity, the field of suicidology, the study of suicidal or self-destructive behavior, is not a new one. Throughout history, every society and culture has demonstrated concern with death and has devised methods to cope with the fear and trauma associated with it. As early as the Greek ages, philosophers argued whether a man had a right to take his own life. At various times since, societies have either condemned or approved suicidal behavior.

Suicide prevention, an important aspect of suicidology, also has deep roots. In 1621, Robert Burton, in his famous *Anatomy of Melancholy,* spoke of the "prognostics of melancholy or signs of things to come." He described how these prognostic signs (referred to by suicidologists today as *prodromal clues*) typically exist for a few days to a few weeks before the suicide attempt is made. Furthermore, he pointed out that recognition of these signs could save lives.

In 1897, the famous sociologist, Émile Durkheim, in his treatise *Le Suicide,* advanced the theory of social causation as an important factor in determining suicidal behavior. He believed that man's responses to his environment, including suicidal behavior, were more explainable in terms of social forces rather than psychological factors.

However, early attention to suicidal behavior was not limited to theorists such as Durkheim. In the early 1900s, for example, the Vienna, Austria, Police Department established a welfare division which handled all suicides and suicide attempts. Following an attempt, a summons was served on the attempter. If it was ignored, a second summons was issued. If it also went unanswered, a social worker was sent to investigate and to prepare an evaluation. In 1928, 2,373 cases were handled by this division. Over 1,000 were hospitalized for treatment, and an additional 544 were seen as outpatients. Considered a public service function, the program also provided employment, housing, and financial counseling—problem areas closely associated with suicidal behavior.

Other historical perspectives included those of the ancient Greeks. While most believed that taking one's life was improper, some felt it could be justified in certain circumstances. For example, the Epicureans, a philosophical group in early Greek culture, believed that life was to be enjoyed but recognized that, when it became impossible to achieve this goal, suicide was an appropriate way to hasten the inevitable. Similarly, in early Roman times, suicide was considered an offense only if one took his life to avoid trial or, by his death, caused another party to suffer a loss.

However, with the advent of Christianity, viewpoints toward suicidal behavior began to change. In 693 A.D., the Council of Toledo imposed excommunication upon suicides and denied them a Christian burial. By the eleventh century, suicide had become a recognized public problem and laws were passed to control it. Guided by Christian values, the courts regarded suicide as "murder of oneself" and, therefore, viewed suicide or a suicide attempt as a criminal act for which not only the one committing suicide, but also his entire family, could be punished.

These views have continued to exist in one form or another into modern times. For example, laws against suicidal behavior existed in England until 1961. Between 1946 and 1955, nearly 6,000 suicide attempters were arrested and over 5,000 were found guilty and sentenced to either jail or prison. The United States also had laws against suicide and suicide attempts until the 1960s. As late as 1964, nine states still declared attempted suicide a crime and eighteen others had laws against "aiding and abetting" a suicide attempter.

Not only did these laws label suicidal behavior as criminal but, more important, they also prevented the achievement of accurate statistics. In most jurisdictions where suicide was regarded as criminal behavior, the admissibility of evidence at a coroner's inquest followed the rules of criminal evidence (such as prohibition against hearsay), and this also prevented an accurate accounting of suicide attempts.

In the past, financial penalties have also been associated with suicide. For many years, insurance companies included suicide clauses in their policies which called for the return of premiums paid rather than the face value of the policy, as in other deaths. Current policies, however, specify full payment, but only if the insurance has been in force for a sufficient time.

Another reason for the stigma associated with suicidal behavior is the common myth that suicide is a psychotic act. Therefore, many families prefer to cover up anything which might point to suicide saying that "we have to admit that he is dead, but we don't have to admit that he was crazy."

Until recently, these legal, financial, and ethical prohibitions, as well as the associated stigma, greatly retarded a realistic study of suicidal behavior. In the United States, three psychologists, Farberow, Schneidman, and Litman, became interested in suicide notes found on file in the Los Angeles County Coroner's office. Their study of these notes and the circumstances surrounding the deaths of those who had written them convinced them that suicide was a major public health and mental health problem deserving of further study. They also became convinced that suicide was an individual matter which could be prevented in most cases if warning clues had been recognized (Schneidman, et al. 1970).

As a result of their efforts, the first Suicide Prevention Center was opened on the grounds of Los Angeles County Hospital in 1960. Gradually, awareness of its existence spread, and referrals of persons who were giving either verbal or behavioral clues of suicidal intent began coming in. The telephone as a means of contact became popular; by 1970 over 99 percent of first contacts were by phone.

By the mid-sixties, the concept of the suicide prevention center had gained in popularity. Funding was made available from many sources, including the National Institute of Mental Health, to establish more suicide prevention centers in other cities. Many of these centers have now discovered that their phones are utilized for all crises and, consequently, they have broadened their services to *crisis intervention.*

The Suicide Attempter

Schneidman has divided those who attempt suicide into four groups, based on the manner in which they approach the attempt.

Those in the first group do not intend to die. Their gestures are often dramatic and persistent with the principal aim of conveying a message to someone that they do not like what is happening and that they want something done about it immediately. This person may take a quantity of aspirin and then immediately tell someone so he can be rushed to a hospital; or he may climb to the top of a high water tower and threaten to jump unless some clearly stated condition is met.

Because these kinds of attempts are often attention getting, there is a danger that those who deal with them may ignore their seriousness or even make fun of them. For example, emergency room personnel often regard those who make this type of suicide attempt as intruding into their busy and "real" lifesaving activities. However, if this type of suicidal behavior is not taken seriously, the person may be goaded into a more serious attempt to convince others that he is not kidding.

Another reason for taking these attempts seriously is that these are the people who, if they die, often have a surprised look on their faces.

The prisoner who ties a sheet around his neck and jumps from his cell bunk when he hears the jailer approaching may underestimate the time required for the jailer to reach him. The recruit, maneuvering on the water tower may misjudge the tower's slipperiness and fall to his death. Although the officer may judge the potential lethality of the act as low, it is important for him to refer these people to mental health professionals so that intervention in any persistent pattern of this suicidal behavior can begin.

The second group is the "gamblers." These people have reached the point at which they are willing to let fate or some other person determine whether they live or die. Examples include those who play Russian roulette. Although these people may have given up some control to outside persons or situations, they remain uncertain as to whether they wish to live or die and often wish to do both at the same time.

In these cases, suicide prevention depends on recognizing the coexistence of the wishes to live and die and throwing support to the side of life. It is important to help the troubled person realize that there are more satisfying alternatives to suicide and that, even though he may feel intolerably miserable at this time, things will change and, with help, he will be able to overcome these feelings. One technique which the authors have found useful in these situations is confronting the attempter with what his contemplated suicide may mean to those he loves, especially any children he may have. Sometimes he will claim that "the kids will be better off without me." He should then be told emphatically that the children will not be better off; that they need him, and that children of a parent who commits suicide are often left with deep psychological scars. It is also helpful to point out the underlying anger by asking, "Do you really hate them that much?" This approach firmly closes the door on the use of rationalizations by the attempted suicide and gives him time to see other ways of handling his problems.

The third group includes those who seriously intend to die, but unforeseen factors intervene and save their lives. One of the authors recalls a retired sergeant who became very depressed and decided to commit suicide. When his wife and son left one morning, he connected a hose to the car exhaust, closed the garage door, and started the car. However, his son had used the car the night before and it soon ran out of gas. He then went back in the house to look for his son's rifle but, upon locating it, discovered that there was no ammunition. He then proceeded to the kitchen where he found some poisonous liquid under the sink. When he tried to drink it, he became sick and vomited.

At this point, his married daughter arrived at the house. Knowing that she usually left the keys in her car, he hid while she entered the front door and then sneaked out the back, started the car and sped away. Down the road, he ran the auto into a concrete abutment at a speed estimated at ninety miles an hour. The car was a total wreck, but he had only a broken leg. There is no question that this man was trying very hard to die but that fate had intervened. Despite the seriousness of their attempts, these people often welcome rescue and are later grateful that they were saved.

The fourth group consists of the successful attempters. These persons might also have been saved if someone had been alert enough to detect some of their early clues to this contemplated behavior. Recently, a young professor at a local university bought a gun, went into the desert, and shot himself. From later talks with his graduate students and fellow faculty members, it became apparent that he had given many clues of his intention.

Yet, as Schneidman has pointed out, we are often loathe to suspect suicidal intentions in those with whom we are close or who possess some type of status. For example, Farberow has pointed out that many physicians who commit suicide could be saved if they were treated like ordinary citizens in distress and hospitalized or referred to other appropriate treatment centers. The same situation exists in suicides among police officers. Fellow officers are often reluctant to admit the possibility of suicidal behavior and are even more hesitant to broach the matter to the officer himself (Schneidman, et al. 1970).

Each of these groups of suicide attempters presents clues prior to the attempt. Whether or not the suicide is successful, later investigation will usually reveal that these clues were present.

Clues to Suicidal Behavior

Schneidman has classified the clues to contemplated suicidal behavior into four broad categories—verbal, behavioral, situational, and syndromatic (Schneidman, et al. 1970).

Verbal Clues

Verbal clues can be direct or indirect. For example, a direct verbal clue is the statement "I'm going to kill myself" or "I'm going to take my car up the mountain and run it and me off the cliff." Less clear than these are indirect verbal clues or "coded" messages. In our clinic, a depressed young man appeared one day and asked, "How does one leave his body to the medical school?" Other examples include: "Well, I'll never have to worry about that anymore" or "You won't have to put up with my complaining much longer." Vague statements by a person that he might "do something" or expressions of "getting out of control" also can suggest suicidal intent.

When a person gives verbal clues, the officer should not be afraid to bring the question of suicide into the open. Some may hesitate because they are afraid that their questions might suggest this act to someone who has not really considered it. However, this is unlikely and, if suicide hasn't been on this person's mind, inquiring about it is not going to trigger it. Posing a direct question regarding suicidal thoughts will often help the formation of a trusting relationship because the person contemplating suicide will be relieved to find that others are able to understand what he has been thinking.

Behavioral Clues

Behavioral clues also may be direct or indirect. Direct clues include a history of a prior attempt. The officer should be especially alert if the prior attempt was almost lethal or if there has been more than one attempt. However, any history of past attempts, regardless of their potential lethality, should call attention to a suicidal risk.

Indirect behavioral clues to suicidal intent may include the sudden making of a will, the giving away of prized possessions, or the sending home of clothing and things needed for daily living. A few years ago, a skeleton of a young man was found by road crews working on an army reservation. Investigation revealed that the skeleton was that of a young lieutenant who had vanished from the base fifteen years earlier and had been listed as a deserter. Investigators managed to reconstruct the last few days of his life, even though many years had passed.

Two or three days before his disappearance, he had withdrawn all of his money from a local bank. Some he had lent, without security, to a friend who wanted to purchase a new car. He had sent the rest home to his father along with a footlocker containing his best clothes and prized possessions. He had then bought a revolver from a pawn shop, gone out in the desert, and shot himself. The rusted gun was found with his skeleton.

Although he had no history of depression or suicidal behavior and had given no direct verbal clues, his behaviors contained warning signs which might have led to the saving of his life if someone had noticed them.

Situational Communications

In addition to verbal and behavioral clues, situational communications often indicate contemplated suicidal behavior. Some situations are so stressful that they may lead to desperate attempts to escape them through suicidal behavior. For example, although most prisoners manage to do time without cracking up, others find it intolerable and will try to get out of jail or prison through suicide attempts. Although most of these attempts are clearly manipulative and are usually not fatal, they should not be ignored.

In a recent study of suicidal behavior in jails, the authors found that six out of eight prisoners transferred from the county jail to the psychiatric service of the county hospital because of suicidal behavior admitted that the motivation for their behavior had been to get out of jail and into the hospital. While all six stated that they did not intend to kill themselves, they all emphatically threatened to "do a better job next time" if forced to return to jail. After being returned to jail, four of the six made additional suicide attempts (Beigel and Russell 1972).

Other situations which may constitute serious emotional emergencies leading to suicide attempts include hospitalization, the possibility of major surgery, the discovery of a malignancy or terminal illness, and the loss of a job or loved one.

Syndromatic Communications

Schneidman describes a fourth category of clues known as syndromatic communications. These are a group of symptoms which, if they appeared singly, would not lead to concern. However, as the number seen in a single individual increases, the concern for possible suicidal behavior should also increase.

SLEEP DIFFICULTY

In nearly every study of suicidal patients, this symptom is mentioned prominently. It may be difficulty in falling asleep or, if the person falls asleep readily, he may awake in the middle of the night and be unable to go back to sleep. He may experience frequent and horrible night-mares as he sleeps fitfully and awakens at the slightest sound.

LOSS OF WEIGHT

Any appreciable loss of weight over a short period of time in the absence of a known physical cause, such as dieting or severe illness, may be significant.

FEARFULNESS

The person who is contemplating suicide may express vague fears of losing control. If this person had a previous depression which included a suicide attempt, he might say, "I don't want to end up that way again."

FATIGUE

Complaints of always being tired may be accompanied by posture and movements which communicate a feeling of great effort.

LOSS OF INTERESTS

These may include loss of interest in hobbies, work, social contacts, and/or sex. The more general the loss of interest, the more serious the depression and the more likely a possible suicide attempt.

IRRITABILITY

Continuing irritability, particularly in the absence of provocation and directed toward those whom an individual ostensibly loves.

FEELINGS OF SELF-DEPRECATION

The person who begins to describe himself as "worthless, bad, evil, and a failure" and who resists attempts to convince him that the opposite is true might be a suicide threat.

FEELINGS OF HOPELESSNESS

When an individual regards his situation and perhaps even himself as "hopeless," it is possible that he is not far away from seeing that there is no way out other than through his own death.

CHANGES IN DRINKING PATTERNS

When drinking patterns begin to change either through increased drinking, drinking alone or drinking at odd times, an acute state of depression may be present. Accidental suicides are often associated with changes in drinking patterns, since increased alcohol use combined with taking pills can be a lethal combination even though the person did not intend to die.

Helpful Hints to the Law Enforcement Officer

Establishing a relationship with the proposed suicide attempter, identification and clarification of this person's focal problem, evaluation of suicide potential, assessment of the strengths and resources available to the individual, implementation of rescue operations, if necessary, and referral to appropriate agencies are the critical aspects of suicide prevention which may occur in sequence or at the same time. The law enforcement officer who comes in contact with a potential suicide attempter should have a basic knowledge of these important aspects of suicide prevention.

The Relationship

When an officer is confronted with suicidal ideation, he should be patient, interested, self-assured, hopeful, and knowledgeable. By assuming this attitude and behavior, he communicates to the potential suicide attempter that he has done the right thing by letting the officer know that he is contemplating suicide. He should be accepted without challenge or criticism and allowed to tell his story in his own way while the officer listens.

Any contact with a proposed attempter initiated through a telephone call also requires certain clear approaches. First, the call should be answered with clear identification of the agency and the officer's name. As soon as it is known that the caller is suicidal, a request for the name and telephone number should be made. When some callers refuse to give their names, the officer should calmly accept this refusal, for the moment, and proceed with the conversation. However, at some later appropriate time, names and phone numbers of interested persons such as family members, physicians, or close friends who might be possible resources should be obtained. Since the immediate goal is to gather information to be used in evaluating suicide potential, getting into a discussion or argument about whether the caller is going to reveal his name will be counterproductive.

Identification and Clarification of the Local Problem

In conversations with officers, suicide attempters may often display a profound sense of confusion, chaos, and disorganization. Because they are often unclear about their main problems and get lost in details, one of the most important services which the officer can perform is to help them recognize what their central problems are and to place them in proper perspective.

For example, a woman called the police department, voicing many complaints including feeling of worthlessness, despair, and inadequacy. She said that she was not a good mother because she could not manage her housework and that her family would be better off without her. Careful initial listening by the officer followed by some specific questioning helped the officer to learn that her main problem was her relationship with her husband. When the officer reflected this back to her with authority, she was able to organize herself better and to address this specific problem more effectively.

Evaluation of Suicide Potential

Suicide potential refers to the probability that a person might kill himself in the immediate or relatively near future. It is important that as soon as the officer begins to talk with someone who is contemplating suicide, he should start to evaluate the suicide potential in order to make an accurate assessment of the immediate lethal risk. This is extremely important because the officer's plan of action will depend upon this evaluation.

Statistics indicate that the suicide rate rises with increasing age and that men are more likely to kill themselves than women. All other things being equal, a communication from an older male, therefore, tends to be more dangerous than one from a young female. However, young people do kill themselves although their original aim may have been to manipulate others rather than to die. Therefore, age and sex offer only a general framework for evaluating suicide potential. Each case must receive further appraisal according to other criteria.

One of these is the suicide plan. Three main elements should be considered in appraising the plan. These are: (1) the lethality of the proposed method; (2) the availability of the means; and (3) the specificity of the plan's details. Methods involving a gun, jumping, or hanging are usually more lethal than pills or wrist cutting. Furthermore, if the gun is at hand, the threat must be taken more seriously than when a person talks about shooting himself but does not have a gun. If a person describes specific details, indicating that he has spent time making preparations such as changing a will, writing suicide notes, collecting pills, buying a gun, and setting a time, the seriousness increases markedly. In addition, if the plan is bizarre and the details are apparently irrational, it is quite possible that the officer is dealing with a psychotic person, and this also increases potential lethality.

Information about the precipitating stress is also useful in evaluating potential. Typical precipitating stresses include losses such as the loss of a loved one by death, divorce, or separation; the loss of a job, money, prestige, or status; the loss of health through sickness, surgery, or an accident; or the threat of prosecution for criminal involvement or exposure for some reported misdeed. Occasionally, increased anxiety and tension may be associated with success, such as a job promotion with increased responsibilities.

The officer must evaluate the stress from the caller's point of view and not from his own or society's. What an officer might consider a minimal stress may be felt as especially severe by the caller.

The specific clues to suicidal behavior described in the previous section also serve as criteria for evaluating suicidal potential. The officer should keep in mind how these symptoms compare to the stress which he has found out about. For example, if the symptoms are severe but the stress precipitating them appears to be minor, then either the story may be incomplete or the individual may be chronically unstable, with a history of prior crises similar to this one.

The stress and symptoms must also be evaluated in relation to the individual's life-style. For example, the officer should evaluate whether the suicidal behavior is acute or chronic. If the officer discovers that serious attempts have been made in the past, the current situation must be rated as potentially more dangerous. On the other hand, if undergoing a severe stress, a person with no prior history of suicide attempts may also be a high risk.

In forming a plan of action, the officer should assess the available relationships of the potential suicide attempter. If he discovers that the suicidal person has severed all communications with others, then potential danger is increased.

Finally, it is also useful for the officer to inquire tactfully into the medical status of the potential suicide. For example, if the person is suffering from a chronic illness which has changed his self-image, suicide potential may be greater.

In summary, no single criterion need be alarming by itself, with the possible exception of the person who has a very lethal and specific plan for suicide. Rather, the evaluation of suicide potential should be based on the general pattern which develops after an examination of all criteria in the context of a specific person. For example, feelings of exhaustion and loss of resources will have different implications in two persons of different ages. A twenty-five-year-old married man stated that he was tired, depressed, and was having vague ideas about committing suicide by driving into a freeway abutment. There was no history of prior suicidal behavior. He reported difficulty in his marriage and talked of separation but was still in contact with his wife and working at his job which he had had for many years. This case was considered a low suicide risk.

In contrast, a high risk was a sixty-four-year-old man with a history of alcoholism who reported that he had made a serious suicide attempt one year ago and was saved when someone unexpectedly walked in and found him unconscious. He had a history of three failures in marriage and many job changes. He further said that his physical health had been failing, that he had no family left, and that he was thinking of killing himself with the gun he had in the house.

Assessment of Resources

In handling the person who is contemplating suicide, it is as important to assess his resources in the environment in which he lives as it is to evaluate specific aspects of his thinking and behavior. For example, although an individual may present many negative feelings and acts which indicate suicidal intent, this intent may be lessened by positive factors, such as a continued relationship with a loved one or even a positive reaction to an initial interview with the officer.

The discovery that the person is already in contact with a treatment agency or therapist may also lessen concerns about suicide potential. Finally, the presence of loved ones, particularly family and relatives, and their willingness to remain with a troubled person will also decrease suicide potential.

Rescue Operations and Referral Procedures

The officer's response to a specific situation will be determined by his evaluation of the suicide risk and the information he has obtained about available resources. In general, those situations which the officer rates as having high suicide potential in the presence of few resources will require immediate intervention. If the person is on the telephone, the officer should attempt to keep him on the line until a police unit arrives at the scene. This person should be immediately taken to a hospital for a professional evaluation unless family or close friends are present who will help bring the situation under control. In either case, those in control should be instructed not to leave the person alone.

Some situations encountered by the police are of low or medium risk, and initially, can be handled very satisfactorily by a sympathetic and understanding listener who provides telephone counseling. However, an attempt should also be made to refer this person to an appropriate agency, such as a suicide prevention center or a mental health clinic for continuing care. Consequently, the officer should be familiar with agencies in the community and know their hours of operation and telephone numbers. He should offer to make an appointment and should follow up by informing the person, if possible, while he or she is still on the line. Although the call may not be judged serious in terms of immediate suicide potential, the caller still has serious life problems which need help. A failure to respond may eventually lead to a more serious cry for help.

In the rare situation in which someone calls in the midst of a suicide attempt, the police should obtain only as much information as is necessary to identify the caller. A police unit should be immediately sent to the scene. If an individual is calling about another person, the informant should be instructed either to take the suicide attempter to a nearby emergency room or to call an ambulance.

The following are suggestions about general and community resources usually available during these situations. One or more of these resources should be considered by the officer.

The family is often a neglected resource during this crisis. The attempter should be encouraged to discuss his problems with his family. If it is important that someone be with this person during the crisis, family members should be called and told of the situation even though the attempter may express reluctance. However, he should be first informed that his family will be called.

Close friends may be used in the same way as families. For example, the caller or the attempter can be encouraged to have a friend stay with him during a difficult period. The friend may also be helpful in talking things out and giving him support.

People often turn to their *family doctors* for help because physicians are seen as supportive authority figures. If the potential suicide attempter has a good relationship with his physician, he should be encouraged to discuss his problems with him. Physicians can also be helpful when medication or hospitalization is required. If the potential attempter is religious, the involvement of a *clergyman* may be helpful.

In addition to people, the resources of *the community and its agencies* may be useful. The hospital emergency room, the suicide prevention center, the community mental health center or a social work agency, a private therapist, and/or a psychiatric hospital are appropriate helpful resources. When the officer considers utilizing one of them, he should recognize that his responsibility does not end until he has made certain that the attempter has been turned over to its care.

The following are examples of typical calls handled by a police station in which suicidal behavior or suicidal ideation was prominent. Following a description of the telephone call, we will suggest how the problem might be handled. These examples have been chosen for teaching purposes, and not all calls fall within these rather well-defined areas.

Case Example. A woman between thirty and forty years old called one night saying that she didn't understand why she felt so depressed. She said she was alone, complained of not being able to sleep, and of having troubled thoughts and feelings. She mentioned that she had thought about killing herself, but that she didn't really want to even though she had been having these thoughts for years. On the telephone, she sounded agitated, depressed, and somewhat hysterical. She was demanding and asked what could be done for her right now because she felt that she would not be able to get through the night. Upon further questioning, the officer was able to determine that many of these episodes had occurred before.

In such a situation, it is best for the officer to listen patiently and to wait for an opportunity to point out that things often look worse at night, but that it is not the best time to get help. The woman should be advised to call her doctor, a social service agency, or a mental health clinic in the morning to make an appointment. The officer should take her number and call her back the next morning to reinforce his suggestion. At the same time, he can suggest that she call a close friend or relative to come over and spend the night with her.

Case Example. A woman who sounds between twenty and thirty-five calls the police station but will not identify herself. She asks the officer what can anyone do for a person who doesn't want to live anymore. Although she sounds in control, she alludes vaguely to a long-standing problem. She demands that the officer do something about her problem.

The officer should point out to her that she has a responsibility to cooperate if she really wants help. He should tell her that it is important for him to know more about her situation and who she is before he can help her. If she mentions that she has a therapist and who he is, she should be referred back to the therapist. The officer can also tell the woman that he will call and notify the therapist that the woman has called. Although she may initially express resistance, it is likely that she will accept the officer's direction.

Case Example. A woman, perhaps in her early fifties, calls one evening to complain that she is very depressed and feels that no one is interested in her. During the phone call, she talks about her many physical problems and complains that her doctor is not helping her enough and that her husband is not giving her enough attention. She states that she feels her life is over and that there is no point in continuing to live.

She should be encouraged to talk with her husband and to tell him how she is feeling. If this is not feasible, either because he is not at home or because she is unwilling, she should be encouraged to call her family physician and talk to him. The officer may also offer to call her physician. If none of these resources is immediately available, she should be referred to a suicide prevention center or an appropriate mental health facility.

Case Example. A young man, probably in his early twenties, calls the police station. He is evasive and reluctant to give his name. He talks about a problem which he does not identify, but states that he is calling for help because he has reached the point where the only solution to his problem is to kill himself. He describes impulsive suicide plans, such as smashing his car on the freeway or cutting himself with a razor blade.

In this situation, it is important for the officer to be supportive. He may commend the young man for having done the right thing in calling as a beginning effort to get help. The officer should give the young man a list of helping resources. In this discussion, it is important to talk with him about which resource he might feel most comfortable contacting. Any assistance which the officer can give him in making this contact will be helpful.

Case Example. A young man in his early thirties calls one evening to complain that his life is a mess because of his bungling. He talks about having gotten himself in such a jam, financially and with his family, that he now feels the only way out is to kill himself.

The officer will often be able to identify a specific recent setback in this person's life. Once he has uncovered this recent stress, he should tell the caller that he is reacting to this specific stress and that he needs help with this particular problem. The caller should be reminded that he was able to function well before this setback and that he is probably suffering from a temporary depression, for which he needs professional help.

Case Example. A man, age fifty, calls one evening and sounds very depressed and discouraged. He is apologetic about calling and troubling the officer. He complains about a physical problem which has prevented him from working and states that he now feels that this problem is beyond help. He expresses many sad feelings about being old and a burden upon others. When asked about his suicidal thoughts, he reveals a specific plan for killing himself.

A police unit should be dispatched and contact maintained with the individual until the unit arrives. He should be told that help is available and on the way. After the unit arrives, family, friends, and other resources should be mobilized and involved.

Case Example. A family member or friend calls the police one evening about someone who is depressed and withdrawn. The caller is further concerned at having learned of this person's plan to kill himself and has even discussed its specifics. The caller is asking how serious the situation is and what to do.

This caller should be advised by the officer to contact the potential suicide immediately and explain that he or she is concerned and trying to get help. The caller should be told to encourage the potential suicide attempter to call a suicide prevention center or another appropriate agency. The initial caller should be kept in contact and asked to continue to inform the officer about what is happening.

Case Example. This caller is a neighbor who is concerned about someone but is reluctant to be identified or become involved by assuming any responsibility. Instead, the officer is asked do something for the person he or she is concerned about. Furthermore, the caller is vague about the disturbing situation.

In these cases, the officer should get as much information as possible and should tell the caller that it is important to take some steps, such as letting the potential suicide know of his or her concern.

It should also be pointed out to the caller that it is unrealistic for the officer to contact the person about whom the caller is concerned without being able to tell that person who notified him. If the caller is still reluctant to be identified, then it is even more important for the officer to emphasize that it is the caller's responsibility to become involved.

Case Example. In this situation, a physician, minister, or mental health professional in a position of responsibility calls about someone who needs immediate rescue to prevent a suicide. The officer should get only as much information as he needs to dispatch a unit quickly. He should ask the professional's opinion about what should be done after the potential suicide attempter is taken into protective custody.

Case Example. In this case, a caller informs the police that a neighbor or family member is being physically restrained from attempting suicide at that very moment and cannot be left unattended.

This caller should be advised immediately to take the person to the nearest hospital. If the caller cannot manage alone, a unit should be dispatched. In the meantime, the officer should emphasize that any harmful drugs or objects should be removed and that someone should always remain with the potential suicide.

In each of these examples, the officer has a responsibility to obtain as much information as possible and to maintain contact with the situation until it has been resolved. He must avoid empty reassurances and superficial platitudes, which will only convey to the person seeking help that the officer does not understand the problem and does not have any real empathy. If the officer conveys this impression, it is likely that the person who is contemplating suicide will not be able to form a trusting relationship with the officer. Possibly he will then break off communication and make a suicide attempt.

Police Response to an Ongoing Suicide Call

A police officer responding to an ongoing suicide call should keep the following in mind:

1. *Take the proper mental attitude.* Many times it is difficult for the police officer to take an appropriate mental attitude, since the officer may see the behavior of the person attempting suicide as manipulative. Perhaps the officer has been called to assist this person before and feels the person does not really want to commit suicide. However, every suicide threat or attempt should be taken seriously. Assume the proper

mental attitude by reminding yourself that every human life has dignity and that your responsibility is to help this person regardless of his behavior. This is what is meant by the proper mental attitude.

2. *Secure the scene and assess the threats to your own safety, the safety of others, and the safety of the suicide attempter.* In securing the scene, try to keep as many people as possible away from the immediate action. Frequently, ongoing suicide scenes resemble a three ring circus, with squad cars, an ambulance, a fire department truck, and neighbors in close proximity. Dispense with all that is not needed and try to keep other people clear of the immediate area. Do not be surprised when onlookers try to thwart your efforts by either making fun of the attempter, or by urging him to go ahead with the attempt.

3. *Introduce yourself and your organization, using name and title ("I am Officer Smith of the City Police Department").* This is important because it assists the attempter in relating to you. Ask what he likes to be called. Do not assume that because, for example, his name is Kenneth, he likes to be called Kenny or even Kenneth. This may be the name that the person with whom he is very angry or disappointed addresses him, and using it will create an unnecessary obstacle. This is especially true when dealing with juveniles since they may interpret your use of a nickname or even a first name as condescending. You might say, "Your name is Richard Smith; do you mind if I call you Richard?" or "What do your friends call you? What would you like me to call you?"

4. *Give plenty of reassurance.* Continually emphasize that you are there to help, that you can help, that there is hope, and that there are other alternatives to suicide. Many times it is useful to say something such as, "In my experience as a police officer, I have seen people who have been as unhappy as you and yet down the road, they're glad that they didn't do it." Remember that suicide prevention consists of helping the person to find alternatives to the suicidal act. The attempter is in this situation because he has not found alternatives and sees life as hopeless.

5. *Try and determine the main theme.* Usually, one of two major themes will predominate. Either the person is angry at someone and wants that person to pay for whatever was done to him, or he sees life as hopeless. You can deal more directly with the problem if you know which of these themes predominates. For example, if the attempter is angry at a specific person and wants that individual to pay for whatever has been done to him, you might point out to him that there is no magic replay of the suicide act. If he has guessed wrong and they are really

not going to feel sorry, then he missed the boat. Many people in this stressful situation show magical thinking; for example, a suicide attempter may talk about making her husband pay for all the harm that he has done as if she were going to be around at her funeral to see how sorry he is going to be. You have to point out that she won't be around and he may not be feeling this way at all.

If a person is feeling hopeless, helpless, unworthy, and inadequate, it is sometimes helpful to point out that he can always kill himself if talking with you doesn't work.

"But, just talk to me and let's see if we can work something out; you can always commit suicide just like right now, but let's see if we can work something out first." Sometimes these approaches will be successful, but at other times you may have to confront the person with the true consequences of the proposed act. For example, a mother or father may say that "the children will be better off without me." You can say, once again, "In my experiences as a police officer, this is not true ... I have seen children whose parents committed suicide and they are left with deep emotional scars." Then, judging the ability of the person to handle the guilt, you might say to him or her, "Do you really hate the children that much?" Remember that if one thing doesn't work, try another. If something you try doesn't work or seems to aggravate the situation, quickly back off. It is amazing sometimes what will work and what won't. For example, in New Orleans, a man had jumped into one of the canals. People nearby threw him life lines but he refused to grab them. He was getting weaker as he dog-paddled to keep to the surface, shouting out that he was going to drown and life wasn't worth living. Suddenly, a rookie cop arriving on the scene drew his revolver, aimed at the individual in the water and shouted, "Come out of there or I'll blow your Goddamn head off," whereupon the man grasped the line and allowed himself to be pulled ashore. You never know what will work. You have to be flexible.

6. *Comply with any requests if at all possible.* For example, the one attempting suicide may say, "Get that damn SWAT guy off the roof" or "Get those officers away from my front door." Grant this request. This does not mean that officers should give up trying to maneuver into more advantageous positions should quick action become necessary. But if something is annoying the person, or if he wants a Coke or a glass of water, grant the wish. Try to show that you understand where he is coming from and that nothing he has done so far cannot be undone.

Many times people in this situation feel they have gone too far and must go through with the act. Some even fear that they may go to jail if they don't kill themselves. Do not deceive them but frequently reinforce the idea that nothing has happened that cannot be undone. If they have done something which can't be undone (for example, if they have killed somebody), then point out that at least they can stop from doing any more harm or making the situation worse.

7. *Remember that the one attempting suicide is in control.* The attempter has seized ultimate control over his life. If you threaten this control directly or indirectly, you may precipitate completion of the act. Someone with a gun to his head or on the edge of a roof ready to jump is in full command of the situation. Remember, also, if he has a hostage and is threatening the hostage in addition to himself, with a gun to the head of the hostage, he has control. Your job is to take the control from this person in an unobstrusive way by showing your sincere desire to help him out of the situation.

8. *After the crisis is over, reassure the person.* Tell him that he did the right thing. If he surrenders the gun, comes down from the roof, or otherwise neutralizes the situation, be quick to praise him for a wise decision. He may disagree with you, but the fact that he allowed you to convince him otherwise shows that he is probably relieved at the outcome.

Response to a Suicide Scene That Has Been Interrupted Before Police Arrival

If a police officer responding to a suicide scene finds that the attempt has been aborted, either voluntarily or through the use of force, the officer should introduce himself by name, rank, and organization, reassuring people that he is there to help and being certain that the necessary medical facilities are available to assist if needed. If the person has to go to the hospital, then he should tell the family where he is going and that it probably will be best if one of them were to follow in their own car or ride in a police car because the medical personnel at the hospital will have questions only they can answer. It may also be necessary (according to the statutes of the particular state) for an eyewitness to sign a petition for involuntary commitment, if indicated. At the very least, the hospital will welcome the opportunity to obtain background information on the subject. The officer should also make inquiries as to what preceded the event, whether there was a previous history, and what the family sees in terms of the future. This will enable him to complete his report more fully and accurately.

Response to a Successful Suicide

If the officer responds to a suicide which had been successful, he must, of course, secure the scene. In larger departments, he will then call homicide and they will take over the investigation. In smaller departments, he himself may have to make the investigation.

The officer should remember that to many people suicide is a stigma, an act which brings disgrace on the family. Even though the majority of suicides leave suicide notes, the note may have been withheld from the police or even destroyed. There are many reasons for this, including social stigma, financial penalties in insurance policies, or perhaps a desire to keep the true nature of the act from other members of the family.

The officer always should be alert for suicidal acts in which there has been an attempt to conceal the nature of the act. For example, in a southwestern city some years ago, a body was found in a deserted shack in an isolated area. There was no furniture in the shack, and the body was hanging from a rope tied to a beam in the ceiling. The beam was too high for the individual to have reached it without standing on something. The case might have been labeled homicide except an alert detective noted that the dirt floor under the body was still a little damp. Further investigation revealed that the suicide had ingeniously managed to hang himself by stepping on two big blocks of ice. He intended that his body would be found after the ice had thoroughly melted, leaving no trace as to how the body was suspended from the beam. The motivation for the disguise of the act was that he wanted to leave considerable insurance to his wife and children.

Another caution for the officer investigating a successful suicide by strangulation or hanging is to remember that it may have been an act of sexual bondage and not suicide.

Summary

Suicidal behavior is a public health and mental health problem of major dimensions. It occurs among the rich, the poor, the young, and the old; among members of all races and religious backgrounds, and within all professions and occupations—even policemen. At the same time, it is an individual matter and can be prevented if one is trained to recognize the clues to suicidal behavior which most potential attempters display before making an attempt or successfully completing the act.

Police responsibility involves understanding the personalities of those who are most likely to attempt suicide, knowledge of the various clues to contemplated suicidal behavior, and awareness of those principles of suicide prevention that will allow an officer to respond appropriately to both telephone calls and emergency situations.

BIBLIOGRAPHY

BEIGEL, A., and RUSSELL, H. E. 1972. "Suicide Attempts in Jails: Prognostic Considerations." *Hospital and Community Psychiatry* 23:361–363.

BURTON, RICHARD. 1961. *The Anatomy of Melancholy.* ed. F. Dell and P. Jourdan-Smith. London: J. M. Dent and Sons.

FARBEROW, N. L., and SCHNEIDMAN, E. S. 1961. *The Cry for Help.* New York: McGraw-Hill.

GELLER, A. M., and ATKINS, A. 1978. "Cognitive and Personality Factors in Suicidal Behavior." *Journal of Consulting and Clinical Psychology* 46:860–868.

HATTON, CORRINE LOING, ed. 1977. *Suicide: Assessment and Intervention.* New York: Appleton-Century-Crofts.

HENDIN, H. 1963. "The Psychodynamics of Suicide." *Journal of Nervous and Mental Disease* 136:236–44.

LESTER, D., BECK, A. T., and MITCHELL, B. 1978. "Extrapolation from Attempted Suicides to Completed Suicides." *Journal of Abnormal Psychology* 88:78–80.

MARIS, RONALD W. 1981. *Pathways to Suicide: A Survey of Self-Destructive Behaviors.* Baltimore: Johns Hopkins University Press.

MURPHY, G. E., CLENDENIN, W. W., and DARVISH, H. S. 1972. "The Role of the Police in Suicide Prevention." *Life-Threatening Behavior* 1:96–105.

SCHNEIDMAN, E. S. 1967. *Essay in Self-Destruction.* New York: Science House.

SCHNEIDMAN, E. S., FARBEROW, N. L., and LITMAN, R. E. 1970. *The Psychology of Suicide.* New York: Science House.

PART V

Behavioral Aspects of Crisis Situations

Chapter 16

Behavioral Aspects of Disaster

THE PAST SEVEN chapters have focused on a small number of people who demonstrate different kinds of behavior, often in association with mental illness. It is important for the police officer to recognize that even healthy or normal individuals can demonstrate abnormal behavior as an acute reaction to overwhelming environmental stress.

In police work, the most common events associated with overwhelming environmental stress occur in disaster situations. Fires, floods, tornadoes, earthquakes, and auto accidents are examples of this type of acute stress situation which can lead to nonfunctional behavior in someone who is otherwise healthy.

The ability of the officer to deal effectively with the behavioral aspects of these disaster situations will depend on his understanding of the types of reactions which may occur, the factors which lead to the behavior associated with them, and the specific intervention tools he has available.

Historical Background

Much of our knowledge about stress and its effects, particularly during disasters, has come from military experiences. During the Civil War, medical personnel first observed and recorded the principle that environmental stresses may produce symptoms of abnormal behavior in soldiers. Surgeons of both the North and the South described a condition *(nostalgia)* which seemed responsible for considerable ineffectiveness. Soldiers afflicted with this disorder showed many symptoms of emotional instability, including nervousness, anxiety, discontent, and passive-aggressive behavior. In this group, there was a higher degree of AWOLs and other disciplinary problems. The medical personnel realized that these symptoms were a result of a pathological interaction between the soldier and his environment. They made note of this in their journals, but the war soon ended, and the lesson which they had learned was soon forgotten.

When World War I began, the military again discovered soldiers, especially in the combat area, with similar symptoms. This time the diagnosis offered was *shell shock,* a term coined by Lieutenant Colonel Mott, a British medical officer. He believed that these observed symptoms were a result of a brain concussion of varying severity secondary to the effects of exploding shells. However, later observers noted that not all soldiers exposed to combat developed these symptoms and that, furthermore, some of those with shell shock had not had any exposure to combat and had not been anywhere near an exploding shell. Consequently, the strictly physical explanation for their ineffectiveness was discarded, and these individuals were considered emotional casualties of the war.

The British and the French noticed that, when these casualties were evacuated to rear-echelon medical installations, only a few ever returned to combat duty. However, if they were treated up front, a majority could be returned to full combat duty within twenty-four to forty-eight hours. The treatment was relatively simple and emphasized food, rest, and emotional support, along with a firm expectation from the treating officer, repeatedly conveyed to the soldier, that the soldier would be all right in a few hours and able to return to his group.

These well-documented experiences during World War I were quickly forgotten and, at the start of World War II, the military was again found lacking in knowledge about the effects of battle stress. When the first full-scale battles in which Americans participated resulted in a large number of unanticipated psychological casualties, these casualties were evacuated to rear-line medical installations, contrary to what experience had taught during the latter stages of World War I. Many of the soldiers thus evacuated did not recover and ended up with medical discharges and diagnoses of psychoneurosis or psychosis.

However, as the war continued, American psychiatrists became more skilled in treating war neuroses, using hypnosis and drug-induced interviews to relieve anxiety and restore health. The value of treatment on the front lines was rediscovered and psychiatrists were again assigned to combat positions. Then the high level of psychological casualties decreased (Glass 1953).

From these wartime experiences, two basic principles emerged: (1) treat victims up front as much as possible; and (2) return them to duty as soon as possible. These principles have direct application to civilian disaster situations, including floods, tornadoes, fires, industrial accidents, and auto accidents.

The Four Phases of Disaster Reactions

Studies of disasters have led to a description of four distinct phases which can be anticipated in any reaction to a major stress situation. These are: (1) period of warning; (2) impact; (3) immediate reaction; and (4) delayed response (American Psychiatric Association 1964). An understanding of these four phases will enable the police officer to apply effectively those principles and techniques of psychological first aid that we will describe later.

The Warning Period

Warning of an impending disaster is desirable. However, this warning might have a destructive or disorganizing effect on individual behavior. While some people function at a high level of effectiveness in the face of danger, others may respond to a warning signal as if a disaster had already occurred and become completely helpless.

This latter group usually consists of two types of people: those who have experienced a previous or similar disaster in which they were helpless and for whom the warning signal rekindles earlier helpless feelings; and those who will always be helpless in the face of any danger or threat. These people are susceptible to panic and must not be left to their own devices or they will communicate their panic to others.

The Impact Period

When disaster strikes, people will experience many frightening feelings. Although patterns of behavior have been well established, the initial impact will be stunned inactivity. It has generally been shown that, for about the first fifteen minutes, no one will be able to act effectively. Approximately fifteen minutes after a disaster has occurred, about 25 percent of the people will be able to resume effective behavior and, within one hour, another 60 percent will be capable of effective functioning. Most of the remaining 15 percent will take several hours to several weeks before they will be able to function effectively. A few may never recover.

Immediate Reaction after Impact

The period immediately following a disaster or stress situation is critical because this is when ineffective behavior is most costly. In contrast, effective behavior can save lives, relieve suffering, and decrease confusion.

Period of Delayed Response

When the community or the person is no longer in immediate danger, the situation can be evaluated and action taken to meet needs. However, although the immediate danger is over, some may have a delayed reaction. The person who was observed functioning effectively immediately after the disaster may no longer be doing so. Instead, he may now demonstrate signs of emotional disturbance, including anxiety or depression. Therefore, some people may require continued observation to insure that they do not have a delayed reaction to a disaster.

Normal and Abnormal Behavioral Reactions

The police officer may often have to set priorities as to whom he gives psychological first aid most immediately. It is, therefore, important for him to distinguish between normal behavioral reactions to stress or disasters and abnormal reactions.

He should recognize first that the presence of fear, anxiety, indecisiveness, confusion, and even temporary disorientation can be normal reactions. Their presence does not necessarily mean that an abnormal reaction is occurring. Abnormal reactions are more complex and can be divided into four general categories.

First, there is the individual who is in a complete *panic.* In addition to the symptoms and signs listed above, judgment and reasoning have completely disappeared. The person who simply tries to escape a dangerous situation is not necessarily in a state of panic. The panicked individual attempts to leave, in an unreasonable manner and without any judgment. It is important that this person be immediately identified and isolated from others before they are affected by his reaction.

The second category of abnormal behavioral reactions is the depressed group. These people are slowed down, numbed, and dazed. The individual with a depressed reaction may sit in the midst of utter chaos, gazing vacantly into space and unable to respond. This is probably the most frequent abnormal behavioral reaction, and people suffering from it usually respond very quickly to psychological first aid.

The third category is the *overactive reaction.* At first, this may look like panic, but the critical difference is that the affected person does not try to leave the situation but rather begins markedly increased physical activity. He may talk rapidly, joke inappropriately, or make endless suggestions of little value. If his hyperactivity can be controlled, he may eventually prove to be very helpful in dealing with the disaster. Consequently, anything he is given to do that will work off excess activity will be helpful. After he has settled down, he can be assigned to constructive tasks.

Finally, the last category of abnormal behavioral reactions to stress or disaster situations includes the *abnormal body reactions.* In these cases, the physical reactions to stress are severely incapacitating and may include severe nausea and vomiting that will not stop or hysterical blindness or paralysis.

Long-Term Psychological Effects

Long-term disabilities arising from disaster situations occur infrequently. Studies which have been completed on our returning Vietnam veterans clearly support the need for continued counseling to those who may suffer long-term effects from severe stress situations. These effects may not be apparent until much later, when hospitalization may be required.

Those who have long-term reactions to disaster situations are more likely to have had acute reactions to other disasters in the past. Consequently, it is important for a police officer to find out, if possible, whether a person with an acute reaction during a current disaster has been involved in another situation in the past and to learn more about his reaction at that time and what was done about it.

Helpful Hints to the Law Enforcement Officer

Similar to the physical first aid which an officer gives to someone who has been injured in an auto accident, he can also apply psychological first aid to those whom he encounters with acute emotional reactions to disaster situations. His principal goal is to return the greatest number of people to effective functioning in the shortest time. In responding to stress or disaster situations, the officer should keep in mind the following principles:

1. He should respect every person's right to his own feelings. Just because the officer has responded appropriately, he should not expect that everyone else will. He should realize that there will be as many different reactions as there are different people because each person is unique. A psychological casualty is not an inferior or cowardly person.

2. The officer should remember that emotional disability secondary to a disaster situation is as real as physical disability. No one would expect a soldier who has had both of his legs shot off to buck up and go back into the fray. Similarly, the police officer should not expect people who have had a severe emotional reaction to pull themselves together and carry on.

3. The officer should remember that every physically injured person will have some emotional reaction to his injury. Furthermore, some people may have severe emotional reactions to minor injuries because of their personal significance. For example, the artist who has cut his finger may have a more severe reaction than a lawyer with the same injury. Occasionally, the major reason for a severe reaction is not as obvious and may relate to a symbolic event or an unconscious fear.

Because of this fear, a person may distort the seriousness of the injury, consequently increasing his emotional reaction. Finally, it is important for the police officer to recognize that there is often more strength in people than may initially appear. Although this may seem contradictory to the first principle, which states that a person's feelings should be recognized and accepted, it is not. The officer should direct his support to the individual's strength. If he can mobilize this strength, he can significantly reduce the emotional reaction to a disaster.

4. In handling a disaster situation, the officer must remain calm if he is to be effective. He must keep his wits about him so that he does not inadvertently compound the disaster situation and the emotional reactions of others to it.

Consequently, he should also remember *not* to do the following when encountering those with acute emotional reactions to stress situations. He should not strike, slap, or hit anyone. He should remember that it will not do any good to tell someone to "snap out of it" or to "use their will power." Statements such as these will only increase feelings of inadequacy, with which the person may be already overwhelmed. Finally, he must not upset anyone with pity, blame, or ridicule since these will also increase feelings of inadequacy.

5. The police officer should establish, as soon as possible, some form of communication with the person, either verbal or nonverbal. In this regard, it is helpful to remember what a mother does with a hurt child who comes in from the playground crying. The good mother will take the child onto her lap, comfort him, and ask him what happened. As he sobs out his story, she may put ice or some medicine on his bruise and get him a Band-Aid while continually reassuring him that everything will be all right. This is a good example because, in disaster situations, many people regress to childlike behavior.

While the officer may not take a person onto his lap, he certainly can put his arm around him, ask him what happened, and help him ventilate his feelings about the situation. In doing so, the officer is not interested in the truth or falsehood of any statements but, rather, is trying to get the person to talk about his feelings.

6. After establishing communication, the next important thing a police officer can do is to get the person to engage in constructive activity. This will reduce physical tension as well as divert him from thinking about his own problems. By enabling him to serve others, he can restore his feelings of adequacy. After this physical release has been achieved, he should be encouraged to rest and pay attention to his own needs, such as hot food or dry clothing. Throughout his handling of this person,

the officer should convey to him firmly the expectation that he will shortly be all right.

7. Remember that to suffer together is to suffer less. The officer should try and get the person back to his family and friends as soon as possible. If there has been a tornado, for example, and people have been rushed to hospitals, the officer should try to maintain a list of who went where so that he can assist survivors to find their loved ones.

8. Finally, the officer should always be aware of his own feelings. It is natural to feel resentment, anger, and hostility toward those who do not seem to be physically injured and contribute nothing to help the situation. The officer must not allow these feelings to interfere with his ability to help others during a disaster.

Summary

This chapter has described reactions to acute stress and disaster situations. Emotional casualties are often more frequent than physical disabilities. By recognizing this, the officer can have an important influence on reducing abnormal behavior reactions to disaster situations. Not only can he save lives and relieve suffering, but, perhaps more importantly, he can also help people get back on their feet as quickly as possible so that they can assist him in the many tasks demanded by the disaster situation.

BIBLIOGRAPHY

AMERICAN PSYCHIATRIC ASSOCIATION. 1964. *First Aid for Psychological Disasters.* Washington, D. C.: American Psychiatric Association.

COHEN, RAQUEL E. 1980. *Handbook for Mental Health Care of Disaster Victims.* Baltimore: Johns Hopkins University Press.

GARB, S., and ENG, E. 1969. *Disaster Handbook.* New York: Springer.

GLASS, A. J. March 16–18, 1953. "Psychotherapy in the Combat Zone." In *Proceedings of Symposium on Stress.* Washington, D. C.: Army Medical Graduate School, Walter Reed Medical Center.

HANSON, S. 1979. "Natural Disaster: Long Range Impact on Human Response to Future Disaster Threats." *Environment and Behavior* 11:268–284.

HOCKING, F. 1970. "Extreme Environmental Stress and Its Significance for Psychopathology." *American Journal of Psychotherapy* 24:4–26.

WOLFENSTEIN, MARTHA. 1977. *Disaster: A Psychological Essay.* New York: Arno Press.

Chapter 17

Behavioral Aspects of Riots and Riot Control

DURING HIS WORK, the police officer must often handle large crowds, some of which are peaceful while others are not. Both disasters, as described in the previous chapter, and civil unrest can lead to behavioral changes in individuals and/or large crowds which will present problems to the officer.

Without knowledge of those psychological principles associated with riot behavior and riot control, it will be difficult for the officer to handle crowd behavior effectively. With knowledge, however, he will be able to plot a course of action which will have the best chance of preventing violence or panic, or of controlling such an outbreak if it has already begun.

In this chapter, we will discuss characteristics of crowds and mobs; underlying factors that influence their behavior and countermeasures the police officer can take to control it; techniques employed by mobs in mob action; types of panic-producing situations that might occur and the actions which can be taken to prevent them; and the type of mental preparation required of officers before undertaking civil disturbance duty. Finally, we will present a code of conduct for the police officer which can serve as a guide to his behavior during civil disturbances.

Characteristics of Crowds and Mobs

It is important to distinguish between a crowd and a mob, since the majority of gatherings do not present any special problems to the police. A crowd is a large number of people temporarily congregated without organization, who think and act as individuals. A crowd may be a *physical crowd* or a *psychological crowd.* An example of the former would be people in a shopping center who have gathered together accidentally without a specific organization or purpose other than shopping. In contrast, the psychological crowd exists when there is a common interest. This type of crowd can be further described as either *casual* or *intentional.* An example of the casual crowd is a gathering at an accident or a fire. In contrast, the intentional psychological crowd might be found at a sporting event, a political rally, or a funeral. It is the intentional psychological crowd which is most susceptible to transformation into a mob.

A mob is a crowd whose members, influenced by stimuli of intense excitement or agitation, lose their sense of reason and respect for law and follow leaders into lawless acts of violence and destruction. It is helpful to classify mobs according to the behavior and motivation of its members.

The *aggressive mob* riots and terrorizes (for example, race riots, lynchings, and prison uprisings). The *escape mob* is in a state of panic or blind flight. Members of an escape mob lose their power of reasoning and may cause their own destruction (for example, fleeing from a disaster). An *acquisitive mob* is motivated by a desire to acquire something (for example, looters following in the wake of an aggressive mob). Finally, a *dispersed mob* may quickly join together, accomplish an act, and then disperse again. This mob's objective is to create simultaneous disturbances as diversions from the actions of a principal mob (for example, setting fires to incite additional violence, or sniping).

The Riot Process

Having defined the types of crowds that exist, characterizing how a crowd may turn into a mob, and describing the types of mobs, we will now turn to the riot process and describe it in detail.

Precipitating Incident

Almost anything can serve as the precipitating incident to a riot. It might be a forceful apprehension by an officer or a routine traffic stop. It may not be an act but only a rumor which leads people to pour into the streets in a state of agitated anger.

It may not be a single event, but rather a series of previous incidents and/or rumors that have occurred to set the stage for the final incident which triggers the riot's start. For example, during the summer of 1980, residents of Miami, Florida engaged in several days of civil disturbance. The precipitating incident occurred when several policemen were acquitted in court of charges stemming from a case of alleged police brutality in which a black man had died.

Although this was the immediate precipitating incident, the roots of this riot actually had been developing over several years and may have even dated back to the riots of 1968. For several days, the weather had been unusually hot. For several months, economic conditions had been worsening, with a resulting increase in black unemployment. More important, there had been several incidents of alleged police brutality toward blacks in recent years, with the growing belief that nothing would ever be done about it by either the police or the local government. All of these events, prior to the precipitating incident, created an emotional climate conducive to the spontaneous eruption of violence after an incident which would normally not have created this extreme difficulty.

Studies have shown that, in many cases, the riot process can be stopped at this point if the mayor or another important official immediately visits the area, talks to the people, and promises to listen to and redress their grievances. An example of this occurred when John Lindsay, then Mayor of New York City, walked the streets of Harlem in 1968, speaking with people and thereby carrying out an important part of riot prevention.

Confrontation

During the second phase, the police must avoid either overreaction or underreaction. Many confrontations exhaust the energy of the riot participants and nothing further happens. However, in some situations, a *keynoting process* may begin. This occurs when the angriest members of a crowd, or perhaps a single more militant individual, urge more violent action.

To counter this, moderate community leaders may try to persuade the crowd to disband, promising that a committee will be formed to channel the protest to the city hall. If these leaders prevail, the crowd will disband and the riot will be over; but if the militants or the hostile keynoters win, the riot will escalate to the next stage.

Roman Holiday

The *Roman Holiday* phase usually involves young people who are angry, hostile, and impulsive. Although their actions may have been planned in advance, a spontaneous reaction is more likely. They may begin to break windows, overturn cars or set them afire, and engage in other destructive events.

During this stage, it is again important for the police not to over- or underreact. If they respond with excessive force, tales by the victims to the news media will reach dissident communities and lead to further escalation. On the other hand, a permissive attitude may be considered as a go-ahead signal, and the result is the same. When this phase is not handled properly, more people, both adults and children, begin to take part in looting and stealing. Firebombs and guns may be brought into play, and the riot may escalate into open conflict.

Open Conflict

This phase becomes combat in the city, as exemplified by the 1968 riots in Washington, D.C., the 1980 riots in Miami, Florida, and the 1981 disturbances in some British cities. The police must now use force to contain the riot and restore order. Moderate to intense sniper fire occurs. Firebombing increases and is used as a selective weapon by the rioters.

The police respond by using automatic weapons. The National Guard is often called in. A dissident community, especially if agitated by militants, may arm itself and assemble its own firepower. Eventually, the establishment usually wins, since the odds are always in its favor because of its greater resources.

The Individual Rioter

Although rioting is mob action, the individual is still the basic unit of the mob. We must ask: Why do individuals participate in mob action? What is it about the mob that leads people to lose control and commit acts which they would not do under other circumstances? To help answer these questions we will discuss several underlying factors that affect individual behavior in a mob.

The first is *anonymity*. A person tends to lose his identity in the mob since he feels that he will not be blamed for his actions. Because he sees the things he does as only a small part of a larger picture of violence and destruction, his sense of anonymity is increased.

A second factor is the *impersonality of group behavior*. This may be understood better by recalling the football player who bears no personal grudges against his rival, but will "do or die for Old Notre Dame," or the soldier who bears no personal animosity against the enemy soldier he may shoot.

The impersonality of mob behavior is also demonstrated when one member of a race or group is not seen as an individual but as a stereotype. The sniper who puts the figure of a police officer in the crosshairs of his high-powered rifle scope may hate, but he hates the police symbol, not the individual officer he is about to try to kill. It does not matter to this sniper that the officer in his sights may have a wife and children or that he may be one of the fairest officers on the force. Neither would it matter if he was one of the most hated officers. The sniper stereotypes him as a "pig" and kills him with an impersonal attitude.

Because of the intense emotions present during a riot, members of the mob tend to suspend their own normally critical judgment and react impulsively to the suggestion of a dominant member. Police officers can counter this kind of negative *suggestibility* by suggesting an alternate course of action to the mob. For example, during the 1967 march on Washington, when agitators were trying to incite tired mob members to continue the disturbances at the Pentagon, undercover police officers infiltrated the crowd and encouraged people to take advantage of waiting buses to rest their tired feet. The mob responded positively to this countermeasure and left the area.

Closely allied to suggestibility is *contagion*. The reader is probably more familiar with this term in a medical sense, such as a contagious disease resulting from the transmission of a virus from the sick to the healthy. Similarly, ideas and feelings can be contagious. People become emotionally stimulated by the feelings and ideas of others, although they have not shared the experiences from which they originate.

Imitation is another factor. The urge to do what others are doing is very strong when large numbers of people are gathered together. Group identity grows and draws people closer psychologically. Contrary to popular belief, hostility is not eliminated or reduced by having a good fight or by letting off steam through violent acts. This behavior merely solidifies hostile feelings and develops increased hatred within the mob. As open violence increases, more destruction is likely to follow.

Novelty may also encourage individual participation in a mob. Many who lead dull and uninteresting lives may view a riot as a break in their daily routine and react with enthusiasm. The riot gives these people an opportunity to do some things they have always wanted to do but didn't dare. A less harmful circumstance is the college panty-raid, when many students join in this novel activity to relieve the boredom of studying.

The Riot-Prone Personality

From the personality disorders discussed in chapter 6, it is evident that some people might be more apt than others to become involved in a riot. For example, the passive-aggressive person, with underlying feelings of hostility and aggression, may need only a small provocation to release these feelings against others. The paranoid person—chronically angry, hostile, and suspicious—will take advantage of an opportunity to act out these feelings. The psychopath is not only riot-prone but is often an instigator and leader of riots, especially in jails and prisons. On the street, he may engage in riot behavior as a mask for criminal activity or for the attention he receives as a militant leader. Finally, the emotionally immature person may engage in riots because of his tendency toward immature, acting-out behavior. He is suggestible, and may be a follow-the-leader type, welcoming the opportunity to release hostility through destructive action. In the mob, he gains courage to do things that he would not do alone.

Techniques of Agitators

To counter the behavior of agitators, it is important for the police officer to understand the principal techniques they use in starting or continuing to incite mob action.

The Emotion-Producing Rumor

Police engaged in civil disturbance duty should have an intelligence unit aimed at picking up and controlling rumors, since the adept agitator will use rumors to increase the tempo of a disorder or to change an orderly demonstration into a violent one. Police must be aware of these rumors and put out factual information to defuse them.

Propaganda

Newspaper, radio, television, and magazine propaganda are used by agitators to aggravate existing prejudices and grievances. In this way, they can bring a crowd together at a particular location or time and incite emotions by using propaganda to intensify real or imagined inequities. Aroused in this way, the crowd is ripe for transformation into a violent mob.

The police can effectively counter propaganda through up-to-date, factual information, especially about their own actions or those of other controlling forces, such as the National Guard. The mayor of a community may help by publishing proclamations that give the public concise information and instructions.

Forceful Harangue

As a well-trained speaker, the experienced agitator uses emotionally loaded words and phrases to appeal to local needs, fears, and prejudices. Emphatic movements, such as waving of the arms, help to influence people to abandon their critical reasoning and to engage in actions which they would rebel against or condemn under normal circumstances.

The police may act by apprehending the speaker (which has the risk of making him a martyr) or dispersing the crowd (which is sometimes quite difficult). The mayor of one large American city undermined the planned actions of an agitator by meeting him at the airport with a courtesy car and appearing on the platform to introduce him. This implied association with the establishment created distrust among those who were prepared to hear and follow the militant.

The Appearance of an Irritating Person or Symbolic Object

A crowd may be brought to a fever pitch by the appearance of an object, such as a flag, or a particular person for whom the crowd has antipathy. This is sometimes difficult to combat, since it often occurs accidentally. If this happens, the person or object should be removed as quickly as possible, especially if it can be done without further exciting the crowd. When there is information ahead of time that the appearance of a particular individual might trigger a disturbance, the appearance should be cancelled. In 1960, President Eisenhower's trip to Japan was cancelled because of the danger of civil unrest which, it was felt, his presence in Japan at that time might trigger because of existing anti-American feeling.

Acts of Violence

Acts of violence, when they occur, can be successfully played upon by agitators to begin a chain reaction leading to further violence. Although we have been discussing techniques by which trained agitators can incite crowds, many disturbances are triggered by amateur agitators who seize a spur-of-the-moment opportunity. The following example, taken from the pages of the *Arizona Daily Star* of July 30, 1973, is an illustration:

Dallas, Texas: Quiet returned to downtown Dallas Sunday after a protest march led to a night of rock throwing, burning and looting.

Police said forty-eight businesses were damaged in the melee which erupted during a march to protest the fatal shooting of a twelve-year-old Mexican–American boy by a policeman.

A large force of city and state policemen and sheriff's deputies quelled the violence after about three hours. At least five policemen were injured, none seriously.

The Dallas City Council met in emergency session after the incident and issued a statement both supporting the police and saying it joins with all Dallas citizens in understanding the outrage and sorrow of the Mexican–American community.

A police spokesman said there will be some inciting to riot charges filed today.

The march to the City Hall had been peaceful, according to a police spokes-man Sunday, until a black woman grabbed a microphone in an unmarked police car and began shouting, "Kill the Pigs!"

The woman was one of thirty-nine arrested. In all, forty-eight businesses sustained damage from glass breakage or looting. Police said estimates of total damage are expected to be high.

Panic may also occur when police begin to move in. The police must be prepared to size up panic-producing situations and to take active steps to prevent a panic or to control the mob's actions when panic starts. Panic has been described as *blind flight.* It develops when the mob perceives a threat to survival, and it spreads rapidly. This per-ceived threat may be physical and/or psychological; real or imagined. It is usually regarded as so imminent that the mob views flight as the only possible escape.

In a riot, the presence or threat of riot-control agents, such as tear gas, may be enough to spark a panic reaction. The mob becomes irrational and fearful, seeking only to get away from the danger. Escape routes become clogged, and the physical pressure of those in the back causes those in front to be crushed, smothered, or trampled. More panic is then produced, and a vicious cycle begins.

Police personnel may counter panic reactions by the following tech-niques: (1) get up-to-date, factual information to the people and keep it coming; (2) provide escape routes and inform the crowd or mob where these routes are; and (3) keep these routes open and make sure that front-to-rear communication is maintained.

Sufficient communications equipment must be provided and alter-nate means for backup should be at hand in case the main communica-tions equipment and/or personnel are ineffective. Despite any difficul-ties, police must be alert to prevent these incidents.

Helpful Hints to the Law Enforcement Officer

Having described the types of behaviors and techniques, both group and individual, associated with riot behavior, it is now important to turn to those techniques which law enforcement must employ if it is success-fully to contain and control this behavior. Like the individual and group activities which are a part of riot behavior, riot control involves actions of the individual police officer and the police as a whole.

Self-Control

The individual police officer and the police as a group must not lose self-control when dealing with riots. A professional, businesslike detachment, accompanied by impartiality and the sharp execution of orders, will enhance the police image and contribute to orderly restoration of law and order. Only force necessary to control a situation should be used, since excessive force in a sensitive situation will destroy what has been previously gained and seriously affect future accomplishments.

Alertness

Policemen, especially those in command positions, must be alert so that they can detect rapid changes in the course of a disturbance. Just as soldiers prepare for the sounds and sights of battle through desensitizing techniques such as infiltration courses and mock enemy villages, police personnel should be prepared for the sounds and sights of riots and other civil disturbances.

At the Southern Arizona Law Enforcement Institute, two techniques have been useful in training officers and recruits to maintain their alertness. The first technique involves a two-hour class on "maintaining your cool," in which the emotionality of certain words and their ability to provoke highly charged emotional reactions are presented. Recruits are told to look at the person on their right and think of the most insulting thing to call or say to the other. Then both are asked to stand and the first recruit is asked to say it to the other's face using the nastiest tone possible. Then the second person is asked to respond in the nastiest way possible to this insult. This exercise dramatically points out the emotional power of words and makes the recruits more alert to their own reactions to name-calling and verbal baiting. Developing an alertness to their own reactions will help officers maintain their cool during riots when they are called names or are insulted.

The second technique is an attempt to simulate the sights and sounds of battle. During this exercise, one-half of the recruit class is required to handle a disturbance staged by the other half. Depending on the actions of the "police," the disturbance becomes either aggravated or quieted down. After the exercise, a critique is held to discuss the actions of the "crowd" and "police" to determine which actions led to which results. A valuable part of the exercise is that recruits can see how both sides tend to get carried away by their emotions. Alerting officers to this aspect of riot behavior is important in increasing riot control effectiveness.

Community Support

Acquiring and maintaining community support is an important factor in riot control. To maintain community support, the police must act competently and professionally. As Craig has pointed out, "The key to the real support of the police is to be found in the development of enhanced competence among police officers. The competent police officer performs effectively under any and all conditions. Competency is more important than philosophy in police–community relations" (Craig 1969).

Furthermore, competency is color-blind. For example, in the black ghetto of an eastern city which experienced serious rioting, there was a "ten most wanted list" of unpopular police officers. Although only five of the eighty-two officers on the police force were black, two of the ten most hated were black. The two most respected officers were white and had been judged among the most competent by their supervisors and fellow officers.

Another example of how competence can promote community support and help in riot control is illustrated by the following example. In one large eastern city, a police officer who was at the top of a promotion list and due to be promoted to supervision was not noted for his liberalism. However, since no disciplinary action had ever been entered in his record, there was no reason to deny his promotion. Consequently, with considerable doubt, he was promoted and assigned to the ghetto. To everyone's surprise he did his job effectively and became one of the ghetto's favorite cops, an officer whom they could rely on for firm and impartial law enforcement. He gave the black citizens protection, respected them as individuals, and responded to their needs. That is really all these residents wanted, just like other residents of the city.

As competency promotes and maintains community support, police incompetency destroys community support. The report of the National Advisory Commission on Civil Disorders gives many examples of how the incompetency of a police officer can aggravate an already tense situation and, in some cases, spark further disturbances. These examples include the officer who allowed a black teenage prisoner to be handcuffed and, while lying on the ground, to be kicked in the face by a white man. No arrest was made.

In another example, the police in an eastern city were expecting a riot and were testing their tear gas guns on a firing range situated in the middle of a black residential area. When the wind blew the gas into their homes, the residents were understandably enraged. Even if such incidents are excusable because of pressure existing at the time, they cannot be tolerated if the police are to maintain the support of the community.

The Use of Humor

The value of humor is often overlooked as an effective police tactic in crowd control. It can be used in the control of sit-ins, marches, and other mobile demonstrations; in handling confrontations between mobs and control forces that have not yet reached a stage of violence; in dispersing groups to minimize animosity; in reducing hostility when it is necessary to make selected or mass arrests at a demonstration; or in the general prevention of hostility secondary to an issue which has led to a demonstration (Coates 1972).

Where possible, the police should direct the humor against themselves to reduce some of the hostility harbored by the demonstrators toward them. The humor should be verbal rather than visual. If the humor is effective, it tends to be contagious, with one laugh facilitating the next. Although initial attempts to use a light touch on a crowd may not be well received, repeated attempts may have a cumulative effect. However, heavy-handed humor should be avoided and, in most situations, ethnic humor is definitely out of place.

These positive benefits of humor in riot control suggest that police departments might identify officers for duty who demonstrate an ability to handle crowds with wit and humor.

Police Policy

Most law enforcement authorities have policies that are the basis for their handling of crowds or mobs. They should be reexamined frequently to evaluate their effectiveness. For example, a common police practice during riots is to order all men on twenty-four-hour-alert and to increase the on-duty time to twelve hours or longer. However, the efficacy of this practice is questionable. A tired policeman is a poor policeman, especially when faced with the stress of a civil disorder. How long can a police officer stay on the street, facing a hostile and potentially violent crowd, without losing his control? A police sergeant commented, "When my men are fresh, they toss off the insults and jeering with good humor. After an hour or two, their patience begins to wear thin. Give them another couple of hours and they're probably ready to bust heads."

Some other common practices seem equally ill-advised. For example, in anticipation of trouble with student demonstrators, twenty or more deputies were brought to the scene in a school bus. They were confined in the bus in the hot sun for three to four hours, awaiting a possible call to action. Fortunately, the call never came, and the deputies were driven back to the sheriff's office. One can speculate what frame of mind these men were in after about an hour on the hot bus. Had the call to action come, they might have used more force than necessary to control the demonstration.

Law enforcement authorities should plan policies which will reduce the physical and emotional stress of riot duty. A place for the officer to rest in comfort while on call should be set up immediately with drinks and sandwiches available. If possible, this should be provided by a local civic organization. This will indicate to the officer that he has community support.

A sense of group identity supports effective action. It is advisable for law enforcement authorities to arrange for officers who are coming off street duty during civil disturbances to spend time with other officers. This will enable them to share experiences, fostering an esprit de corps.

Since most officers are trained to work individually, more training must be provided to help them work as a team during civil disorders. The attainment of this goal requires constant practice. The police should plan regular team meetings, even if a riot is not imminent.

The Police Officer's Code of Conduct

As a summary, we will suggest a code of conduct for the police officer during civil disturbances and riots. This should be a guide to professional behavior not only during these conflicts but also in other stressful situations.

1. Remember that you are a professional law enforcement officer. Take pride in your ability to act professionally under any and all conditions.

2. Remember that your most powerful weapons are psychological ones—patience, tolerance, good humor, tact, and the ability to set an example by your own conduct.

3. Remember that it is your uniform and your position, as symbols of the establishment, which some people react to negatively. Do not take threats, insults, or abuses personally.

4. Do not look upon all situations as a challenge to your ability as a police officer. No one expects you to take unnecessary chances or to prove anything.

5. Try to learn all you can about how a person functions in a group, especially under conditions of stress. The more you know about this type of behavior, the better you will be able to predict, control, and alter it.

6. Don't overestimate your endurance threshhold. A tired policeman is a poor policeman, especially during civil disturbance duty.

7. Have faith in others. You are not alone. There is a whole system behind you with local officials and other responsible citizens working to restore order.

8. Remember that all riots must end sometime and that the task of restoring affected areas must begin. Therefore, do not do anything during the stress of the disturbance that would jeopardize either your or the department's position in carrying out this task.

Summary

In this chapter, we have presented many of the principles which influence the behavior of crowds and mobs. We have also discussed the underlying factors which influence people to participate and the characteristics of those who emerge as leaders of these mobs. Finally, we have suggested techniques for law enforcement to use in controlling mobs as well as a code of conduct for the police officer.

BIBLIOGRAPHY

COATES, J. F. 1972. "Wit and Humor: A Neglected Aid in Crowd and Mob Control." *International Journal of Offender Therapy and Comparative Criminology* 16:184–191.

CRAIG, D. 1969. "The Police in the Middle of the Conflict." *Journal of Crime and Delinquency* 15:387–392.

KREPS, G. A. 1973. "Change in Crisis-Relevant Organizations: Police Departments and Civil Disturbances." *American Behavioral Scientist* 16:356–367.

Report of the National Advisory Commission on Civil Disorders. 1970. Washington, D.C.: U.S. Government Printing Office.

SPIEGEL, J. 1968. *Toward a Theory of Collective Violence.* Waltham, Mass.: Brandeis University Press.

SWAN, LLEWELYN ALEX. 1980. *The Politics of Riot Behavior.* Washington, D.C.: University Press of America.

Chapter 18

Behavioral Aspects of Hostage Situations

HOSTAGE TAKING has been called a "mushrooming growth industry" (Gallagher and Bemsberg 1978). What this means for the police officer is that no matter where he works, his chances of confronting a hostage situation in today's violent and unstable world are mounting daily. This chapter will elaborate why this subject is important to the police officer. It will provide a definition of pertinent terms; suggest a philosophy for conducting hostage negotiations; describe the various types of hostage negotiations and review the psychological characteristics of those that engage in hostage taking; and review hostage negotiation techniques and strategies, including the moral dilemmas presented to the police in certain negotiation responses, the effect of the incident on hostage victims, and the effect of the hostage negotiation process on the negotiator(s).

Importance to the Police Officer

Since the early 1970s, hostage taking by criminals and political extremists has increased, and every indication is that the frequency of hostage incidents will continue to rise. In the United States during 1976, there were 207 cases involving 291 hostages (Table 1).

TABLE 1

Hostage Situations in 1976*

Total Cases	207
Total Hostages	291
Cases in which People Were Killed	10
Number of Hostages Killed	10
Cases in which Injuries Occurred	18
Number Subjects	344
Number Subjects Killed	3
Cases Involving Gunfire	17
Political Hostage Cases	0
Cases in which Money Was Demanded	91
Ransom	28
Robbery	63
Cases for Transportation	90
Cases Involving Sex	38
Hoaxes	1
Ransom Demanded	$4,260,000
Ransom Paid	$1,344,300
Ransom Received	$918,860
Money Obtained from Robbery	$338,425

*From material presented by Dr. Richard Kobetz, during IACP course on Hostage Negotiation, San Diego, California, 1977.

None of these involved political terrorism. By 1979, there were 52 proven terrorist incidents which resulted in 8 dead and 24 injured (Quainton 1980).

This dramatic increase in political terrorism associated with hostage taking reinforces the need for police officers to be familiar with the tactics of political terrorists. The methods of terrorists are being employed more frequently by criminals and others in situations where local police are responsible for intervention. Therefore, while political terrorism is still not an everyday occurrence, local police must handle armed robbery attempts where hostages are being seized with distressing regularity to aid flight, respond to jail and prison riots where hostages are being taken to insure compliance with prisoner demands, and react to family fights and other crisis situations where victims are seized for no other reasons than to prove a point or increase attention.

In addition to the influence of political terrorism, the increase in hostage taking may result from a number of other factors. First, there has been a sharp increase in the number of felonies. Twenty years ago, only 10 percent of all murders happened during another crime; today, almost 30 percent of murder victims die in this way (Lunde 1975). This increase in felonies is partially a result of the spread of shopping centers, jewelery stores, and other lucrative targets for criminal activities. When the growing number of holdups of these targets is coupled with the increasing speed of police response, the opportunity is created for a hostage situation to develop at almost any time.

With the development of federal, state, and county computerized record systems, patrol officers can identify wanted persons through routine checks. This is likely to increase the possibility of dealing with a barricaded subject or a hostage situation.

Another factor may be the increase in the number of previously violent people who are released to the community because prisons, jails, and mental health facilities no longer have the space or programs to handle them. Finally, the increase in hostage taking may be caused by deteriorating economic conditions, associated with high unemployment. Those who find themselves without jobs and are thus incapable of supporting their families often become desperate as their feeling of being trapped increases. Faced with a hopeless situation, they often resort to hostage taking as a last desperate attempt to fight their way out.

Definition of Terms

A *hostage situation* exists when a person seizes another person against the latter's will and holds him to enforce certain demands. This can apply to a few or to many people.

A *barricaded subject* is a person who barricades himself in defiance of law enforcement authorities.

All hostage situations, at one time or another, can include barricaded subjects. However, all barricaded subjects cannot be considered in hostage situations because, in most cases, the barricaded subject has not taken any hostages. Police tactics and techniques in handling both of these incidences are quite similar.

Negotiation is the bargaining process between principals. In this case, the principals are the hostage takers and the law enforcement authorities.

A *negotiator,* if used, is the person who mediates between the principals. The negotiator does not have the power of decision, which often allows him to buy time since the demands of the hostage taker and the responses of the police authorities must be relayed back and forth. The absence of decision-making authority also relieves the negotiator from the responsibility of any negative or unfavorable decisions by police authorities that have to be relayed to the hostage takers.

The Philosophy of Hostage Negotiation

Prior to the last decade, police response to hostage situations and barricaded subjects was typically to assemble all available personnel and firepower, deliver an ultimatum to the hostage taker or barricaded subject to surrender, and then, after an interval of time (the length of which most generally depended upon the patience of the commander at the scene), order a full scale assault. The criminal was sure to be overcome in this unequal contest, but, unfortunately, one or more hostages, innocent bystanders, and sometimes even police officers would be killed or injured. These casualties, while mourned, were considered the necessary price of the mission (Pierson 1980).

Today, barricaded subjects and hostage situations are approached by police departments with a very different philosophy. The method involves handling these potentially explosive situations by bargaining rather than force, with logic and common sense instead of bullets and tear gas.

Whenever a barricaded subject or hostage situation exists, the police may respond by: (1) containing and attempting to negotiate; (2) containing and demanding surrender; (3) using chemical agents to force surrender; (4) using snipers or sharpshooters to neutralize the subjects; or (5) using special weapons and tactic teams (SWAT) to resolve the situation. If responses (3), (4), or (5) are tried and fail, it is impossible to go back to responses (1) and (2). Therefore, attempting to contain and negotiate the release of the hostages or the surrender of the barricaded subject is the preferred method. Optimally, police today try to return the hostage or hostages unharmed and to take the criminal or criminals into custody (Fuselier 1981).

Confronting Hostage Situations

Types of Hostage Situations

Hostage situations may occur under the following conditions:

1. Criminals may plan from the outset to use hostages to ensure their escape, to gain ransom money, or for some other purpose as part of their criminal act.

2. Criminals may not plan to take hostages, but are trapped inside an establishment they intended to rob. A quick response precludes escape, and they seize hostages as their way out. (This is probably the most common situation faced by law enforcement officers.)

3. Hostage situations may arise in jails or prisons. Prisoners seize hostages to highlight their demands for change (better food, more visits) or to assist in an escape. Sometimes, a mentally disturbed prisoner may seize hostages for reasons associated with his particular mental disturbance. Often prisoners may seize hostages to espouse a particular point of view (the Symbionese Liberation Army).

4. A psychotic person may seize hostages in response to his delusional thinking (to right a perceived wrong or carry out a secret mission). A severely depressed person may conclude that the only logical answer to life's pain is murder-suicide, usually involving family members. The individual with an explosive personality may hold his family hostage after destroying the contents of the house in a rage reaction.

5. Normal people who are under severe stress and become intoxicated may take a hostage. A parent may take a child hostage in a custody dispute, believing that the other parent is unfit and that this is the only way he or she can keep or regain custody of the child.

6. Hostages may be taken by political terrorists, usually for the purpose of getting publicity for their cause, forcing the release of certain political prisoners, or gaining revenge. Their demands go far beyond the authority of local police departments and usually cannot be handled by local police. The likelihood of hostages being killed is much higher when they are held by terrorists, since the terrorists have probably discussed the possibility or even the desirability of killing the hostages and may be prepared to die as martyrs.

Personalities Involved in Different Hostage Situations

All hostage takers have some kind of emotional problem. Bolz notes the resemblance that hostage cases bear to suicide attempts; the person is fearful, desperate, depressed, impulsive, angry. It was this assumption that allowed a (New York Police Department) hostage negotiation team to believe they could talk their way out of almost any seige, because "just as every suicide attempt could be successful if the subject had really wanted death, every hostage holder could have killed his captives before the police even arrived to negotiate" (Bolz and Hershey 1979). The following illustrate different hostage situations.

THE CRIMINAL HOSTAGE TAKER WHO PLANS TO TAKE HOSTAGES

Since the psychopath (antisocial personality disorder) is so often found among criminals, it is not surprising that he sometimes plans to take hostages as a part of his criminal activity, most often for ransom or to enhance bargaining power. Familiarity with the characteristics of the psychopath (chapter 9) should assist the negotiator in handling hostage situations involving this type of personality.

The psychopath is the classic manipulator and con artist who may be very adept in eliciting the *Stockholm Syndrome* (sympathy for the hostage taker) in the hostages. Even more important, however, is his lack of real feelings for people. This insensitivity, coupled with his sometimes sadistic and impulsive behavior, may make the situation very dangerous for the hostages.

It is best to appeal to the psychopath in terms of what profits him the most. It is important to remember that the psychopath can't stand prosperity. Even when things are going well for him, he needs to stir up trouble. It follows that he needs frequent stimulation, which the negotiator should provide through frequent contacts and challenging problem-solving situations. Without these, the psychopath may turn his attention to the hostages. It is possible that, if one or more of the hostages are women, they may be raped.

While some criminals may not be diagnosed as antisocial personality disorders, the majority of them still fall into one of the other diagnostic entities listed under personality disorders. This means that they are not psychotic and generally do not suffer from the neurotic symptoms of tension and anxiety except under very stressful conditions. Therefore, since they are in touch with reality, it is probable that a police negotiator can convince them that their own best interests lie in surrender rather than in harming the hostages or prolonging the hostage situation.

THE CRIMINAL WHO DOESN'T PLAN TO TAKE HOSTAGES

Criminals engaged in a felony crime who seize hostages when things go sour and the police arrive too soon are usually preoccupied with escape. If escape is blocked, they become concerned primarily with their own safety. With hostages, they may be fearful of terminating the situation since they may be shot by the police.

These criminals are usually not psychotic. They are probably familiar with the police and know what to expect. Negotiations in these cases should be oriented towards helping the hostage takers see the advisability of surrendering so that they do not further jeopardize themselves by additional charges. Their personal safety upon surrender should be assured.

PRISONERS

"It is an unfortunate fact in our society that some prisons tend to be the garbage heaps into which the worst and most violent among us are discarded" (Hassel 1975). When a riot or hostage situation occurs in jails or prisons, a psychopath is almost always one of the leaders. Hostages taken are most often correctional personnel or volunteers who happen to be in the prison at the time the riot begins. In some cases, the seizure of volunteers or professionals is a part of the riot plan.

Since these prisoners are desperate, and feelings, particularly against the guards, may run high, the threat to any hostages of injury or even death is great. The situation is further complicated since prisoners usually demand freedom. Many correctional institutions have a firm policy that no inmate will leave the institution by taking hostages. Thus, the primary demand cannot be met under any circumstances. Demands for better food, living conditions, or amnesty for the rioters can be negotiated.

In contrast to civilian police action in hostage situations outside of correctional institutions where early confrontation is avoided, authorities believe that quick, forceful action on the part of correction and other law enforcement personnel is advisable so that the disturbance can be quelled before the rioting prisoners can organize and strong leaders emerge to take over the riot. If early intervention is impossible, the disturbance should be contained in the smallest possible area.

Efforts should be made in jails and prisons to identify inmates who are known psychopaths. These inmates can then be monitored whenever tensions are running high so that they can be promptly removed at the first hint of any disturbance. This is critical, since they are often the instigators of the disturbance or add fuel to the situation once the riot begins. Finally, they are likely to be chosen by the inmates as their spokesmen in any negotiations, thus complicating the proceedings.

THE MENTALLY DISTURBED HOSTAGE TAKER

In this instance, the hostage taker is psychotic or borderline psychotic. If he is a paranoid schizophrenic, he may have seized the hostages to right a perceived wrong or to carry out a delusion. If psychotically depressed, he can be very dangerous because of inadequate, unworthy, and hopeless feelings which convince him that he is unfit to live. Not only is the potential for suicide extremely high, but the hostage taker may decide to take some or all of the hostages with him. He may also kill any police officers that offer him the opportunity. In such situations the hostages are often members of his own family or persons well known to him. He may believe that he is actually doing these people a favor by saving them from a sinful or terrible life. Often delusional thinking will have a strong, religious component, such as in a murder-suicide in Tucson in 1978, where a wife killed her husband and their three children so they could leave this world and meet their "Sun God."

Negotiating with these disturbed people is very difficult. Although it is generally recommended that the department psychologist not be involved as a negotiator in hostage situations, consideration must be given to employing this person as the negotiator in these cases. His clinical experience in dealing with the mentally disturbed may allow him to respond more effectively to the many nuances of behavior and emotions characteristic of these people.

While the senior author (H. E. R.) is trained in hostage negotiations and has been the negotiator in several cases, other police psychologists have been reluctant or opposed to being involved directly in negotiations even in these situations. We do not share their concern. Sometimes barricaded subjects do not wish to speak to police officers; sometimes they are quite willing to speak to a doctor, especially if the doctor has presented his identity in such a way as to be nonthreatening to their mental health. Just as policemen represent safety and protection to many people, a doctor represents for many, including hostage takers, someone who is concerned for the welfare of others and who would not allow actions by the police (or anybody else) to be harmful to the hostage taker. Further, the mental health professional may be able to offer hospitalization or some direct relief, other than jail, to the barricaded subject or hostage taker.

THOSE WITH SEVERE STRESS REACTIONS

All of us have a breaking point, and all of us sometimes display stupid, impulsive, and ineffective behavior under sufficient stress. For example, a person who has been a good husband, father, provider, and citizen may lose his job. Additional things go wrong. He becomes depressed, irritable, and perhaps he begins to drink a little too much. One day, after going to an interview with high expectations of finally getting work, the job does not materialize. He arrives home that night and is met by a wife who also is laboring under the stress of his unemployment and financial insecurity, as well as her own problems. An argument ensues, he has a couple more drinks, throws a beer bottle through the window in a fit of anger, and then grabs a gun. He yells at her to "get the hell out," that he's "going to take care of everything." She won't have to worry any more about it. She hastily leaves as he begins to smash up the furniture. She calls the police. All of a sudden he looks out his window and finds he has started World War III. SWAT is there, police cruisers are all over with fire and rescue, all the neighbors are out, everything has gone to hell.

The negotiator should realize that what is needed here is time for the person to cool down. Sometimes it is advisable to do nothing and let him sleep it off. There is always a risk in this decision, especially if he has made some veiled or actual suicidal or homicidal threats. Some officers, however, feel compelled to take action, thus starting a whole chain of unnecessary events that increase the potential for violence, injury, or even death to those involved. The police officer should never take action just because he thinks action is called for.

POLITICAL TERRORISTS

Many terrorists and terrorist organizations, both in the United States and in foreign countries, borrow from Marxist philosophy. All significant acts of the Marxist revolutionary must be measured against the only moral reality—that this action contributes to the revolution. "The conventional mores such as truth, honesty, and the values reflected in the Ten Commandments are dismissed as bourgeois morality and are considered merely imperialistic devices to maintain the status quo" (Hassel 1975, pp. 55–58).

According to Strentz (1980), among the members of terrorist groups, the leader usually exhibits some type of *paranoia.* With such a personality, argument and logic are futile. Any questioning of his beliefs indicates that the questioner does not understand, is one of the enemies plotting against him, or seeking to discredit his ideas. Often his paranoia is well hidden, and on the surface he is self-confident and very commanding. Thus, he is likely to emerge as the leader. Police involvement with this person is infrequent because he usually operates behind the scenes.

Another type of person involved in terrorist organizations is the *activist-operator,* who usually has an antisocial, psychopathic personality. Frequently he is a former soldier, current soldier-of-fortune, or an ex-convict with a long and varied rap sheet. He is an opportunist. He may have been recruited from a prison population by the wily leader who will allow the opportunist to take the spotlight while he remains the power behind the throne. The activist-operator, in turn, sees this situation as an opportunity to lead a hedonistic life with support from the leader and the organization which he views as naive and completely within his own control. He thus becomes the muscle and field commander for the terrorist group.

A third personality type in most terrorist organizations is the idealist dedicated to a better world, who usually is assigned the duties of a *gofer.* While he is the least psychologically disturbed, "he's a guilt ridden hitchhiker who thumbs a ride on every cause from Christianity to Communism. He's a fanatic, needing a Stalin (or a Christ) to worship and die for. He's a mortal enemy of things as they are, and he insists on sacrificing himself for a dream impossible to obtain" (Hoffer 1951).

Since terrorists often take hostages to gain publicity, the hostages are better protected if the media are kept away from the terrorists, depriving them of the publicity needed for martyrdom. The terrorist view is that a sacrifice without the cooperation of the press is useless. Experience indicates that a terrorist rarely will make a private sacrifice of his life. If the terrorist knows that the media will not present his death as an act of sacrifice, but rather as the act of a deranged criminal, he may modify demands, thus allowing the psychological advantage to revert to the law enforcement negotiator.

Initial Response to the Hostage Situation

The patrol officer is often the first to encounter hostage situations, since most develop impulsively during the commission of a felony, in the settling of a family dispute, or from a deranged person call. The patrol officer should consider immediate intervention if the hostage taker has not gained physical control of the crime scene and victims (IACP Training Key 234, 1976). In these cases, the patrol officer must exercise caution for the safety of the hostages. Immediate intervention by patrol officers is not appropriate if the suspects controls the crime area and the hostages. Patrol action would needlessly endanger the lives of the hostages, the hostage taker, and, possibly, the police officers themselves. Patrol's objective is to analyze and stabilize the incident and notify the appropriate supervisor that a hostage incident has developed.

Attitudinal problems may arise with some officers in these situations. "Put a cop on the job for a number of years, give him some success, and then put a bulletproof vest on him, and he sometimes begins to think he cannot be hurt. And that can be a deadly misjudgment" (Bolz and Hershey 1979). Pierson (1980) refers to this attitude as "tombstone courage," noting that many officers feel pressured to act in an emergency, even if they are not sure of what the proper action is. The officer who fails to exhaust every other alternative before unnecessarily confronting an armed subject who is posing no immediate threat to his or another's life is a good example of "tombstone courage." Frequently, such officers have been called heroes, most often posthumously decorated.

If trained negotiators are available, they should be brought to the scene. In many small departments, however, or in cases where negotiators cannot arrive on the scene for some time, the patrol officer with his supervisor may have to establish negotiations and carry out the process.

Steps in Establishing Hostage Negotiations

Negotiation principles are not easy for many police officers to learn. Typically, the police officer has been trained to assist those in danger by eliminating the threat as soon as possible. In a hostage situation, however, he is confronted by a situation where he cannot quickly direct the outcome of the event. His primary job is to preserve the status quo until a trained negotiator is available to resolve the issue. His initial goals are to establish a working relationship with the hostage taker, obtain information about the incident, set the stage for further negotiations, and consume time (IACP Training Key 235, 1976).

The essential ingredient in all hostage negotiations is the establishment of effective communication between the negotiator and the hostage taker. First, the police officer must elicit enough information so that he and his superiors can understand the situation fully and thus work with the hostage taker. The three essential questions regarding the hostage takers which must be answered in the initial stage are: "Who are they?" "What do they want?" and "What will they take?"

Effective communication in hostage situations between the hostage taker and the police officer requires a common language. The hostage taker will be considering carefully every word that the officer speaks. If the officer does not remember what he says or does not express himself appropriately, there may be room for misinterpretation by the hostage taker which could be disastrous. Any questions asked by the police officer or the negotiator should be framed to discourage a "yes" or "no" reply from the hostage taker. Asking questions in a way which encourages conversation permits the buying of time and increases the likelihood of being able to establish rapport with the hostage taker.

The officer must be very attentive at all times. This is difficult in a hostage situation because the officer is naturally apprehensive, fearing for his own life and the lives of the hostages. He will also be trying to observe everything that he can about the details of the incident. The officer should remember that the hostage taker will interpret the attentiveness and the sincerity of the negotiating officer by the way he acts. Nonverbal communication may be even more important than verbal communication.

Why should the hostage taker be willing to talk to the police? He needs somebody to relate to. He will accept the police officer if he is convinced of the officer's sincerity and that the officer won't set him up. He recognizes that he needs the officer to obtain an agreeable settlement, especially in those cases where the hostage taker did not intend to get into this situation in the first place. In all probability, he is quite frightened and confused. He knows he needs some help if he has any hope of getting out of the situation.

Negotiation procedures will differ with each situation, depending on the purpose of the hostage taking, whether the hostages are in immediate danger of injury or death, how many suspects are involved, what type of weapons they have, and where the situation is located. However, regardless of the specifics of any hostage situation, there are general guidelines that can be followed in most cases.

Access to the Hostage Taker

After the situation has been somewhat stabilized, the police officer who is acting as a temporary negotiator should make initial contact with the suspect by phone, bullhorn, or the loudspeaker on a patrol car. He should identify himself by name, rank, and department and ask if anybody requires medical assistance.

No attempt should be made to disguise the true identity of the police officer or the department mental health professional (if he is involved in direct negotiations). Any deception at this point is likely to fail and seriously impair the development of the trust required in the negotiation process. This could needlessly endanger the lives of the hostages, the negotiator, and perhaps other police officers. The same hostage taker, particularly if the matter arose from a family dispute, may present the same hostage-taking situation to officers a few months later. One hostage taker, deceived by a police sergeant in negotiating his surrender, told the sergeant afterwards, "You better hope I never get into this situation again, because the next time I won't trust any of you bastard cops and I'll blow the first one away that sets foot on my property."

After the police gain access to the hostage taker, the next step is to establish a dialogue. What does he want? What does he have in mind? How can the situation be resolved? An article on "Communication Techniques in Hostage Situations" by Special Agent Robert Fitzpatrick of the FBI Academy (1980) contains some valuable suggestions for establishing the dialogue.

Know everything you can about the personality of the hostage taker. Is he normal, abnormal, or depressed? Remember, the depressed hostage taker is a powder keg and may present the greatest threat, not only to the hostages but also to the negotiator and other police, since he may be willing to commit suicide by using murder as a strategy to force police to kill him.

Gather all facts together about the hostages. Who are they? Are there any medical or psychiatric problems among them? Are there any with special training or skills that might be useful in resolving this situation?

What Not to Do

There are three common mistakes that negotiating officers must avoid. The first is to lose patience. Based on an analysis of twenty-nine different hostage incidents reported by twenty-three different law enforcement negotiators, Mirabella and Trudeau (1981) concluded that the average time for a hostage negotiation is twelve hours. Prior knowledge and acceptance of this twelve-hour average can and will assist law enforcement in the reduction of anxiety, in the premature use of force, and in the logistical planning and management of hostage incidents.

The second mistake is taking precipitate action. Despite outside pressure on the police to resolve the situation quickly and the natural tendency for situations to create impatience because they are stressful, police must resist the tendency to act prematurely even if negotiations seem to have fallen apart. There may be ups and downs in the negotiating process, and these should not be seen as a signal (or an excuse) to break off further attempts to negotiate.

A third critical mistake is for the negotiator to make value judgments about the hostage taker. Successful negotiation requires that the negotiator remain objective and concentrate on maintaining a dialogue with the hostage taker which will eventually resolve the incident without violence (IACP Training Key 235, 1976).

Although no two hostage situations are alike, and flexibility in negotiations is the major requirement of an effective negotiator, there are certain set rules that should be followed.

1. Do not give weapons or ammunition to the hostages.

2. Never give any additional hostages or exchange hostages. Above all, never exchange a police officer for a hostage. This is not because of any premium placed on the officer relative to any other hostage, but simply because the introduction of a police officer as a hostage can create complexities and problems that are not needed in an already complex and problematic situation (for example, how his fellow officers will feel knowing that one of their own is a hostage; the hostage takers may have a special hostility to police officers).

3. Never give anything without receiving something. When demands are met, you exchange something (for example, food or cigarettes for one of the hostages).

4. Prior to each face-to-face meeting, the negotiator should receive a promise from the captors that the negotiator will not be harmed. Bolz and Hershey (1979) emphasize, "If the perpetrators say they will not hurt you, our experience indicates that you can count on it."

5. If there is more than one captor, try to reach agreement at the start on who will represent the group so that the negotiator does not speak to more than one perpetrator at a time.

Deception and Lying

As stated earlier, the negotiator should avoid lying to deceive the hostage taker. However, if it is possible to lull the perpetrator into a sense of security which enables members of the Tactical Force to step in quickly and neutralize him, then this should be done. We agree with Bolz and Hershey (1979) that "there is no honor owed to anyone holding an innocent party against his will."

In other situations, the commanding officer at the scene may deem it best not to inform the negotiator of tactical plans so that the negotiator can maintain integrity in dealing with the hostage taker without the problem of deliberately making false statements. This also enables the negotiator to disclaim responsibility in case something goes wrong. For example, if the negotiator has told the hostage taker that the demanded money is on the way, and later this is proved false, the negotiator can claim that he was only relaying information given to him: he didn't lie, they did.

Mobile Situations

It is undesirable to permit hostage takers and their hostages to leave the contained area and become mobile. However, to obtain freedom, the hostage taker may demand to leave the area—sometimes in a police car, plane, or helicopter. Even though authorities may wish to close this door, it is quite possible that, without any hope of escape, the hostage taker may be more likely to kill his victims and himself. This is particularly true of political terrorists. Therefore, tactical advantages may accrue to the authorities by allowing the suspect and the hostages to leave the scene (for example, sharpshooters may get a chance to neutralize the hostage taker, particularly if there is only one, or the hostages may have an opportunity to escape during the mobile phase). Law enforcement agencies should have contingency plans in the event that the hostage situation does enter a mobile stage.

What if a Hostage Is Killed?

If a hostage is killed, the situation should not automatically be considered nonnegotiable. It is possible that the hostage taker did not really mean to take a life. Even if he did, the goal of the hostage negotiator is to save the lives of those hostages still remaining. Therefore, while the death of a hostage complicates the picture, it does not rule out further negotiations.

If it seems appropriate, the negotiator may tell the hostage taker that even though there has been an injury or death, he can only worsen the situation by continuing in this manner and that the only chance he has of resolving the situation in his favor is to show evidence of good faith from this moment on.

In most hostage situations, the time most dangerous to the safety of the hostages is the first half hour after the incident begins because this is when the hostage taker is most likely to be emotionally unstable. From his point of view, everything is deteriorating rapidly. As he sees all the forces which he has unwittingly set in motion converging upon him, he may panic. The negotiator's approach must be low-keyed in an attempt to diffuse this panic. The negotiator should reassure the hostage taker that nobody is going to rush in after him. The key to the resolution of the situation is communication. Conversation serves not only to calm and stabilize the hostage taker but also to wear him down. As pointed out by Taylor (1979), "wearing a man down means giving him enough time to become physically tired and emotionally subdued, so that he sees clearly that his best chance to resolve his crisis is to let his hostages go and, finally, to surrender."

Communication with the Hostages

Although negotiators usually intentionally downplay the importance of the hostages when dealing with the hostage taker, in many situations there are contacts with the hostages. The hostages may question the competence of the police, interfere with negotiations, and/or take control of the communications between the suspect and the police (Mirabella and Trudeau 1981). Therefore, techniques of hostage management are important.

The same techniques used to decrease the hostage taker's anxiety can be used to reassure, calm, and instruct the hostages. Bolz and Hershey (1979) suggest that if the following information is given to the hostages, it will maximize their chances of emerging safely, without bodily harm.

1. Don't be a hero; accept your situation and be prepared to wait.

2. The first (fifteen to forty-five) minutes are the most dangerous for all concerned; follow the instructions of your captor; the longer you are together, the less likely the captor will be to hurt you.

3. Don't speak unless spoken to and only if necessary; try to be friendly if possible, but not phony.

4. Try to get rest; sit if you can; if the situation goes on for a long period of time, try to sleep if you can.

5. Don't make suggestions to the hostage taker; if your suggestion goes wrong, he or she may think you planned it that way.

6. Don't try to escape unless you are absolutely sure you can make it; even then, rethink it before you try.

7. If anyone needs special medication, inform your captors.

8. Be aware of everything you see and hear. Try to remember the number of captors, their descriptions and conversations, the weapons they have, and the number and identities of other hostages; you may be released and your information will help the police.

9. If you are permitted to speak on the phone, be prepared to answer "yes" or "no" to questions asked by the police.

10. Don't be argumentative to captors or other hostages; express a cooperative attitude.

11. Don't turn your back on your captors unless directed to do so, but don't stare at them either. Eye contact can be good. People are less likely to harm someone they are looking at.

12. Be patient. Even though the police may appear to be doing nothing, they are engaged in a complete program designed to rescue you unharmed as soon as possible.

13. If you believe a rescue is taking place, or you hear noise or shooting, hit the floor and stay down. Keep your hands on your head. Do not make any fast moves.

After It is All Over

Whether the captor surrenders or is overpowered, how the negotiator deals with him afterwards is as important as how he dealt with him when the negotiator was under the pressure of knowing a gun was pointed at the head of the hostage. The negotiator should talk with the hostage taker quietly, just as he did when the pressure was on. Praise him for being cooperative in letting the hostages go. Tell him he made the right choice in surrendering. Any roughness, violence, or verbal putdown is inadvisable, since there is a chance the police may deal with him again, especially if the situation involves a mental case or a family fight (Danto 1978).

The Selection of Hostage Negotiators

How does one select an effective hostage negotiator? The most important characteristic is to really care about people. This person must be able to make people comfortable, to communicate effectively with them, and to create in them a feeling of trust (they really matter and won't be deceived).

The stressful nature of the job demands that the negotiator be psychologically stable and able to perform well under stress. He must possess a sense of humor—he'll need it. He must convey, physically and psychologically, what in the military is referred to as "command presence." This translates in civilian terms to an appearance of maturity and effectiveness, someone who commands respect. As a manipulator he must be flexible and adaptable under stress conditions, but he cannot be a "bull shit artist" because the hostage taker will quickly see through insincerity.

Finally, as Cooper (1977) has stated, "Experienced negotiators are agreed that success in their endeavors is dependent to a large extent upon the creation of a bond of trust with the hostage taker. Such a bond is not easy to forge and there is much evidence to suggest that it tends to be personal to the individual negotiator rather than attaching to the institution or interest he represents."

Moral Dilemmas for the Police

Hostage situations often present moral dilemmas to police administrators and commanders. For example, is a visit or phone call from the President, Governor, or other important official to the hostage taker in response to his demands a precedent to be avoided, or is it negotiable? Should promises made under duress to a hostage taker in return for surrender be honored after apprehension? Should hostage takers be permitted to leave the original site of the hostage incident, especially if they go outside the original jurisdiction? If a clear shot is available at a hostage taker about to leave the jurisdiction in accordance with negotiation promises, should that shot be taken? Would the steps taken to terminate a hostage incident be different if the hostage was an illustrious public official or personality rather than an ordinary citizen who just happened to be in the wrong place at the wrong time? Do all lives in jail or prison hostage situations (for example, the lives of murderers, pimps, rapists, robbers, and those on death row) have equal priority?

These questions have no clear-cut answers, since they involve moral issues and personal value judgments. It should only be noted that when a police commander is faced with any of these issues, he must consider the precedent set by whatever action he chooses.

Effects of the Hostage Experience

Effects On Victims

At 10:15 A.M. on Thursday, August 23, 1973, the quiet routine of the Sveriges Kredit Bank in Stockholm, Sweden was destroyed by the chatter of a submachine gun. As clouds of plaster and glass settled around the sixty stunned occupants, a heavily armed, lone gunman called out in English, "The party has just begun." The "party" was to continue for 131 hours, permanently affecting the lives of four young hostages and giving birth to a psychological phenomenon subsequently called the *Stockholm Syndrome* (Strentz 1979).

This syndrome describes the automatic, unconscious, emotional response to the trauma of becoming a hostage victim. It consists of the following three stages of behavior: (1) the hostages begin to identify with their captors and to have positive feelings toward them; (2) the hostages begin to have negative feelings toward the authorities; and (3) since the Stockholm Syndrome is a two-way street, under the right conditions, the hostage takers begin to develop positive feelings toward their hostages.

Strentz (1979), who has studied hostage situations and interviewed many victims, finds that hostages typically go through four stages: denial, delusions of reprieve, busywork, and taking stock. The first and immediate defense mechanism employed by hostages is *denial*. They react as if the traumatic incident is not happening to them. Gradually they begin to accept their situation but find relief for their anxiety by viewing the situation as temporary, believing that the police will soon come to their rescue *(delusions of reprieve)*. If freedom does not occur soon, many hostages become engaged in *busywork*, such as methodically counting and recounting windows or knitting. Sooner or later, all hostages begin to reflect upon their past life *(taking stock)*, vowing to change for the better.

While the vast majority of hostages experience this sequence of emotional events, the Stockholm Syndrome occurs only in a few because time is the critical factor in its development.

Strentz describes the Stockholm Syndrome as a regression to a very elementary level of development. The hostage is like the infant who cannot feed himself, who cannot speak, and who has no locomotion. Like the infant, the hostage is in a state of extreme dependency and fright. The infant has a mother who sees to his needs. As these needs are met by the mother, the infant begins to love her for fulfilling these needs. So it is with the hostage—his every need, in fact, his very life, is a gift from his captor. He is now as dependent as he was when he was an infant, once again with a controlling, all-powerful adult, and threatened by the outside world. The weapons the police deploy against the hostage taker are also deployed against him. Since he is extremely dependent upon a powerful adult figure, the behavior that worked when he was a dependent infant surfaces as a coping device. He identifies with his captor as a means of self-protection, sometimes even going so far as adopting the values and philosophy of his captor.

Most hostage takers, including terrorists, cannot inflict pain or death on another human being unless the victim is dehumanized. When a captor and his hostages are locked together in a relatively small space, a process of humanization usually begins. The hostages gain empathy while maintaining dignity, lessening the aggression of the captors.

However, if the hostages are held in isolation by being locked in another room or have been hooded, tied, gagged, or forced to face the wall away from the hostage taker in the same room, then the captor has dehumanized the hostages, making it easier for him to kill them. As long as the hostages are isolated from their captor in any of these ways, the Stockholm Syndrome will not develop, regardless of the time involved.

Fuselier (1981) notes that the Stockholm Syndrome has both a positive and negative impact on hostage negotiations. The stronger the Stockholm Syndrome, the less likely it is that the hostage taker will kill the hostages, especially if the Syndrome has advanced to the third stage. On the other hand, information coming from the hostages may be falsified, either consciously or unconsciously. Hostages may act counter to the commands of the police during an assault. It is possible for the Syndrome to be so strong that the hostage offers himself as a human shield for his captor. There are also documented incidents of released hostages making their way back through the barricades to reenter the hostage situation. Finally, the Syndrome may affect the performance of the negotiator, especially if a hostage fails to seize an opportunity to escape or attempts to interfere with the negotiator's efforts.

In spite of these negative aspects, however, the negotiator should attempt to foster the Stockholm Syndrome for the purpose of achieving the safe release of the hostages. Since reaching the third stage (the hostage taker's development of positive feelings toward the hostages) may save lives, the negotiator should attempt to humanize the hostages for the hostage taker in every possible way. For example, he may ask the hostage taker to get information on the names of the hostages, the names of their relatives or children, or their medical condition. He can ask the hostage taker to allow the hostages to talk on the phone. He can discuss with the hostage taker some of the family responsibilities of the hostages. Any action which the negotiator can take to emphasize to the hostage taker that the hostage is a human being may assist in developing feelings of empathy for the hostages by their captor.

Just as a crime victim's problems do not end with the capture of the offender, so too the tribulations of hostage victims do not end with the termination of the hostage situation. Experience suggests that these victims go through stages similar to those of rape victims: the immediate stage, the psuedo-adjustment stage, and the resolution and integration stage (chapter 10). They also demonstrate some of the same feelings seen in other crime victims, such as self-blame, guilt, fear, and anger.

Middendorff (1974) makes the interesting observation that there are actually three victims in every hostage situation: the hostage; the indirect hostage, such as a family or airline; and the co-victim, such as the state, represented by the police. After the termination of a hostage situation, Middendorff urges that attention be given to all three victims in hostage situations.

Finally, the debriefing of the hostage victim by a law enforcement aide and a psychologist or a psychiatrist (if available) is critical. The victim should understand that these interviews are accepted routine and, afterwards, should be given a number to call twenty-four hours a day if the need arises.

Effects On Negotiators

Research has demonstrated the variety of emotions experienced by negotiators, including anger towards suspects and hostages, empathy and sorrow, boredom, fatigue, and discomfort (Mirabella and Trudeau 1974). All police negotiators also pay a personal price when they attempt to induce the Stockholm Syndrome. "Hostages will curse him as they did in Stockholm in August in 1973. They will call the police cowards and actively side with the subject in trying to achieve a solution to their plight, a solution not necessarily in their best interest or in the best interest of the community . . . a hostile hostage is a price that law enforcement must pay for a living hostage" (Strentz 1979).

The Tucson Police Department Hostage Negotiation Team has been involved in numerous situations involving hostages and barricaded subjects without losing a hostage. Bolz and Hershey (1979) have observed that the first time a hostage is killed will present significant psychological problems to the negotiating team and others at the scene.

Summary

The primary objective in any hostage situation is to negotiate the safe release of the hostages and to ensure that nobody gets injured or killed, including the hostages, the police officers (and other emergency personnel present), innocent bystanders, and the hostage takers. We have described the types of hostage situations that occur, the personalities likely to be involved in each type of situation, hostage negotiation techniques, and the characteristics of successful negotiators. We have discussed the effects of hostage taking upon the victims and the negotiators.

Up to 1981, the New York City Police Department Hostage Negotiating Team has handled more than 180 situations without losing a hostage, policeman, or perpetrator during the hostage situation. This testifies to the effectiveness of the approach described in this chapter and to the importance of negotiation as the most humane, compassionate, and effective way to handle hostage-taking situations and barricaded subjects. Negotiation saves lives, prevents needless bloodshed, and represents professional police work at its very best.

BIBLIOGRAPHY

BOLZ, F., and HERSHEY, E. 1979. *Hostage Cop*. New York: Rawson Wade.

COOPER, H. H. A. 1977. "Pacta Sunt Servanda: Good Faith Negotiations With Hostage Takers." *International Association of Chiefs of Police Training Program* 1–24.

DANTO, B. L. November 1978. "Managing the Man With the Gun." *FBI Law Enforcement Bulletin* 3–9.

FITZPATRICK, R. 1980. "Communication Techniques in Hostage Negotiations, part I." Unpublished article. Quantico, Va.: FBI Academy.

FUSELIER, G. W. June 1981. "A Practical Overview of Hostage Negotiations, part I." *FBI Law Enforcement Bulletin* 2–6.

FUSELIER, G. W. July 1981. "A Practical Overview of Hostage Negotiations, Conclusion." *FBI Law Enforcement Bulletin* 10–15.

GALLAGHER, R., and BEMSBERG, C. 1978. *Hostage Negotiation for Police*. Schiller Park, Ill.: Motorola Teleprograms.

HASSEL, C. V. September 1975. "The Hostage Situation: Exploring the Motivation and Cause." *The Police Chief* 55–58.

HOFFER, E. 1951. *The True Believer*. New York: Harper & Row.

IACP *Training Key #234*. 1976. Professional Standards Division. Gaithersburg, Md.: International Association of Chiefs of Police. 1–6.

IACP *Training Key #235*. 1976. Professional Standards Division. Gaithersburg, Md.: International Association of Chiefs of Police. 1–6.

LUNDE, D. T. July 1975. "Our Murder Boom." *Psychology Today* 35–42.

MIDDENDORFF, W. April 1974. "The 'Victimology' of the Taking of Hostages." *Kriminalistik* 1–7.

MIRABELLA, R. W., and TRUDEAU, J. May 1981. "Managing Hostage Negotiations." *The Police Chief* 45–47.

PIERSON, T. September 1980. "An Approach to Barricaded Subjects." *Law and Order* 40–42.

QUAINTON, A. C. E. May 1980. "Combating Terrorism: A Strategy of Partnership." *The Police Chief* 22–24.

STRENTZ, T. April 1979. "Law Enforcement Policy and Ego Defenses of the Hostage." *FBI Law Enforcement Bulletin* 2–12.

STRENTZ, T. 1980. "The Terrorist Organizational Profile: A Psychological Evaluation." Unpublished article. Quantico, Va.: FBI Academy. 1–29.

TAYLOR, L. B. April 22, 1979. "Bargaining for Lives: The Deadly Gamble of Hostage Negotiations." *Family Weekly* 6–8.

Chapter 19

Behavioral Aspects of Conflict Situations

POLICE officers frequently must respond to calls involving people in conflict. Whether these situations involve family differences or neighborhood arguments, all of the conflict management skills of the officer are required to achieve a satisfactory resolution without escalating the situation or harming one of the participants—including the officer.

Family Disputes

Involvement in a family dispute is an all too common experience for most police officers. Research conducted by the Oakland, California, Police Department showed that in the first six months of 1970, officers responded to more than 16,000 family disturbance calls requiring more than 8,000 man hours; 25 percent of all assignments were returned calls to family disputes (Oakland Police Department 1971).

More important, these calls often result in placing an officer's life in jeopardy. Twenty-two percent of all policemen killed nationally and about 40 percent of those injured were involved in handling a family dispute at the time. Approximately one-third of all homicides and other assaults take place in the family. Family disturbances are also frequently associated with suicide and child abuse.

Prior to 1966, no law enforcement agency in the United States had a training program designed to teach officers to intervene effectively in family disputes. The original family crisis intervention study was implemented in 1967 by Dr. Morton Bard, with his training of "family cops" in the New York City Police Department. During the 1970s, many departments saw the need for this training, and other programs were initiated. Although the training methods differed among the programs, the goals were similar: (1) to improve police capability of restoring order in the family during a crisis, while at the same time minimizing the chances of police or citizen injuries; (2) to assist families in resolving the tensions that can lead to disputes by referring them to appropriate community social health and mental health agencies; (3) to reduce the number of repeat calls from chronically fighting families by providing solutions before serious physical injuries result (there is a much higher risk of injury arising from incidents characterized by a history of repeat calls); (4) to enhance police–community relations by providing excellent services to families in crisis; and (5) to establish a liaison between the police and other community agencies which provide specialized services to families in crisis so that the necessity for future police intervention can be reduced.

Police training programs for the handling of domestic disputes should be a minimum of forty hours, preferably eighty hours. The following subjects should be covered: (1) necessary tactics and practices to ensure the safety of the officer and the family; (2) interviewing techniques emphasizing how to observe both verbal and nonverbal communication patterns and to assess content; (3) characteristics of a stable family relationship and factors causing a stable situation to deteriorate; (4) aspects of human behavior that can have a special impact on the family, such as alcoholism and job loss; (5) social, legal, medical, and mental health agencies that are available within the community to accept referrals, the procedures for referral, the type of cases each agency handles, the agency's requirements for eligibility for its services, and the hours the agency is open; and (6) role playing of typical family dispute situations, using volunteers as well as officer trainees.

Handling Family Disputes

In order to deal effectively with family disputes, officers must prevent injury, restore order, and assist the disputants in finding lasting solutions so as to eliminate the need for repeated police call backs. The officer's approach to family fights is one of problem-solving and crisis management—not arrest and prosecution.

In diffusing a family conflict, officers should follow these basic procedures:

1. Be alert to the high danger potential of a family conflict and approach it with full safety precautions.

2. Prevent injury. Once inside, officers should position themselves between the two (or more) parties in conflict. Be alert for any objects that might be used as weapons (real weapons, such as guns or knives, or potential weapons, such as pots and pans).

3. Separate the disputants from each other. If possible, each person in the argument should be kept out of the hearing and visual range of the other. If this cannot be done, then the officers should insist that one person speak at a time.

4. Introduce yourselves, using full name and title, and address both parties of the dispute as Mr. and Mrs. This is important because it aids in creating a tone of politeness which may serve to calm the highly emotionally-charged atmosphere of the conflict up to the time of the officers' arrival.

5. Avoid overt threats, and convey the clear impression that you are there to assist in solving the problem, not necessarily to arrest somebody or even to decide who is right or wrong. The traditional approach, before family crisis training for police officers was available, was to warn the family, "If I have to come back again, somebody's ass is going to jail." Officers arrive at a family fight with the authority invested in their role. There is usually little need to stress this authority since it speaks for itself.

6. Try to create an atmosphere favorable for discussion by removing your hat, sitting down, asking the disputants to sit down, turning down their radio, and looking directly at them. All of these actions will demonstrate to the disputants that you expect to discuss the situation, rather than the fighting between them.

7. Take steps to exclude outsiders unless there is someone present who can be useful in resolving the fight or calming the participants.

8. Demonstrate firmness, but indicate you are open to discussion and

have a fair attitude toward all participants. One side or the other will often try to use or exploit the officers, especially if he or she is the one who called the officer to the residence.

9. Ask diversionary reality questions to tone down the hostility and anger of the disputants, assisting them in making contact with reality. For example, the officer might ask how many people are living here, or where the children are.

10. Find out the facts. Officers should identify the facts of the family disturbance (whether a crime has been committed, whether there are court orders involved, who was the caller).

11. Reinforce calm behavior, and make every effort to allow the parties to back down gracefully and save face.

12. Make every effort to resolve the conflict which led to the dispute.

The following techniques can be used to resolve family disputes (Goldstein et al. 1977).

MEDIATION

An officer's goal in mediation is to help the disputants solve their own crisis rather than in trying to solve it for them. It involves the following steps:

1. The officer informs the disputants that they must solve their problems themselves, but he is there to help.
2. The officer avoids suggesting solutions. Instead, he solicits suggestions from the disputants as to how they think their problems can be solved.
3. The officer checks any proposal with the other disputants until there is acceptance or compromise.
4. The officer avoids criticizing the disputants and encourages them to follow through on the agreed upon solution.

NEGOTIATION

In negotiation, the officer suggests solutions, compromises, or other means for dealing effectively with the crisis. He helps the disputants bargain but remains neutral.

For example, if two officers are present in a husband and wife dispute, one officer might suggest a solution as he talks with the husband, while the other officer does the same as he talks with the wife. Then the two officers can bring the two disputants together and help them negotiate a solution or compromise.

COUNSELING

Counseling a husband and wife in a family dispute takes time, training, and experience. The problems leading to family fights do not occur overnight. They are often long-standing and will not be easily resolved, especially during the stress of the crisis. The officer may have to be satisfied with helping the disputants to acknowledge that they have a problem and encouraging them to get help.

REFERRAL

If the disputants need help, a referral to a community agency may be appropriate. The greatest problem associated with referrals is the frequent nonavailability of community agencies at the time of critical need. Family disputes often occur late at night, early in the morning, on weekends, and on holidays, when most community agencies are not open. As a result, police officers must know the resources available in the particular community, their hours of availability, the services offered, and the eligibility requirements of those agencies most frequently used.

When referring someone, the officer should remember he is involving a third party whom the disputants do not know and may not wish to contact. Therefore, he may have to overcome some resistance to following his referral suggestion. This will be easier if the officer lets the disputants know that he understands their problem and their feelings about it and tells them that the chances are good that the agency can help. The officer should give the disputants all appropriate referral information in writing and make sure that they understand it. He may offer to call the agency to facilitate the referral. If this is not appropriate, the officer should obtain a commitment that they will contact the agency at the earliest possible opportunity. A later follow-up call to the disputants may also be advisable and may assist in a successful referral.

ARBITRATION

If the officer has tried mediation, negotiation, and counseling, and has suggested referral, but none of these has been acceptable to the disputants, then he may have to impose a solution directly. Since this will be his solution, he must realize that this is the least desirable method for resolving family disputes and results in the highest number of return calls. Therefore, arbitration should be used only as a last resort.

In arbitration, the officer should first think of all the possible solutions to the problem and review in his head the strengths and weaknesses of each. He must be aware of any of his biases that may effect his consideration of the possible solutions. Having reviewed all the solutions he can think of, he chooses the one he feels is best and, if possible, discusses it with his partner. He (or he and his partner) makes the final decision and tells the disputants to follow it—and spells out the consequences if they do not.

Legal Aspects

Police departments presently are besieged by legal and civic groups demanding stronger police action in domestic confrontations. The courts also are beginning to examine the problem.

Recently, action was brought against the New York City Police Department, as well as probation and family court personnel, alleging that police officers intervening in domestic disputes did not make arrests even if physical evidence of an assault was present (*Bruno* v. *Codd* 1977). In another case, the Oakland, California, Police Department was accused of an inadequate response to women in general, and black women in particular, who were victims of domestic violence (*Scott* v. *Hart* 1977). In this case, plaintiffs alleged that they were deprived of equal protection when police failed to respond to calls from women who were assaulted by their spouses, former spouses, or boyfriends while responding to calls from those assaulted in nondomestic situations.

Traditionally, police have maintained a policy of nonarrest in domestic violence cases whenever possible. Although this policy was never intended or perceived to be discriminatory, these recent court actions suggest that police will have to take a careful look at their policies and be ready to defend them or amend them.

Landlord–Tenant Disputes

Police are usually called in these disputes because nobody else is available, but they have little or no training in the complexities of landlord–tenant law. As a result, the officer often sees this as a waste of time, and the citizen is disappointed because the officer does not have a legal solution. However, these calls cannot be ignored by the police, since they often lead to violence and other serious criminal offenses. Most disputants seeking police assistance lack the motivation, sophistication, or money to seek a lawful settlement.

The most common abuses perpetrated by landlords are: lockout of a tenant, usually accompanied by the lock-in of the tenant's possessions; seizures of a tenant's property; removal of doors or windows; trespassing (the landlord enters the tenant's premises without permission); and termination of services (the tenant's gas, electricity, or water is cut off).

Abuses most commonly perpetrated by tenants are: destruction of the landlord's property, refusal to pay rent, and accumulation of garbage.

Handling Landlord–Tenant Disputes

Effective handling of landlord–tenant disputes requires that the officer know and understand the applicable penal code provisions. This will enable the officer to intervene, not by making an arrest but rather by explaining to the parties involved what conduct is not lawful and suggesting alternate lawful solutions. For example, if the landlord has locked out the tenant, the officer can explain that a lockout is unlawful and suggest that the landlord consult his attorney or go to the small claims court. If the landlord is unwilling to desist, the officer can make it clear to him that the tenant can initiate criminal proceedings.

The Oakland, California, Police Department has established a landlord–tenant intervention unit to achieve a settlement of landlord–tenant disputes by referring the parties to other agencies, such as the small claims court. Early settlement is a priority, since it deters violence that might otherwise occur. The establishment of this unit followed a sixteen-month experimental landlord–tenant dispute settlement program, in which the Department found that effective police involvement in landlord–tenant disputes prevented both minor and serious offenses, some violent, that might have occurred had the parties been left to themselves.

Officers can be trained to identify the causes of landlord–tenant disputes, to refer these disputants to the proper agencies for resolution, and, in some cases, to achieve a settlement without the necessity of referral.

The Community Mediation Service

Another innovative approach to handling a variety of disputes that have usually required police intervention or can lead to serious crime is the community mediation services of the Pima County (Arizona) Victim Witness Program. The objectives of this services are: (1) to present viable alternatives to resolve disputes involving families, neighbors, and landlords without violence; and (2) to settle a problem quickly, in order to reduce repeated law enforcement involvement.

Most people do not want to take friends or relatives to court, lose time from work, pay a fine, or go to jail. This program is an organized effort to assist police by providing another place where both parties involved in a dispute can sit down in a nonthreatening environment with a mediator and talk about ways to reach an agreement. It takes the police officer out of the mediation role while providing a specialized referral resource.

Summary

In this chapter, we have discussed conflict situations and their management. It is important for the police officer who is called upon to handle these situations to recognize that he is not expected to act as a proxy psychologist but to preserve the peace, prevent injury, and assist people in a crisis to find solutions to their problems. However, because so much of his work involves dealing with people in crisis situations, the police officer has a significant opportunity to contribute to the mental health and safety of the community by learning how to perform effective conflict management through mediation, negotiation, counseling, referral, and arbitration.

BIBLIOGRAPHY

BARD, M. 1970. *Training Police as Specialists in Family Crisis Intervention.* Washington, D. C.: National Institute of Law Enforcement and Criminal Justice.

BARD, M., and ZACKER, J. 1973. "Effects of Conflict Management Training on Police Performance." *Journal of Applied Psychology* 2:202–208.

Bruno v. *Codd.* 1977. 90 Misc. 2- Adv. Sh. 1047. 396 NYS. 2d 974.

GOLDSTEIN, A. P., MONTI, P. J., SARDINO, T. J., and GREEN, D. J. 1977. *Police Crisis Intervention*, Kalamazoo, Mich.: Behaviordelia.

NIERENBERG, G. I. 1968. *The Art of Negotiating.* New York: Cornerstone Library.

OAKLAND POLICE DEPARTMENT. January 18, 1971. "Information Bulletin—Family Crisis Intervention Program."

Scott v. *Hart.* 1977. No. C76-2395, N.D. Cal.

STEINMETZ, S. K., and STRAUS, M. A. 1974. *Violence in the Family.* New York: Dodd, Mead

Chapter 20

Behavioral Aspects of Crisis Intervention with Victims

WHY SHOULD police officers be interested in victims? First, because of the high amount of unreported crime and unsuccessfully prosecuted crime, it is important for officers to understand why victims do not report or cooperate as effectively as they might. What the officer feels is uncooperativeness is actually the result of other serious problems. Victims may be fearful, hostile, confused, or ignorant of what to do. The officer who is first to arrive on the scene and interact with the victims sets the whole tone for the follow-up activities of other investigative officers. His knowing how to handle victims and witnesses will not only lead to a more positive attitude by victims toward the police but also can facilitate their cooperating more fully with the prosecution and testifying in court if necessary.

Second, studies of victims of crippling accidents or sudden fatal illnesses have revealed much information about how victims of catastrophies may react. A review of the emotional changes experienced by crime victims suggests that they have similar reactions (Flint 1975).

Although the police officer is not a mental health professional, he is often the first person to contact the victim during the crisis. Since the victim is extremely vulnerable, the officer's actions can be of great help, not only in handling the immediate effects of the crisis but also in the final resolution and integration of the experience.

The Psychology of Victimization

People are victimized in various ways. When people become victims as a result of chance events or circumstances over which they believe they have no control, such as crime, they usually feel helpless.

Society also plays a role in how victims often feel. For example, when a child comes home from school and tells his parents that the teacher was mean and made him sit in the corner, a common parental response is to inquire, "What did you do to deserve it?" From experiences such as this, many people grow up thinking that if something bad happens, perhaps they deserved it—bad things do not happen to good people. Therefore, if something bad happens, the victim must have precipitated it.

Society sometimes regards victimization as contagious. Being a victim, many people believe, happens to somebody else. Often, people don't wish to associate with those to whom bad things happen because it may rub off.

All of these beliefs may contribute to the feelings of self-blame that most victims experience. The burglary victim, for example, tells himself, "If only I had had those locks replaced." The rape victim asks, "Why did I ever go to that bar in the first place?"

Some of this self-blame may be displaced onto the police officer. "Where were you when I needed you?" or "This is what you're paid to prevent" are examples of a victim's attempt to avoid self-blame.

As a result of the feelings of helplessness and loss of control over one's own life, anger at the offender would be a natural reaction. However, the victim may be too fearful either to directly express the anger or acknowledge it to himself. This is understandable when one considers that the victim has been placed in great danger by the offender and may be hesitant to express anger because of the fear of retaliation.

The victim may handle this anger in several ways. It may be directed against the group to which the offender belongs (for example, blacks, hippies, or juveniles). It may be directed against the self, in which case depression may result.

As the victim searches to make sense out of nonsensical acts, he may use rationalization. He may ask over and over again, "Why would anybody do such a thing as this?"

Finally, victims often use denial. Like heart attack victims who may deny that they are experiencing an attack by thinking it is heartburn or a muscle strain, crime victims often behave as if the crime has not occurred. A car theft victim may walk blocks trying to find his car before willing to admit that it probably has been stolen. The rape victim may deny its impact by appearing very cool and collected as if the experience has made no impression.

Crisis Intervention with Victims

The emotional reactions experienced by victims become crises when existing defenses and problem-solving techniques are not adequate, and the victim feels helpless and unable to cope. Effective crisis intervention by the officer can be of immeasurable assistance in the criminal investigation while at the same time helping to prevent serious emotional consequences to the victim.

Crisis Intervention Techniques

Silbert (1976) has described a ten-point checklist of techniques for officers to use in the field management of victim situations.

1. *The officer should introduce himself by full name and title.* This is important in any police encounter with victims, since it offers the victim a choice of calling the officer by name or rank. This gives the victim a certain amount of control over the situation and may be the first small step that the victim can take toward regaining a sense of mastery over what has happened.

2. *Briefly verify the crime.* This should be done quickly without a detailed discussion. Obtain only necessary information, such as the type of crime being dealt with, whether it involved a weapon, how many people were involved, and whether the criminal had transportation.

The officer may explain to the victim that another officer will be interested later in the details, but right now he needs only this basic information. He might remark, "Do you think you can help me?" giving the victim another choice.

3. *Recognize the victim's ordeal, and reassure him of his immediate safety.* Since victims are often confused and unable to appreciate the presence of the police and what it means for their safety, even though there may be several squad cars with emergency lights flashing, it may be necessary for the officer to constantly reassure the victim that "it is safe now," "the police are here," "we have officers in the area," "you are safe." Repeating the word *safe* is important, since it brings the victim back to the reality of the moment instead of allowing him to ruminate about what has happened.

The reassurance of safety is also important because the victim, with feelings of guilt and self-blame, may view the police officer with mixed emotions—glad to see him as a protector, but also afraid of him as a punisher or blamer. The officer who shows empathy immediately will help counter any negative feelings of the victim toward the officer.

The officer should remember that to the victim the ordeal is important, no matter how routine the officer may consider the case. Even if it is the officer's third purse snatching of the day, he must realize that to each of the victims the crime is unique. To convey empathy, he might say, "You've been through a terrible ordeal; I know it's been a terrible shock to you. You're safe now."

4. *Verify the victim's physical well-being.* All injuries may not be visible, particularly in victims of assault. Elderly victims may have vague or nonspecific complaints. Police officers should verify the victim's well-being immediately or as soon as the victim is calmed down sufficiently to assist. If hospitalization is required, an ambulance should be called, and the officer should administer whatever emergency first aid is required.

5. *Solicit the victim's help in identifying the suspect.* Demanding that the victim identify or describe the suspect immediately may cause further trauma rather than solicit useful information. Victims of crimes, particularly those involving assault, have experienced a loss of control over their environment. The officer can help a victim overcome any emotional block resulting from this loss of control by offering the victim choices. Instead of demanding or simply asking what the suspect looked like, the officer might want to consider the following: "I'd like to ask you a few questions about what happened and then I'll explain what we're

going to do. I need your help with one thing right now . . . finding the suspect. There are other officers waiting to look for him right now. The more information you can give me now, the better chance we have of finding him. Do you think you can calm down enough just to help with this? Good."

These words have several effects. First, the frequent use of the word *now* helps to reinforce present reality for the victim. The crime is over; he is safe. The officer needs the information now to help the officers in the field. Soliciting the victim's help in identifying the suspect in this manner offers a choice, because the officer asks for help rather than demands it. When the officer asks if he is calm enough to help, he again offers a choice. When he responds to the victim's affirmative nod with "Good!" he is reinforcing positive behavior.

6. *Diffuse crisis emotions.* The officer should set up a calm atmosphere, modulate his voice, be an active listener, and introduce reality slowly.

7. *Establish elements of the crime.* After the initial moments of crisis have passed, it is time for the officer to begin establishing the exact elements of the crime so that he may fill out his report. He should be flexible in filling out the report so that he doesn't give the victim the impression he is making demands that the victim must perform.

The victim should be allowed to proceed at his own pace in telling what has happened. The officer should provide encouragement and reassurance and continue to offer the victim a choice. He should ask "Can I make notes while I'm asking the questions?" or "I have to fill out this report. Would it be all right if I make notes and write down your answers on this report form?"

8. *Keep the choices simple.* The availability of choices is such an important tool in psychological first aid that it is important that they not be complicated. The proper response for a simple choice is "yes" or "no." Choices which require more complicated answers are less effective.

9. *Explain procedures that will follow.* Police officers tend to forget that although they are familiar with the procedures that follow, the victim is not. In crisis situations, understanding what will happen and why is especially important because the feeling of helplessness is so predominent. Even if the victim does not ask what will happen next, it is important for the officer to say that a follow-up detective will call as the case progresses. The officer should answer any of the victim's questions. Even though justification may not be necessary, an explanation is always helpful.

10. *Preserve the crime scene and collect physical evidence.* This procedure is standard and will not be discussed further.

Nonverbal Intervention Techniques

Sometimes what is said is less important than the way it is said. Nonverbal communications often determine how words are interpretated. Some of the most important features of nonverbal communication are:

BODY POSTURE

The way we position our bodies tells a lot about how interested we really are in what the speaker is saying. If we incline our heads and sometimes the whole upper part of our body towards the speaker, this indicates that we're really listening. On the other hand, if we lean back, we may communicate disinterest. The victim may judge the officer's attitude from this nonverbal message.

In handling victims, officers should sit down, if at all possible, and encourage the victim to sit down. Sitting down helps to reduce tension and relaxes the victim.

DISTANCING

One should maintain an optimal distance when talking to the victim. If one stands too close or too far away, the conversation is likely to be uncomfortable. The officer should stand close enough to express feelings of empathy and interest yet far enough back to avoid threatening the victim. The farther away one stands, the greater the feeling of formality and disinterest. The police officer must judge the victim's responses to determine whether the distance is too great or too small.

EYE CONTACT

Because of feelings of guilt and self-blame, a victim will often avoid eye contact. If the officer keeps looking directly at the victim's eyes, there is usually an improvement in the victim's response. Eye contact communicates encouragement and support. If the officer is looking around the room or at his notebook, this may indicate disinterest and perhaps even impatience. If he has to write something, he should look up frequently and make eye contact, especially when asking questions.

TOUCHING

Touching can be crucial in diffusing a crisis or instigating further upset. Officers should be careful about touching victims, particularly those who have experienced a sexual assault. They may place a hand close to the victim—for example, on a table. This allows the victim a choice. Officers should not draw back if the victim touches them for emotional support.

Verbal Techniques

The importance of nonverbal behavior does not decrease the importance of verbal techniques.

VOCALIZATION

Victims often speak hesitantly and softly or not at all. As a result, it is important for the officer not to overwhelm the victim with his voice. The officer should speak softly and slowly, avoiding any voice tone or pace which may communicate impatience or lack of interest.

ACTIVE LISTENING

Officers should show that they're really interested, particularly when the victim has an obvious need to ventilate emotions. Allowing silence, offering reflective comments, and providing timely clarifications and summaries are three major tools in active listening.

Allowing silence is extremely important to a victim in crisis since it gives the victim time to collect thoughts and to phrase them comfortably before responding to a question. Victims are often confused and require a moment or two to orient themselves to the question before coming up with an answer. A rape victim may have special difficulty in answering questions that are embarrassing and perhaps regarded as degrading. Officers themselves are often uncomfortable asking these questions. Sometimes the victim's reported uncooperativeness occurs because the officer is uncomfortable and doesn't know how to ask these questions sensitively. The officer who is uncomfortable in asking a rape victim details of the crime should consider acknowledging his discomfort, thus increasing the likelihood that the victim will respond in a helpful manner.

Reflective comments also demonstrate that the officer is actively listening and can encourage the victim to express emotion. Both the

266

content and the feeling of what the victim has said can be reflected back to indicate active listening. For example:

Victim: He jumped right through the window . . . .
Officer: You mean he just burst right in? (reflecting *content*)
Officer: I bet that was frightening. (reflecting *feeling tone*)

Timely clarifications and summaries are another means of demonstrating to the victim that the officer is actively listening. Moreover, timely clarifications and summaries help to tie up random emotions for the victim. These summaries should be done after the victim has finished a segment of a story rather than interrupting repeatedly to clarify. For example, the officer may summarize what was said and then ask, "Do I have it right?"

DIVERSIONARY REALITY QUESTIONS

These questions force victims to deal with reality, thus reducing their distress. They should be simple, realistic, and nonthreatening (for example, "How many people live here?" "How many children are there?").

PERSONALIZING STATEMENTS

Using words such as *I think* or *I feel* will personalize statements and create an environment of empathy for the victim. If officers are accepting of the victim and indicate their acceptance through personalized statements, this reassures the victim. Since the police are often viewed as representatives of society, an understanding approach will reduce the victim's concern about society's reaction. Officers also should capitalize on their prestige as protectors by reassuring victims that they are safe from further occurrences and from retaliation by the perpetrator. This is especially important with rape or assault victims, who are often warned by the offender that he will return to kill them if they report the crime to the police. In such cases, a clear and repeated statement, such as *"In my experience as a police officer,* rapists do not return to the same person," or *"In my experience as a police officer,* burglars do not generally return to the same house," is critical.

STATE THE OBVIOUS

As we have mentioned several times, victims need constant reassurance that the officer is concerned for their safety and that he understands and empathizes with them. Stating "I'm here to help you, you are safe now" or "I know this has been a dreadful experience for you" may seem obvious to the officer, but it is important for the victim to *hear* these words of reassurance.

Accident Victims

Police officers will frequently have to deal with victims of situations other than crimes, such as severe auto accidents and medical emergencies. Although the major responsibility in these situations often falls upon paramedics (or other medical personnel), the policeman should be aware of the following:

RELAXATION

It is important to relax the victim if at all possible. A simple technique which works well is to tell the victim to take a deep breath and let it out slowly. If he is calm and relaxed, the officer will be able to get the victim to relax.

REASSURANCE

Like victims of crime, victims of accidents need continual reassurance that everything possible is being done for them and everything will turn out all right. The officer should not lie, but he should take the opportunity to assure the victim that he is there to help, that the ambulance is on its way, and (in the case of an accident) that others involved are being taken care of. Officers and paramedics have a tendency, while concerning themselves with those showing physical signs of injury at accidents, to ignore other survivors who do not show symptoms. Yet these people may be suffering emotional damage which is very traumatic.

POSITIVE STATEMENTS

The officer should make only positive statements relative to the condition and future of the victims. The fact that a victim may be unconscious does not relieve the officer of this responsibility. Hypnosis research indicates that what is said under these circumstances, even if the victim is unconscious, can have a significant effect on the victim's chance for survival. Avoid statements such as "He'll never make it" or "I've never seen such a bad injury."

The Emotionally Disturbed Citizen

We should remember that the ordinary citizen who may observe a crisis is also a type of victim. The observer, too, can be highly emotional. The officer first may have to calm down an emotional citizen before he will be able to carry out whatever other police duties are necessary. Goldstein et al. (1977) offers several techniques which officers can use effectively to calm citizen emotions in crisis situations.

1. *Show understanding.* By tone of voice, facial expression, and gestures, an officer shows that he understands the feelings the citizen is experiencing and how strongly he is experiencing them. For example, he may say, "It can be awfully frightening when something like this happens . . . you're really feeling very angry and upset."

2. *Be a model.* If the officer responds calmly to the crisis, his appearance of control serves as a model for the citizen involved.

3. *Reassure.* Using reassurance, the officer should give the citizen reasons why he should feel calmer (for example, "I've handled many like this," or "We've got the situation under control"). Reassurance works especially well in calming a situation if the officer has first established himself as a nonhostile authority figure.

4. *Encourage talking.* It is difficult for anybody to yell, scream, cry, fight, or behave emotionally if, at the same time, he is trying to answer questions. Encouraging the person to talk is an effective means of calming him down. Sometimes the police officer may encourage the person to talk about the crisis itself. This can be a form of ventilation. However, if talking about the crisis gets the citizen more agitated, the officer may calm him by asking numerous questions and taking notes at a deliberately slow pace.

5. *Use distraction.* Distraction is useful although its effect may be temporary. Distraction may be accomplished by asking a favor (for example, "May I have a glass of water?"), asking a question totally irrelevant to the situation (for example, "Can you tell me where you got that particular item?"), or asking a question relevant to the crisis situation but opposite to what the citizen is likely to expect (for example, "Do you really want me to take him to jail?").

6. *Use humor.* Humor can assist in keeping the crisis in perspective and can cool tempers in a highly aggressive situation. However, humor must be used cautiously. Because, of the emotional nature of the situation, it may not be appreciated by the citizen. At no time should the officer ever attempt to use ethnic humor.

7. *Repeat or outshout.* Sometimes calmness does not work. When someone is very upset and is only aware of his own feelings, he is often unresponsive to the feelings and presence of others. An officer may have to repeat himself several times or even outshout the citizen to be heard. He may slam a clip board loudly to get attention.

8. *Use physical restraint.* When calm conversation, repetition, and outshouting have not worked, and when there is an threat of physical danger, the officer may physically have to restrain and subdue the highly aggressive citizen. He should use the minimum force required to accomplish this goal.

9. *Use trust in others.* In a crisis, it may be appropriate for an officer to ask someone else to assist him by speaking to the citizen and attempting to calm him. This may be a trusted friend, relative, or neighbor. However, the officer has to be careful in using a trusted acquaintance, first making sure that this person will not aggravate the subject and worsen the crisis.

10. *Temporarily ignore, if there is a more pressing need.* Sometimes the officer can calm the emotional citizen by temporarily ignoring him while handling someone in more acute distress, such as a bleeding accident victim. This reminder of reality may help calm the emotional citizen.

Summary

In this last chapter in the section on crisis situations, we have focused on one of the central figures in any crisis—the victim.

As a result of a crime, an accident, a medical emergency, or any other crisis, any citizen is capable of having a significant emotional response which must be handled by the officer. The skill demonstrated by the officer will reduce emotional trauma for the victim, enhance his cooperation with the police, and lessen the severity of the crisis. Learning the necessary skills requires an understanding of the psychology of the victim and the adoption of the approaches and techniques described in this chapter.

BIBLIOGRAPHY

BRAMMER, L. M. 1973. *The Helping Relationship: Process and Skills.* Englewood Cliffs, N.J.: Prentice-Hall.

FLINT, R. T. 1975. "The Psychology of Victims." Schiller Park, Ill.: Motorola Teleprograms Inc. 1–13.

GOLDSTEIN, A. P., MONTI, P. J., SARDINO, R. J., and GREEN, D. J. 1977. *Police Crisis Intervention.* Kalamazoo, Mich.: Behaviordelia.

KOBETZ, R. W. 1974. *Crisis Intervention and the Police: Selected Readings.* Gaithersburg, Md.: International Association of Chiefs of Police.

MERCHANT, J. J. 1979. "A Model for Police Assistance to Rape Victims." *Journal of Police Science and Administration* 7:45–52.

SILBERT, M. 1976. *Crisis Identification in Management: A Training Manual.* Oakland, Calif.: California Planners.

PART VI

The Stresses of
Police Work

Chapter 21

Job-Related Stress

IN HIS OPENING remarks to one of the first seminars on police work and stress, Karl Goodin, Chief of the Cincinnati Police Department, observed that "policing . . . is one of the most stressful jobs in the occupational picture today." Chief Goodin continued:

I have been a policeman for almost 20 years. During that time, I have seen many of my fellow police officers incapacitated by health problems, heart attacks, ulcers, chronic headaches, mental depression, and even suicide. They have been stricken in numbers that seem unduly large when compared to friends in the business world and in government service agencies other than police.

The situation is a paradoxical one because policemen begin their careers as healthy men . . . they enter the profession as one of the healthiest and most physically fit of any single occupation . . . yet, year after year, we see them struck down at comparatively young ages when early health history would seemingly point to above average longevity.

Figures show that career police officers . . . both active and retired . . . die younger than most other occupational groups and suffer a particular high incidence of health problems. Why? The work is relatively clean; there are no poisonious industrial fumes to breath or noxious chemicals to handle; it is certainly not monotonous when compared to an assembly line functionary. Even though a police officer runs the risk of being killed in the line of duty, that is a relatively minimal risk. His job is actually safer than a goodly number of others such as iron workers or farmers.

Why does he suffer health problems?

Stress is the reason; named time and again by researchers of occupational hazards as a major factor in the police officer's job.

Stress. What causes it? Why is it such a prevalent condition in the law enforcement officer's life? (Goodin 1975).

This chapter will seek to present answers to some of Chief Goodin's questions. It will not present a comprehensive review of the topic. Readers are directed to the Bibliography at the end of the chapter for references to specific areas of interest they may elect to study further. We will limit our discussion to the following: a brief review of the early history of stress research; a set of definitions; stressors in the police environment and in the personal life of the police officer; the psychological and physical symptoms of stress; and ways that police departments and individual officers can reduce the adverse effects of stress.

Historical Background

It was not until the Civil War that environmental stress was recognized as an important etiological factor in certain physical and emotional conditions. During this war, surgeons of both armies became aware of soldiers who presented certain behavioral patterns. They were listed in the sick book excessively, they got into fights, they went AWOL frequently, and they refused to obey rules and regulations. These symptoms (psychological, physical, and behavioral) were the products of a stress reaction and resulted from the pathological interaction between the soldier and his environment. For the first time, physicians realized that people could become unhealthy from the adverse effects of stress in their environment. The military study of stress continued during World War I, World War II, Korea, and Vietnam. Much of what we know today about the impact of stress on police work was first noticed in the combat area.

In civilian medicine, the study of stress was based upon the work of the nineteenth-century French biologist Claude Bernard, who pointed out that the internal environment of our bodies—our blood pressure, heart rate, oxygen level, the amount of red cells in the blood—must maintain consistency and that all of these must shift periodically to meet the demands of life. If adaptation to change in condition does not occur, disease or even death may ensue.

Dr. Bernard's work was extended by the Harvard physiologist Walter D. Cannon, who discovered "the wisdom of the body," describing the internal mechanisms of adjustment in body functions as responses to environmental changes.

Dr. Cannon was especially interested in the emergency reactions of the body—how the body deals with sudden life and death situations. In one classic experiment, he studied the reaction of a cat suddenly confronted by its proverbial enemy, the dog. The cat immediately went into an emergency response. Adrenalin was released into the bloodstream, as was an almost identical hormone called noradrenalin, leading to a variety of physiological reactions. Blood clotting mechanisms were accelerated, more sugar appeared in the blood, rates of circulation and breathing increased, more red blood cells were released from the spleen, the senses became keener, the digestive system went into temporary inactivity, and the sphincters contracted. All of these responses, Dr. Cannon noted, were extremely useful and adaptive because they prepared the body for maximum effort to either fight or flee to insure survival. Dr. Cannon noted that a variety of emergency situations could trigger this pattern of adaptive responses (for example, pain, physical injuries, and intense emotion).

The word *stress* was virtually coined by an Austrian-born physician Hans Selye, presently Professor Emeritus at the University of Montreal and President of the International Institute of Stress. As a young medical student, Selye was impressed with what he called the *sameness of sickness,* what many different patients had in common as they appeared depleted of energy, listless, haggard, and drawn. Later, he demonstrated that these final manifestations of stress were the product of a three-stage process: (1) the stage of alarm; (2) the stage of resistance; and (3) the stage of exhaustion. Together they consituted the *General Adaptation Syndrome* (G.A.S.). Selye pointed out that no living organism can exist in a continuous stage of alarm and that should stress continue, the animal will either develop a disease or die.

Definitions

When we refer to stress, we are talking about the effect that certain environmental features have upon a person. A police officer does not exist in a vacuum but in a social world, surrounded by others significant to him, such as family, friends, fellow police officers, as well as citizens and criminals with whom he interacts during his tour of duty. He is also surrounded by the physical aspects of his environment, indoors and outdoors, which can be stressful or non-stressful.

When we speak of stress as the product of the interaction of the person with his environment, we are really concerned with *stressors* in the environment, anything which produces an autonomic nervous system response in the individual.

What is the autonomic nervous system and how does it work? Simply, the autonomic nervous system controls all hormonal glanduar activity which influences such functions as breathing, blood pressure, and pulse rate.

A person has two nervous systems: the central nervous system, consisting of the brain and the spinal cord; and the autonomic nervous system. Most conscious, voluntary behavior is associated with the central nervous system (for example, reading, writing, and firing a weapon). But while you are reading this page, thinking about the material, perhaps making notes, your body is also engaging in autonomic nervous system activity (breathing, maintaining blood pressure at a certain level, and secreting hormones).

The autonomic nervous system consists of the sympathetic and the parasympathetic divisions. These two divisions work in tandem. The sympathetic division alerts a person and gets ready to make a maximum effort. When an autonomic nervous system response is initiated, the sympathetic is activated; when the stimulus for an autonomic nervous system response is no longer present, the parasympathetic is activated. The autonomic nervous system functions as an emergency response system.

Humans have survived and have dominated this planet because of two features: a superior brain and the autonomic nervous system response mechanism. When primitive man rounded a bend in the trail and came face-to-face with a saber-toothed tiger, immediately the autonomic nervous system responded—more adrenalin was secreted, breathing changed rapidly, digestion dramatically stopped, the spleen produced more red blood cells so that more oxygen could be carried through the body, the sphincter muscles contracted—placing primitive man in an alert position for a maximal effort of running or fighting.

Today, not many policemen worry about meeting saber-toothed tigers during a normal tour of duty, but the autonomic nervous system response is still there, operating the emergency response mechanism. Functioning as needed, it causes bodily changes in the officer's biology.

Instead of saber-toothed tigers, today's police officer may get involved in a dangerous family fight or a bloody and fatal automobile accident. He may face the stress of working under incompetent or hostile supervisors. Each of these stressors in the police officer's environment can evoke an autonomic nervous system response.

Case Example. The police officer starts his day at a certain level of tension. He receives a call to an accident with injuries. He switches on the emergency equipment, going *code 3*. Immediately and simultaneously, his body also goes *code 3* because the autonomic nervous system response has been evoked. He arrives at the accident scene and takes whatever measures are necessary. When he is finished, he goes *code 4*, turns off the emergency equipment, makes his report, and resumes patrol.

The officer's body changes do not turn off as easily. The parasympathetic division of the autonomic nervous system takes longer to come down from its previous level of tension. His tension level hasn't even gone down to the pre-call level when he gets another call.

This time it's a bad family fight. After nearly being knifed by an irate husband, he ends up arresting him and putting him in handcuffs. Once again, he has gone *code 3*, both in his police equipment and his body reactions. Once again, when the emergency is over, his procedures return to *code 4*, but his body does not go *code 4* as easily as the equipment. Hence, his present level of tension, while not as high as a few moments ago, is still considerably higher than before the second call.

And so it goes during the rest of his duty tour. At the end, his tension is not as high as it was on his last call, but it is considerably higher than when he started out that tour of duty.

It is very important for the officer, his family, and counselors who work with police officers to understand this *code 3* biology. The police officer's level of tension may be very high at the end of a tour. He doesn't want to go home if that means listening to more problems. He may want to stay at the station and exchange war stories with other squad members. He may want to join other police officers in a choirboy rehearsal. Biologically, he has a need to release his tension gradually before he is able to go home and assume his role of husband and father.

We believe that police officers themselves have a *code 3* personality. If you ask a hotel clerk, "What kind of night did you have last night?" he may reply, "Wonderful." You ask, "What happened?" He replies, "Nothing happened—there was no one checking in, nobody checked out, nobody rang the phone. I read my book, dozed a little, and had a marvelous night."

You ask a police officer what kind of a night he had and he says, "Wonderful." You then say, "What happened?" He replies, "We had three rapes, two homicides, three shootouts, and five narcotic busts." The police officer likes that kind of action. He has a *code 3* personality.

This personality type strongly resembles the coronary-prone type A behavior pattern first described by Friedman and Rosenman (1974). "Type A behavior is characterized by high striving, achievement, driving competitiveness, time urgency, devotion to work and numerous other activities which involve a tendency to suppress fatigue and stress-related symptoms in order to meet deadlines" (Davidson 1980). Dr. Davidson finds that over 75 percent of American (and Australian) police officers are type A personalities. She believes that it is important to determine whether police work as an occupation attracts type A persons, or whether policing encourages type A behavior in people. She expresses alarm at these findings and suggests that there should be programs concentrating on the facets of police work associated with type A behavior that increase the risk of coronary heart disease.

Stressors in Police Work

Joseph Wambaugh said, "The physical dangers of being a cop are already vastly overrated by TV and movies, while no one pays attention to the more serious emotional dangers on the job that drive cops to divorce, suicide, alcoholism, and drug addiction in greater numbers than any other vocational group" (Eisenberg 1975). Selye (1978) reinforces this view when he remarks, "It may be said without hesitation that, for policemen, the most important stressors are emotional, especially those causing distress."

What are these emotional dangers? What are the stressors in police work?

Those who write about police stress seem to have their own list of job stressors. Terry Eisenberg (1975), a psychologist and a former police officer in the San José Police Department, appears to have the most comprehensive list. It is based upon his own experiences while performing as a patrol officer in a metropolitan area for over two years. He identifies over thirty alleged or implied sources of psychological stress and organizes them into six categories:

1. Intra-organizational practices and characteristics
2. Inter-organizational practices and characteristics
3. Criminal justice system practices and characteristics
4. Public practices and characteristics
5. Police work itself
6. Police officer himself/herself

Intra-Organizational Practices and Characteristics

Eisenberg describes those features within a police organization which may provoke and encourage the development of psychological stress among police personnel, particularly patrol officers. The following conditions represent sources of psychological stress.

POOR SUPERVISION

Because of the paramilitary nature of police organizations, supervision plays an especially important role in the work of the police officer. This is especially true of first-line (sergeant) supervision. The supervisor who is incompetent, who always goes by the book, who is overly demanding, who manipulates others for his own advantage, or who fails to back up his subordinates in delicate and critical situations can substantially contribute to the psychological stress of his subordinates. In too many police agencies, an officer appointed to supervisory status receives no training for his new role. Even if training is offered, it is given sometime after he has already had to assume the role, make decisions, and direct his subordinates. Except perhaps in very large departments, the police officer is quite restricted in his ability to get out from under such a supervisor. As Eisenberg states, "The importance of the supervisor (sergeant) in the life of a patrol officer cannot be underestimated."

ABSENCE OR LACK OF CAREER DEVELOPMENT OPPORTUNITIES

Most police officers start and end their careers as patrolmen; however, most do not anticipate ending their careers as patrolmen when they start. Most aspire to go higher in the organizational chain and would admit to, at least, occasional fleeting fantasies of someday becoming chief. However, promotional opportunities are limited. In addition, the promotional process often lacks objectivity, which generates more frustration. Specialized assignments within the patrolman's rank are also limited and are sometimes awarded on a buddy system.

EXCESSIVE PAPERWORK

The volume of paperwork that the ordinary officer has to contend with is incredible. Much of it, to the officer at least, seems absolutely unnecessary.

OFFENSIVE POLICY

Many times, police officers find certain policies of the department offensive, threatening, and/or unreasonable. Some of these policies center around two important issues: the use of force and minority recruitment. An officer may worry about getting involved in a shooting (or some lesser use of force). Even though he took action he thought was appropriate at the time, he now finds that his action is being censored by command, possibly even being reviewed by the county attorney to determine if criminal charges should be filed. In such cases, the officer sees himself as having fewer rights than the hoods he arrests. This is because, as a police officer, he must answer any and all questions about the incident, even to the extent of having to take a lie detector test. Although this may violate his constitutional rights as a person, failure to consent to these procedures may subject him to punishment or even termination for disobeying departmental rules and regulations.

Department policies concerning minority recruitment may threaten or offend other officers who see the policy as reverse discrimination. Various interest groups may demand certain concessions and threaten to sue in court if their demands are not met. This, of course, elicits hostility toward the special interest group from other officers who may see these demands as unreasonable and selfish and not in the best interest of the department.

Inter-Organizational Practices and Characteristics

Eisenberg's second category refers to those features between or among police agencies which may lead to stress, such as *jurisdictional isolationism.* Law enforcement agencies tend to operate within a particular jurisdiction, and boundary lines between jurisdictions are often jealously guarded. Although mutual aid agreements may exist, each agency is an island unto itself and often does not share information concerning emergency crisis conditions, equipment, and criminal activity with other agencies.

Although police officers in different agencies may get along well together as individuals, particularly at the patrol level, command personnel often do not reflect this cooperation. Further, when an issue depends on loyalty to the organization, even the cooperation between individual officers may disappear. All local police (city, county, state) are quite suspicious of federal law enforcement agencies.

Criminal Justice System Practices and Characteristics

Within this category are stress-related conditions that arise from the actions of agencies within the criminal justice system (for example, adult probation, juvenile probation, juvenile court, parole, corrections facilities, municipal and superior courts). The criminal justice system is often acknowledged by those within it to be anything but a system, even though the agencies share a common mission. Stressors include.

THE INEFFECTIVENESS OF THE CORRECTIONS SYSTEM

The corrections system is seen by most police officers as having failed in its mission either to rehabilitate, punish, or restrain lawbreakers. Police officers continually find themselves arresting the same people for the same offenses. Consequently, a sense of meaninglessness develops along with the feeling that "they don't care, why the hell should I?"

UNFAVORABLE COURT DECISIONS

Certain court decisions over the past few years are considered by law enforcement personnel as too restrictive and antagonistic to the law enforcement mission. Not only do these court decisions seem to overprotect the rights of the criminal at the expense of both the police and the victim, but there are also delays and continuances in the judicial process which further frustrate the police officer. Plea bargaining, a necessity in today's crowded court schedules, is seen by most police officers as a negative procedure in which those guilty of serious crimes are allowed to plead guilty to lesser crimes, thus mitigating or even putting aside their sentence.

Another source of frustration within the courtroom setting involves scheduling the officer's appearance in court which, with rare exceptions, excludes consideration of the officer's on- and off-duty time. Although there is compensation for overtime, appearing in court usually interferes with the officer's personal life. This is particularly stressful when the officer works shifts other than days, because having to appear in court during the day can severely disrupt the officer's sleep and other personal activities.

Once they are in the courtroom, officers are often attacked by the defense attorney. This can make them feel that they are being treated more as criminals than as police officers.

Public Practices and Characteristics

Eisenberg refers to the sources of stress outside of law enforcement and the criminal justice system that can affect police officers. Included are.

DISTORTED AND UNFAVORABLE PRESS ACCOUNTS OF POLICE INCIDENTS

Police officers know the importance of reporting the news to the public, but they become very sensitive after they are burned a few times by irresponsible or malicious reporters. Accounts of a police incident in the local newspaper may be distorted by incompleteness and/or error, both resulting in the department and its members looking bad in the eyes of the public.

UNFAVORABLE MINORITY AND MAJORITY ATTITUDES

Minorities sometimes see the police as oppressors. Allegations of brutality and racism are common. Majority members of the community may complain about slow response time, failure to enforce certain traffic regulations, and insufficient manpower.

DEROGATORY REMARKS BY NEIGHBORS AND OTHERS

This is particularly hard to deal with since it directly affects the officer's wife and children. An officer's children may be referred to as "pigs" or "piglets." Derogatory remarks are sometimes made about the parent's profession, particularly by teenagers who are in the stage of rebelling against authority. If the husband is an officer, his wife may be cornered at neighborhood gatherings and told of the terrible experiences endured by a neighbor or friend by some brutal or nonunderstanding police officer.

THE INEFFECTIVENESS OF REFERRAL AGENCIES

Police officers encounter daily many situations where community services other than police intervention are required. In some jurisdictions, there is a lack of referral agencies; in others the referral agencies that exist are perceived as ineffective. Many helping agencies (other than the police) work only from 8 A.M. to 5 P.M. (and seldom on weekends or holidays).

Demands of Police Work

Included in this category of stressors are.

ROLE CONFLICT

Police work presents the officer with many conflicting roles. Serving the public sometimes conflicts with his mission to enforce the law. Maximizing efficiency in enforcing the law sometimes conflicts with guaranteeing the individual citizen's constitutional rights. The role of the police officer conflicts with the role of father or the role of friend. The public wants the officer to be highly visible when crime or danger threatens; otherwise they would prefer not to see him. These role conflicts in law enforcement work have significant stressor consequences.

SHIFT WORK

Shift work is a major stressor not only in terms of the adverse effects it has upon an officer's family life but also in terms of his personal health. Man functions best when he has a regular work schedule. Changing shifts every month, every three months, or whatever time period the department mandates is very disruptive to biological rhythms. Anyone who has worked "swing" and "graveyard" can testify to the major adjustments in body functioning required. The biological stress of shift work is often expressed in such symptoms as constipation, sleep difficulty, depression, fatigue, and digestive disorders. The change from day shift to swing or midnight also requires numerous personal and occupational adjustments. Related issues, such as court time and holdover assignments, create additional disruptive influences in the officer's life. Shift work also tends to force police families to associate only with each other, since other families are not available for recreation and company during such odd hours.

FEAR AND DANGER

Whether or not a police officer acknowledges it, police work contains dangerous elements that provoke fear and can lead to serious injury, disability, or even death. Although the actual frequency of these incidents is quite low in relation to the number of police contacts throughout the country on any given day, the tension is still there because the officer is aware from the beginning of training that there is no such thing as a routine stop. An officer going down a dark alley in response to a prowler call may never see the prowler, may never even have to draw his gun, but the fear and apprehension remains. The autonomic nervous system is in action. This is a stressor.

CRISIS SITUATIONS

People in the helping professions are subject to *burnout.* A major cause of burnout is the stress of working in crisis situations. Since over 50 percent of the police officer's calls involve dealing with people in crises, he too becomes subject to burnout (chapter 22).

George Kirkham, a criminologist who worked as a police officer for several months, remarks

As a policeman, I found myself forced to deal with other people at their worst, day in and day out—to mediate interpersonal conflict in situations where the disputants were crying, kicking, screaming, threatening, bleeding, drunk, or enraged. Let me assure you that it is quite a different thing to discuss Jones's chronic temper outbursts in a counseling setting, and to face the same man after he has just smashed his wife's face with a fist and is angrily proclaiming his readiness to do the same to you! (Maslach and Jackson 1979).

SENSE OF USELESSNESS

Officers who seriously desire to help people often find themselves frustrated through no fault of their own. They are often unable to successfully resolve the problems of the people with whom they come in contact.

FRAGMENTATION OF POLICE WORK

Police work is like working on a production line, making one contribution to the total product. There are few opportunities for follow-up on a case and little, if any, feedback from other police personnel, such as detectives, on cases that patrol officers were originally involved in.

PEOPLE'S PAIN

The street is full of people suffering physically and mentally. Brutality, pain, and death are normal and usual and, to the police officer, eventually routine. However, no matter how long the officer has been on the force or how much pain he has seen, he still reacts emotionally

286

in dealing with battered children, sexually abused victims, or older people who have been badly beaten.

RAPID CHANGES

The police officer's working environment can change from complete boredom to a life and death struggle in a matter of seconds. Television and movies rarely show the long periods of boredom that exists in police work, the endless patrolling and filling out the proper forms. Yet, at almost any time, an immediate response to a particularly dangerous situation may be required. When an officer has to move that fast and shift gears that rapidly, he's under stress!

RESPONSIBILITY

The police officer must take responsibility for the consequences of his actions. A mistake, even if accidental or unintended, can call for disciplinary action, civil litigation, or even criminal prosecution. The officer must continually be aware of his actions, their appropriateness, and their possible adverse consequences.

Special Types of Police Officers

Under this heading, Eisenberg discusses five types of police officers whose uniqueness adds to the stressors already described in the categories under Police Work Itself.

THE INCOMPETENT

The police officer who manages to get through the required training but is unable really to do the work on the street, is subjected to severe stress far beyond that experienced by the average officer. Some of these incompetents voluntarily leave. A few are eventually discovered and dismissed, but most stay in police work and attempt in various ways, most of them maladaptive, to cope with their own incompetence.

THE FEAR-RIDDEN

Although all police officers experience fear in certain situations, there are officers for whom fear is a constant burden. They are afraid for their own physical well-being. This type of police officer (the *wimp*) usually does something early in his career which shows his lack of courage, and from then on he becomes the object of ridicule and derision from his peers. Nobody wants him for a partner and nobody wants him as backup. The stress on these officers is even greater because their actions deprive them of the support and positive recognition given to other police officers.

THE NONCONFORMIST

Police departments, as paramilitary structures, demand conformity from their members and allow little deviation from established norms. Like the military, law enforcement is more than a job. It is a way of life, a life with others in the police family. If the officer does not conform, or is in some significant way different from his peers, the stress will be severe. The result is exclusion from the company and support of his fellow officers.

THE ETHNIC MINORITY OFFICER

The minority police officer has special pressures. Not only is he exposed to the ordinary stressors common to all police officers but also to the stress associated with rejection and skepticism from citizens of his own ethnic background. Minority officers often have to fight a long, hard battle before they are fully accepted by their fellow officers as equal members of the police family.

THE WOMAN OFFICER

The woman officer is also subject to additional unique stressors beginning with her very first days at the academy. Most women officers feel that they must excel, particularly in the physical and self-defense portion of the training to prove to their male colleagues that they can back them up in time of need. In addition to this pressure to succeed and be accepted, the woman officer has a problem of how to deal with a professional environment in which most of her cohorts are men. She may be exposed to ridicule, sexual innuendos, even sexual harassment.

Some women officers handle this pressure with no trouble. Others sometimes make a mistake of trying to "outmasculine" the men. With this strategy, they not only surrender their femininity, they try their best to hide it. But by not being able to be themselves, they create one of the biggest stressors to their emotional well-being.

It is obvious that we have not exhausted the list of stressors in police work. Even today, we still do not know all the psychological dangers and stressors in police work, or their consequences. What we do know, however, is that police officers must be made aware that this is a high-stress occupation. Selye (1978) has found that policing ranks as one of the most hazardous jobs, even exceeding the formidable stresses and strains of air traffic control work.

A lack of awareness of the impact of stress can be very dangerous because when people are unaware of threats to their well-being, they are less able to cope with the stress that confronts them. To cope successfully with stress on an individual or departmental level, police officers must be made aware of the nature of job stress and of its consequences. Awareness alone will do much to mediate the adverse effect of stressors in police work.

Psychological and Physical Symptoms of Stress

Reiser (1975) states, "It is not the nature of the stress itself that is important, but the person's perception of the event and his emotional response to it." Selye (1978a) also emphasized that "in our life's events, the stressor effects depend not so much upon what we do or what happens to us, but on the way we take it." Each of us may react differently to certain stresses with our own unique pattern of physical and psychological symptoms that tell us we are under stress. Almost any psychological or physical symptom may develop as a result of stress. We are all familiar with the feeling of being uptight—gritted teeth, tense forehead and neck muscles, fluttering eyelids, shallow breathing, cold hands, and butterflies in the stomach. Beyond these common symptoms, the list of physical sequelae of stress is endless. So too is the list of psychological symptoms. We may become irritable, anxious, fearful, tense, and depressed. Each police officer should learn to recognize how his body tells him that he is under stress.

By careful self-observation, the officer can gradually develop an instinctive feeling that tells him when he is running above or below the stress level that corresponds to his own nature. No refined chemical tests or monitors can do more.

Individual Stress Reduction Techniques

Beyond being aware of the job stressors in his environment, what can the police officer do, as an individual, to reduce the adverse effects of job stress?

Anticipation, Avoidance, Rehearsal

Officers should try to anticipate any stressors in their environment, and, if possible, avoid them. If this is not possible, then the police officer should rehearse his response to the anticipated stress. All of us have had the experience of waiting for an important interview to take place. During the wait, we try to anticipate the questions that will be asked and to rehearse our answers to them. Officers may lessen the stress of responding to calls by rehearsing what they will do when they arrive on the scene, recalling similar situations and what they have done in the past that was either effective or noneffective.

Attention to Diet

The diet of the average policeman is a nutritionist's nightmare. It consists of fast foods—donuts, coffee, hamburgers, french fries, and milk shakes—eaten under the most adverse conditions and usually with the background noise of the ever-present police radio. The officer may have to terminate his meal quickly to answer a 10–52 (accident with injuries), in which he will be exposed to sights and smells and tensions hardly condusive to digestion.

The role of diet as a stress reducer cannot be discussed in detail here. However, as an example of the importance of this subject, let us consider just one food, refined sugar, which makes up a large part of what police officers eat.

Cynthia Rhoads (1977), a nutritionist counselor at Pina Community College, states that sugar may be a leading cause of tension in domestic violence. Her research indicates that wife beaters may vent their frustrations violently, not just because of problems at home, but also in association with tension caused by poor eating habits. Here sugar is the prime offender. Not only can wife beaters become the victims of excessive sugar consumption in poorly regulated diets, but policemen also, according to Rhoads, do not respond as effectively as they could to stress because they eat junk food instead of properly balanced meals. Excessive sugar consumption can cause *hypoglycemia,* or low blood sugar. When a person eats too much sugar, the pancreas releases insulin which regulates the body's glucose levels. After the sweets are eliminated, the insulin remains, leaving a sugar deficiency in the body.

Hypoglycemics may display a bewildering array of symptoms, including depression, impotence, alcoholism, violence, dizziness, and headaches. For hypoglycemics, life may be a series of roller coaster highs and lows. The highs correspond with the mid-morning coffee break, when a sweet roll and coffee with sugar brings a blast of energy. This is followed by a feeling of lethargy and fatigue, when the blood sugar level drops.

Two common ways to relieve the symptoms are to eat more sugar, which provides temporary relief, or to release adrenalin into the system. Since violent outbursts stimulate the flow of adrenalin in the body, a hypoglycemic may actually satisfy a critical body need through anger.

If we apply this knowledge to stress and police work, we may conclude that it may be more valuable to refer an officer who has an abnormally high number of citizens' complaints to a physician for a fasting blood sugar test rather than refer him to the Office of Internal Affairs for investigation. His irritability and tendency to use too much force, which may be the basis for most of the citizens' complaints, may be associated with what he is eating rather than with personality factors. It is noteworthy that in the annual day-long seminars on job related stress sponsored by the FOP (Fraternal Order of Police) wives of the Tucson Police Department, a nutritionist is always on the program. Her presentation is always received with interest and followed by demands for further information on the importance of diet in modulating stress reactions.

Exercise Program

It is ironic that a police officer in even the smallest department must pass quite a demanding physical before acceptance, yet few departments seem to pay much attention to maintaining physical fitness after the academy. Numberous studies have shown that police officers are often overweight and out of shape. This can lead to very serious consequences.

For example, in the local sheriff's department, a young deputy was transferred from patrol to detectives. After staying in detectives for about two years, he was transferred back to patrol. The first day on patrol, he was called to a neighborhood disturbance and engaged in a fight with a citizen. The citizen knocked the officer to the ground and managed to break away and dash back into his house where he obtained a .357 Magnum and came out shooting. He wounded the officer before the officer killed him. It developed that this citizen was not a criminal, but rather a very depressed person who had been drinking heavily and expressing suicidal thoughts since his wife had left him. There is a possibility that the citizen chose this way to die, lacking whatever it took to end his own life.

In this example, the deputy at first seemed to be adjusting well to the stress of the shooting. The department psychologist saw him in the hospital when he was recovering from his wound and reported that he seemed to be experiencing no problem. However, a short time later, the deputy left Tucson and flew to Chicago. Upon arriving there, he called the FBI and informed them that he was wanted for murder in Tucson. He persisted with this self-accusation, turning himself into the Chicago police. Finding that he was a deputy, the Chicago police took up a collection and paid for his air fare back to Tucson. However, he got off the plane at one of the stops and did not appear in Tucson until sometime later. When he did appear, he resumed calling the FBI and other law enforcement agencies, saying that he was a murderer and should be placed in prison and punished. Eventually it was necessary to confine him to the psychiatric ward of the county hospital. The psychiatrist in charge stated that the officer was experiencing considerable guilt related to what he perceived as his lack of physical fitness. He told the psychiatrist that if he had maintained his physical fitness while he was in detectives, the citizen could not have pressed him to the ground, broken away, and gone in to get his gun. He was therefore blaming himself for the citizen's death.

We will discuss in more detail in the next chapter this *post-shooting syndrome,* but the point here is that there is a need for police officers to stay in shape so that they will be able to carry out the physical activities that are demanded of them. Each police officer should assume responsibility for his own physical condition and engage in a planned program of physical fitness on a continual basis. The police officer might involve his wife, and perhaps his whole family, in a physical fitness program. The world's least expensive sport is brisk walking. It offers an opportunity for the family to do something together, it doesn't take much money, and it results in everybody's feeling better and becoming much healthier.

Private Time

Everyone needs some time to be alone. Married couples need private time to be alone by themselves. Some of this private time can be spent on an exercise program. Time for reflection and conversation is a must for any officer.

Relaxation

If Americans knew how to exercise properly, how to eat properly, and how to relax, a large part of our health problems would disappear overnight. Most people have never really experienced true relaxation. They perceive relaxation as not being uptight. Relaxation is much more than this. There are books that will teach you how to relax. One of the best is *The Relaxation Response* by Harvey Benson, M.D. (1975). Dr. Benson discusses the principles of relaxation and gives many different exercises that vary from deep muscle relaxation that can be done at home to quick, simple relaxation exercises to be performed at the office and in the car.

Other relaxation techniques can be helpful—for example, listening to soothing music, meditating, or reading an interesting book. Once you learn to relax by one or more of these methods, then practice relaxation several times a day. It needn't take a long time; under certain stressful situations, even a few seconds can suffice. We teach recruits to relax when faced by stress simply by putting the index finger and thumb of each hand together, taking a deep breath, and saying to themselves, "Relax, relax, relax." Troopers tell us this single technique has been very helpful in stressful situations.

Adequate Sleep

Adults do best when they have had not less than seven hours and not more than eight hours of sleep. It is important in forming habits for better health that one pay attention to getting adequate sleep—a factor often overlooked by action-oriented people, particularly in their youth.

In regard to forming habits for better health, Dr. Lester Breslow

(1980) reported an interesting study of seven thousand residents in Alameda County, California, over the past thirty years. The study's purpose was to establish statistical evidence of a link between peoples' daily life-style and health habits and their general health and life expectancy.

Breslow and his colleagues questioned the participants on seven habits they thought might have a relation to health: (1) cigarette smoking; (2) moderate or no use of alcohol versus heavy use; (3) moderate or strenuous exercise versus little or none; (4) seven or eight hours of sleep versus less or more; (5) eating moderately, so as to be neither obese nor too thin; (6) eating breakfast; and (7) eating regularly at certain mealtimes rather than snacking during the day.

The results were striking. Breslow found that "for every age, those who followed seven of the habits had better physical health than those who followed six. Those who followed six had better health than those who followed five . . . and so on, down to those who followed three habits who were found to have better health than those who followed from none to two."

Perhaps even more interesting was the finding that a man of 60 who followed all seven health habits had about the same physical health as a 30-year-old man who followed from zero to two of the habits. The life expectancy findings were equally startling. "We found that a man at age 45 who was following zero to three of the habits can expect to live to be 67 years old, while a man of 45 who follows six to seven of the habits has a life expectancy of 78." The fact that life-style changes can result in an increase of eleven years in terms of life expectancy gives some indication of the health strategy that everyone ought to follow.

Positive Thinking

One of the common elements of most mental illnesses is a negative self-image. Fortunately, most of us are not mentally ill. However, all of us, to a certain extent, engage in negative thinking, programming ourselves for failure or responding negatively to stressors.

All of us do a lot of self-talking. We do this every day, but unfortunately, many times we don't tell ourselves favorable things. We tend to cut ourselves down, to find fault with ourselves. What we have to do is to change this negative self-talk to positive.

It is clear that it is not the stress but how one interprets it that makes the significant difference. Stress can be both positive and negative in its influence. Selye (1978a) has coined the term *eustress* for the good kind of stress that makes you come alive, that challenges you to do your utmost. By positive thinking, you can convert negative stress into positive experience.

. . . I think there's another better way to handle stress which involves taking a different attitude towards the various events in our lives. Attitude determines whether we perceive experiences as pleasant or unpleasant. In adopting the right attitude, one can convert a negative stress into a positive one—something I call a eustress, employing the same prefix for good that occurs in such words as euphoria and euphonia.

The reader may ask whether positive stress also places demands on the body The answer is yes, but far less of a demand. If your attitude is positive, rather than negative, you can change bad stress into good stress.

Another attitude which in conjunction with positive thinking helps relieve stress may be summed up: "Don't sweat the small stuff." This phrase comes from the reported experience of a business executive who told of an earlier time when, as a salesman, he picked up a young hitchhiker along a mountain road. Shortly after picking up the lad, the salesman found himself behind a big truck. Since it was only a two-lane country road, there was no opportunity to pass. Without realizing it, the salesman found himself getting upset because of his inability to pass the slow moving truck. Finally, as his annoyance was reaching a peak and he was considering passing the truck even though it might be dangerous, he looked over at the young hitchhiker who was apparently very relaxed. The young man, noticing his glance, looked back at him and said, "Don't sweat the small stuff." The salesman, now a business executive, states that was one of the most valuable bits of advice he had ever gotten from anybody and, from that time on, he tried to see things in perspective. Remember, none of us, not even police officers, are irreplaceable, so when something seems to get you really uptight, back off, relax, and "don't sweat the small stuff."

Stress Reduction at the Department Level

As we indicated in our discussion of intra-departmental stressors, there is much that the police organization can do to look within itself, identify unnecessary stresses, and eliminate or moderate them. For example, when an officer is being investigated by the Office of Internal Affairs, he is, quite understandably, under great stress, particularly if there is a possiblity of termination or perhaps even criminal prosecution for his actions. In our American tradition, the officer, like any other accused person, must be presumed innocent, yet many departments make no allowance or provision for keeping the officer informed of the investigation's progress. Understandably, there are certain facts about the investigation that perhaps cannot be made available at a particular time. We are not talking about that. We are talking about unnecessarily allowing him, as a Nixon aide once phrased it, to "twist slowly, slowly in the wind" while his fate is being decided.

In the Tucson Police Department, we found it advisable to make certain administrative changes involving the use of *tickler files* to ensure that the investigation and paperwork were proceeding without unnecessary delay. Using these files, we could inform the officer, at any time, of the status of his investigation, thus relieving him of unnecessary stress. Every department would profit from a review of standard operating procedures in order to eliminate or change those that are unnecessary or stress provoking.

Another way for police departments to reduce stress is to work constantly to improve selection procedures so that only those with a high stress tolerance level are hired. After the candidate is hired and placed in the academy, there should be a field training and evaluation program so that selection errors may be terminated before they become permanent employees.

There should be an active in-service training program to acquaint officers with the subject of job-related stress. Police administrators and commanders can assist the officer wives' auxiliary in holding annual stress management seminars for officers' wives.

Supervisors, particularly first-line (sergeants), should be trained to detect signs of adverse stress reactions in their personnel so that they may be assisted or referred for assistance. Many departments now have an in-house mental health professional or have contracted with the private sector to provide counseling services (chapter 23). Officers and their families should be encouraged to take advantage of these services, and confidentiality should be assured. It is helpful if the professional has an office away from the station where he can see his clients so that those who come will not have to make their visits known to others. There is nothing bad about seeking assistance, but it is realistic to recognize that police officers may be suspicious that seeking help may result in a negative entry in their personnel jacket.

Edward C. Donovan, a Boston police officer and president of the

International Law Enforcement Stress Association, believes that the police department mental health professional should enlist the aid of a peer counselor.

> I say this because when you can take the fear and mystery out of the system and getting help when you need it, the people who are in need of help will begin to ask for it.
>
> Peer counseling works in the law enforcement vocation. It works when others don't and for a simple reason. Peer trusts peer but not outsiders. The police vocation is a closed society that will not let outsiders (non-police) in . . . the unwritten rule of suffering in silence about all that passes before your eyes and never speaking to others outside the vocation is seldom broken. So who else can a cop who is in trouble with himself talk to but another cop, someone who knows where he's at and how he's feeling about being there. (Donovan 1978, p. 25)

The experience of the senior author (H.E.R.) as a department psychologist strongly supports Donovan's view. Sergeant Richard Milne, a career officer with over eighteen years of services, has been a part of the Behavioral Science Unit in Tucson since its inception. Sergeant Milne sees far more cases every week than the department psychologist, not only because of the factors brought out by Donovan but also, perhaps, because the department psychologist has a close association with command. Although it is believed the troops trust the psychologist not to break any confidentiality, it is probably easier to relate to Sergeant Milne, who does not have this daily visibility with command. Further, some people undoubtedly think that when they consult "the doctor," this means they are really on the edge of being crazy or having a breakdown. There is probably much less anxiety in approaching Sergeant Milne, at least as a first step.

Another stress reduction program that the department can initiate is psychological screening for special assignments (for example, SWAT, TACT, bomb squad, K–9 unit, and sex crimes unit). An assignment to undercover narcotic work, in particular, is exceptionally stressful. Little has been done in police departments to really study this specialized stress. There are many unanswered questions, such as what personality traits or characteristics are needed when selecting for these special assignments; how to prepare officers psychologically to accept such assignments; and, perhaps even more important, how to assist them in stepping out of these assignments and going back to being a patrol officer. Research in these areas is very much needed.

Given the importance of exercise in stress reduction, departments need to sponsor on-duty exercise programs. In addition, Reiser (1975) suggests that there should be planned rest and recuperation opportunities, with facilities available to officers serving in high-stress divisions and on extra-hazardous assignments.

We have emphasized the importance of diet in stress reduction. Department cafeterias and nutrition staff should be encouraged to comply with up-to-date concepts in nutrition through the food that they provide. Just as candy, pop, and other junk foods have been taken out of many school cafeterias and food dispensing machines, the same could be done in police cafeterias and snack bars.

Summary

This chapter has presented information on the stressors in police work. We have discussed how stress may have a positive or a negative value. How it affects the individual officer is to a large extent up to the officer. It is not the event but how the officer perceives it that determines how much stress he experiences and whether he experiences it positively or negatively. Stress experienced in a positive way can make one tougher and more able to deal with stresses found on the job or in the family.

It is first necessary to identify the stressors and then to note which ones you react to, how they affect you, and what actions you can take to prevent any adverse effect, while retaining the positive results from dealing effectively with the stressor. These stress-reducing actions include: (1) anticipation, avoidance, rehearsal; (2) attention to diet; (3) exercise program; (4) private time; (5) relaxation; (6) adequate sleep; and (7) positive thinking.

Finally, we discussed certain actions the police department can take to reduce or eliminate unnecessary stressors in the police environment. In the next chapter, we shall discuss some special stress situations.

BIBLIOGRAPHY

BENSON, H. 1975. *The Relaxation Response.* New York: William Morrow.
BRESLOW, L. November 3, 1980. "Forming Habits." *Arizona Daily Star.*
DAVIDSON, M. J. 1980. "The Coronary-Prone Type A Behavior Pattern and the Policeman: A Cross Cultural Comparison." *Journal of Police Stress* 1:39–41.

DONOVAN, E. C. 1978. "Need Some Help, Doc?" *Journal of Police Stress* 1:25.

EISENBERG, T. November 1975. "Labor Management Relations and Psychological Stress." *Police Chief* 1954–1964.

FRIEDMAN, M., and ROSENMAN, R. H. 1974. *Type A Behavior and Your Heart*. Greenwich, Conn.: Fawcett.

GOODIN, K. May 8, 1975. "Police Stress." Presented at a Conference on Police Stress. Cincinnati, Ohio: National Institute of Occupational Safety and Health.

MASLACH, C., and JACKSON, S. E. May 1979. "Burned-Out Cops and Their Families." *Psychology Today* 59–62.

REISER, M. May 8, 1975. "Stress, Distress, and Adaptation in Police Work." Presented at a Conference on Police Stress. Cincinnati, Ohio: National Institute of Occupational Safety and Health.

RHOADS, CYNTHIA. November 12, 1977. "Sugar Plays Role in Domestic Violence." *Tucson Citizen*.

RUSSELL, H. E. 1980. "Job Related Stress in Police Work." Unpublished manuscript.

SELYE, H. March 1978(a). "On the Real Benefits of Eustress." *Psychology Today* 60–70.

SELYE, H. 1978. "The Stress of Police Work." *Journal of Police Stress* 1:7–9.

Chapter 22

Special Stress Situations

CERTAIN SITUATIONS and conditions found in police work constitute special stressors and therefore merit attention. We have selected
five of these areas for discussion: the use of deadly force, burnout,
special assignments, marriage, and retirement.

The Use of Deadly Force

Police officials are very aware of the problems inherent in the use of
deadly force. In January 1980, Chief Joseph S. Dominelli, president of
the International Association of Chiefs of Police, said:

> The use of deadly force is the most awesome and frightening duty ever
> imposed upon a police officer in a democratic society. No other occupation
> group, outside of military forces in wartime, is authorized by law to make a
> life and death decision under the split-second pressure of circumstances fac-
> ing the police officer at the time he reaches for his service weapon (Dominelli
> 1980).

300

Statistics indicate that in the United States each year, more than one hundred police officers kill people in the line of duty. Some of these killings are done in self-defense, some are accidental, some are to prevent a serious crime. A few represent serious abuses of police power (Cohen 1980).

On the other side of the ledger, an average of 111 police officers have been killed annually in the performance of their duty during the past five years. Many lose their lives in that split second required by the processes of perception, evaluation, decision, and action which every officer exercises prior to using deadly force (Dominelli 1980).

Not only does the officer have to face the stress involved in the shooting itself, but he also has to worry whether it will be judged a good shooting by investigators and administrators who will review and judge his every action (or lack of action) in the cold, unemotional reality of the next day. In most jurisdictions, the use of deadly force by police is subject to no less than five legal sanctions: (1) civil action in a local or state court; (2) criminal action in a local or state court; (3) federal civil rights action under Section 1983 of Title 42 of the U.S. Code; (4) federal criminal action under Section 242 of Title 18; and (5) departmental disciplinary action. Recently, in Tucson, a police officer was found innocent of manslaughter in a criminal court but was judged liable in a civilian court (along with the city he worked for), losing everything he owned.

Police policies and procedures also may add unnecessary stresses to the officer involved in a shooting. For example, Lieutenant Henderson of the Metropolitan Police Reserve Corps, Washington, D.C., states, "I have a very good friend in the department who back in the 60's killed a man and still has nightmares about it. His biggest problem was the fact that the department kept him in the dark for months about whether they were going to prosecute or not" (Henderson 1980).

Post-Shooting Syndrome

Dr. Michael Roberts, psychologist for the San José, California, Police Department, was one of the first to call attention to the *post-shooting syndrome*. He pointed out that for many new (and even some experienced) officers, the confrontation between the officer and an armed felon that results in the death of the felon, is the ultimate myth of police work. This hero myth comes also from movies, television, and from our cultural fiction involving the bad guy, the marshall, and "high noon."

Even more important, perhaps, is the support that this hero myth receives from the values of the locker room and the war stories told in police bars.

A San José police officer says that most police officers think that sometime they may have to shoot somebody. "Driving around, you think what if this would happen? . . . finally it happens to you and a lot of things you thought would happen don't. You imagine a blazing gun battle after which you go over and roll him over with your foot and blow the smoke from your gun" (Cohen 1980).

What really happened is that, when this officer had to shoot a man, it took four rounds from his .357 Magnum before the suspect dropped. The officer then grabbed some gauze from the first aid kit and tried for fifteen minutes to resuscitate the victim.

In Memphis, Tennessee, in 1978, patrolman John Thomas Cursey killed two holdup men during a liquor store robbery. He shot one man when he turned on him with a gun and the other when he ran. However, the second man did not die instantly. Officer Cursey heard him gasping for breath for several minutes before he died.

A few days after the killings, Cursey's buddies presented him with a fifth of whiskey; over the label they had pasted a police photo of one of the dead bandits sprawled on the liquor store floor. Six months later, Cursey was an alcoholic. He relived the killings night after night in his dreams. He began to drink uncontrollably and was finally fired because of his alcoholism. Afterwards, he couldn't hold any job. The psychologist told the pension board that Cursey was "what I would describe as a stable, hard working, family oriented type of fellow with a good circle of friends. His reaction to the incident was a very severe anxiety and depressive neurosis, insomnia and a lack of concentration" (*Tucson Daily Citizen* 1978).

The etiology of the post-shooting reaction lies in the emotional discontinuity between the officer's expectations about the shooting and the reality of it. The officer's expectation revolves around the fantasy of a heroic, man-to-man confrontation. In reality, most police shootings do not involve a heroic situation. More often, it is a lopsided contest. Furthermore, if the person is not a felon but a disturbed, mentally ill citizen, or if the shooting is accidental, the psychic trauma for the officer may be even more severe.

Some officers involved in shootouts state that they hated all the adulation they received from their fellow officers after the shooting. One officer says, "You can't really talk to someone who hasn't been there. They want to hear the gory details, not about your problems handling it, because it's heavy and it reminds them that it could happen to them" (Cohen 1980).

Most officers are terribly afraid that they might have to shoot some-one, so they are anxious to talk to an officer who has, hoping that whatever gave him the guts to pull the trigger will rub off on them.

The following are some of the adverse reactions that officers involved in shootings may show.

1. *Sensory distortion:* Time slows down, everything is in slow motion.

2. *Flashbacks:* Many things occur that instantly remind you—another shooting, the sight of a body in the street—you live it over and over.

3. *Fear of insanity:* Officers may have this fear because of the symptoms experienced in (1) and (2) above.

4. *Sorrow over depriving a person of life:* After being taught not to kill, it is very difficult to break this cultural and religious prohibition. Even police officers who have previously killed in military combat state that a police shooting is entirely different. Detective Dan Sullivan of the Santa Barbara, Californina, Police Department states that "in a war, that's what you're there for . . . to wipe them out. Police work isn't like that. You are certainly not on a search and destroy mission" (Cohen 1980).

5. *Crying:* This usually happens outside the police environment be-cause the macho image does not permit tears.

6. *Grasping for life:* Officers becoming very concerned about their families, their home life, being loved and accepted by others—a sort of guilt reaction to the shooting.

7. *Nightmares:* One officer reported frequent nightmares in which the suspect keeps coming at him, looming ever larger and ever nearer while the officer frantically pumps bullets into the apparition.

All police psychologists seem in agreement that the trauma of the post-shooting reaction has to be recognized as normal and that the officer should be offered either peer or professional help, perhaps both if indicated.

To remove any stigma from seeking such help, in the Tucson Police Department it is mandatory that any officer involved in a shooting (even if not fatal) be seen by a member of the Behavioral Science Unit within twenty-four hours. The Behavioral Science Unit may recom-mend administrative leave, transfer to another assignment or squad, transfer to another section of the city, or whatever other action seems appropriate in helping the officer to handle this crisis effectively.

Sometimes it is difficult to get officers to express themselves about the shooting. The assurance of confidentiality isn't enough.

Increasingly, officers involved in shootings find themselves before grand juries or in civil or criminal court. These legal proceedings make psychological intervention more difficult because the officer becomes preoccupied with the legal ramifications of what he says to the psychologist rather than trying to express some of his feelings about the shooting. Officers involved in shootings frequently seek immediate legal representation, either through their own lawyer or perhaps a lawyer from the Fraternal Order of Police. In the case of the Tucson Police Department, this may place a stumbling block in the officer's talking to a member of the Behavioral Science Unit unless the confidentiality of the interview is assured not only to the officer but also to his attorney. Even if this is the case, the attorney may decide that it is not in the best legal interest of his client to participate in such sessions.

In a recent experience one of the authors (H.E.R.) was called to the site of a shooting which involved a senior sergeant. This was the fourth time in his career that this sergeant had been involved in a shooting. The first time, he said that the department had the "fall off your horse" philosophy, in which he was given a pat on the back, reassured that he was a good cop, and told to report for duty the next night. For the second shooting he got some time off because he was severely wounded and ended up in the hospital for several months. The third shooting did not actually involve any gunfire, but weapons were drawn. This last shooting, to which the author responded, involved a family fight. A young wife was firing a rifle at the officers and other people in the immediate vicinity. The sergeant was one of three officers who fired in return. The victim did not die but was severely injured and taken to the hospital. Asked about his reaction to the present shooting, where a member of the Behavioral Science Unit was present (in contrast to the other situations where no help was available), he stated, "Just knowing that you were there made the difference . . . it helped."

The officer involved in a shooting is usually not available for or amenable to any therapeutic help until some time has passed. First, he is interviewed by homicide detectives and other personnel (Internal Affairs) about all aspects of the shooting. He is usually very fatigued at the end of this, and while he expresses appreciation at the help being offered he prefers to go home to his wife and family, get some rest, and then come in to talk. At this time, while the officer is undergoing investigation, more attention should be paid to the spouse and other family members of the officer involved. Undoubtedly, this is also a period of great stress for them, and they may profit from help. In addition, any assistance given to them at this time may enable them to be of more help to their loved one who has been directly involved.

The importance of the post-shooting syndrome as a special stress situation was highlighted in a recent meeting of police administrators and psychologists held at the Southwestern Legal Foundation in 1981. Participants agreed that the post-shooting syndrome was a delayed stress reaction common to many officers in all departments and that departments that have not yet given attention to this problem should do so without delay.

A possible procedure would be to assemble officers who had experienced the post-shooting syndrome to discuss their specific reactions in an informal, confidential meeting. Each officer would also be given literature on the subject of post-shooting syndrome to evaluate in terms of his own experiences. These officers would be encouraged to form a peer support group for any officer who later becomes involved in shootings, fatal or nonfatal.

One or two officers from the support group would be on call each twenty-four-hour day and would respond to the scene whenever a shooting occurred. Their immediate purpose would be to offer support to the officers involved and to carry out the following preventative measures:

1. The officer's family should immediately be informed of his condition.

2. The officer should be removed from the scene by the support officer as soon as possible.

3. Although the officer's firearm must be taken as part of the investigation, a new weapon should be immediately furnished to counteract any feelings of rejection or guilt by the officer.

4. The supervisor in charge should prepare material which can be presented to all shifts at briefings. This material should identify the incident, the officers involved, what happened, and what action was taken to put the officer on sick leave, suspension, and so on. These measures should counteract the rumors that spring up and receive wide circulation following any shooting incident involving a police officer. During this briefing, other officers should be advised that an officer has gone through an experience which can be traumatic and that they should be sensitive to the feelings the officer may have. Joking and prying would be ill-advised.

One of the participants at the symposium related how a young officer had fatally shot a woman. The officer was so upset that he was unable to return to duty for a couple of weeks. After receiving counseling from the Behavioral Science Unit, he returned to duty, only to be blown away again when one of his squad members, attempting to be funny, said, "How does it feel to be a *real* lady killer?"

5. The police officer's family, partner, and squad members may also need some counseling to handle this incident. This counseling should be made available in a way that is not offensive to the wife, partner, or squad and will enable them to handle more effectively any questions or comments from outsiders.

Burnout

"Burnout refers to a syndrome of emotional exhaustion and cynicism that frequently occurs among individuals who do 'people work' and who spend considerable time in close encounters with others who are experiencing chronic tension and stress" (Maslach and Jackson 1979).

Career burnout is not unusual, since almost everybody gets burned out to some degree. However, when a person is constantly working in stressful situations and is responsible for the people with whom he is working, he becomes especially susceptible to burnout. Over time, a person working in a constantly stressful situation may begin to dislike and distrust those with whom he has contact. He may wish that they never existed. This can even happen to a professional who is normally sympathetic and very concerned about the welfare of his clients. In addition to feeling negative about his clients, the worker may begin to feel negative about himself and may question whether his work has any meaning or value. This happens to nurses, doctors, psychologists, and others in the helping professions. But what about the police officer who is constantly exposed to powerful and often violent emotional stimuli associated with death, assault, rape, and murder?

He may develop the *John Wayne/Wyatt Earp syndrome,* in which he demonstrates negative feelings and dehumanizing tendencies, lives by the book, and tends to treat the public, both complainants and suspects, as "scumbags" (Chamberlin 1978). As Dr. Monroe-Cook of Michigan State University has observed, "When policemen and women start swaggering, being cool and aloof, displaying their weapons while off duty, and assume a cynical, unemotional attitude, they are into the John Wayne syndrome" (Monroe-Cook 1975).

Burnout may also be accompanied by somatic symptoms, such as ulcers, constant headaches, chronic fatigue, and colds. According to Randal Kunkel, executive director of Potentials Unlimited (Maslach and Jackson 1979), these physical problems also can include routine overindulgence in alcohol, food, sleep, or drugs, and together constitute the first stage of the five-stage burnout syndrome. Stage two includes subtle changes in the person's social life. Humor becomes more biting and personal. He may start to avoid people, particularly those who drain him emotionally. During this stage, burnout starts to affect the family and other close relationships. The burnout candidate starts snapping, nagging, and not paying attention to the children or spouse. In the third stage, the intellectual stage, there is mental boredom, poor concentration, and an increased orientation to the future—the weekend, vacation, or retirement. Feelings of alienation usually signal the start of the fourth stage. Personal or professional goals and headlines lose their meaning, humor is abandoned entirely, and life planning is done defensively. The final stage is marked by depression, withdrawal from other people, reacting to the demands of others as a personal threat, and increased procrastination (Powers 1980).

Donn Hupler, an Albuquerque police officer/counselor traces this progression in a young police officer:

Coming to the profession young, and very inexperienced, the cadet has a wonderous new world opened up to him. It's a world with sharp edges, pain, and human suffering. Before long, he models behavior of slightly more experienced officers and purely out of self-defense becomes a disciple of the John Wayne Syndrome, usually remaining here for several years until such time as his experiencing reaches a plateau and levels off. During this time, he is a hard cookie, nothing reaches him emotionally, and to varying degrees, he shuts down all external show of affect. All of us who have been through it know of course that internally, the wheels keep turning. This defensive mechanism, if not carried too far, is a healthy entity. Abused, however, it becomes a determent to the officer's own health growth and limiting factor in dealing with others. In the final phase of development, the older officer usually finds peace with himself and not only recognizes that people have an honest right to their emotions, but is willing to deal with them rather than seeking the safety of emotional isolation (Hupler 1980).

Hupler notes that most techniques used by police officers to distance themselves from people and their problems have a depersonalizing or dehumanizing quality. "We do not talk about the attractive young woman who was killed in a flaming car, but rather about the dumb bitch that had her thumb in her ear or the 'crispy critter.'" The police vernacular is replete with words that dehumanize (maggot, scumbag, basket case, and so on).

307

Intellectualization is another defense mechanism that helps police officers handle emotionally charged situations. For example, the police officer may say about the woman who died in the flaming car, "She's better off dead . . . with those injuries, she'd have been a vegetable"; or about the suicide, "If I had his problems, I would have blown my head off too."

Police officers also utilize physical distancing to remove themselves from the emotional punishment associated with their work. Officers do not like to be touched. Devices such as sunglasses, an impersonal tone of voice, aloofness, and such statements as "It's not my problem lady," serve the same purpose of keeping others at a distance. In addition, the officer may distance himself further by aggressive gestures, such as resting a hand or elbow on the butt of his gun. In many ways the message comes through that the officer is not really interested and does not want to get involved.

The officer who goes by the book is also defending himself against stress. He cops out from taking responsibility for his decision or action by retreating to "the book" and stating with all the rigidity associated with military regulations, "I've got a job to do, lady," and "That's the way the law is."

Maslach and Jackson (1979) point out that at an institutional (organizational) level, burnout can contribute to low morale, impaired performance, absenteeism, and high job turnover. Even more important, the citizen who is given the runaround or is mistreated by public servants under stress may in turn develop a disrespect and dislike not only for the individual public servant but also for the organization he represents. This can become a significant factor, particularly at budget time, when John Q. Public can express displeasure and dislike by voting the wrong way on issues critical to the police department.

What can be done to prevent or counteract burnout? Although Kunkel addresses the issue from a non-police perspective, two of his suggestions for companies might also be of value to police departments (Powers 1980). First, there should be increased efforts to bridge the gap between personal and professional life through sponsorship of more family activities. Second, a more decentralized administration will encourage more personal initiatives.

Hupler (1980) believes that salary is an important issue. If the salary is not commensurate with the demands of the job, it isn't long before the officer begins to question how his pay stacks up against the emotional punishment of the profession. He also criticizes the rigidity of the system, noting that changes in assignment and more liberal use of "atta-boys" can be helpful.

Hupler also has suggested that officers be allowed a stress day, a day not deducted from ordinary leave time or sick leave but just an extra day now and then for an officer to use when he feels that he just can't buckle on that leather and go out and face the world one more time. This stress day should not steal time from regular leave, which an officer needs for the family vacation and to get away completely from his job.

Special Assignments

It is a common belief among police officers that certain assignments, such as narcotics, homicide, internal affairs, and airborne, present their own special stresses. The following is a brief discussion of some of the special stresses that officers in those assignments encounter. Although there has been little research to counteract them, increased knowledge of these special stresses can itself be preventative.

Narcotics

Assignment as an undercover narcotics agent is one of the most dangerous and stressful jobs in police work. The *narc* must create and play a role that is not only dangerous, but also puts him in daily intimate contact with the dredges of humanity. As one narc remarked, "We associate with the scumbags—humanity at its worse."

Because of the nature of his work, the narc may become very paranoid and have feelings of guilt because of the deception he must practice. He learns to manipulate his way in and out of different situations —a trait useful in a narcotics assignment but one which can present problems if carried over into other assignments. He may feel alienated from other policemen, not only because his true identity is unknown to other officers but also because they do not understand how big the problems are that he faces every day.

The narc believes that except for himself and a few of his colleagues, no one else realizes that the pushers and criminal elements associated with drugs could take over society. As a result, he becomes vulnerable to a *savior complex,* in which he sees himself standing alone against the forces of evil. He begins to resent directives from police administrators and even supervision from his own bosses, feeling that they obstruct him from achieving his goals. He may become convinced that the ends justify the means because of the critical importance and the magnitude of the problem he is dealing with. He may become sarcastic, cynical, chronically angry and hostile, and even scared. He may be intensely frustrated when he sees weeks or even months of dangerous under-cover work finally culminate in an arrest which comes to naught when the arrestees plea bargain their way out of prison.

The hours may create a special stress on his marriage or on his rela-tionship with a girl friend. Neighbors, not knowing the nature of his assignment, may wonder about his wife (or girl friend) who receives this scummy-looking character at all hours of the day and night.

Finally, his freedom and opportunity to talk about his work may be much less than that of his colleagues, further increasing the stress he experiences.

Little research has been done regarding these stresses and, therefore, many questions about the narcotics officer and his assignment remain unanswered. For example, how do we select an officer for such an assignment? What characteristics or traits do we look for? Which ones do we avoid? How long should he remain in this undercover assign-ment? What are the danger signs that he has been there too long? (One narc sergeant states that when his agents begin to write police reports that sound like novels, he regards this as a danger signal, for it tells him that they are no longer thinking of themselves as police officers first and narcs second.) How do you defuse a narc, helping him through the adjustment after coming off an assignment? Are there any assignments that he shouldn't go to from narcotics? Finally, should his wife and family be briefed before he is assigned and when he is coming off assignment? Answers to these questions, based upon careful research, are badly needed.

Homicide

Dr. Parke Fitzhugh, a psychiatrist for the Dade County, Florida Po-lice Department states that "homicide detectives on the average are one of the last groups to seek professional help . . . they're under a great deal of stress, but generally, they've only gotten to me when they've been referred and they're at a crisis." Another homicide detective has said about his work, "I'll get a case today that looks really hot, but the next day, I'll have another one I'll have to chase, the next day, there's another. The detective gets frustrated and demoralized—he has leads on his own cases that he's not able to follow" (*Tucson Daily Citizen* May 9, 1981).

Compounding the strain is the public's demand that violent crimes be solved, particularly if the homicide involves a child or a victim of sexual attack. The homicide detectives sees all the blood and gore that other police officers do not have to deal with at close range or over a long period of time. Often the homicide detective has to make the death notification to the loved ones of the victim. A further unique strain upon the homicide detective is that he must investigate shootings in which other police officers have been involved.

Internal Affairs

The internal affairs officer is pictured by many as a head hunter who gets pleasure out of proving that a fellow officer has committed a criminal act or violated departmental regulations. While this may actually be true of some members assigned to internal affairs, the authors' experiences with numerous detectives assigned this function indicate that the average internal affairs investigator is more desirous of proving the innocence of an accused officer. In small departments where all officers know those assigned to internal affairs, the personal element can be an added stress because there is less social distance. In larger departments, most of the internal affairs personnel are not known as individuals to the officers with whom they come into official contact. Nevertheless, the stress level for the internal affairs investigator is still high, and many ask to be relieved after a year or two on the job.

Airborne Law Enforcement

During the past few years, an increasing number of police departments have added helicopter units. Sultan has stated:

With the advent of this relatively new addition to the armamentarium of law enforcement agencies has come a variety of issues with which police administrators must deal. These include the selection of appropriate personnel as helicopter pilots and observers, training of personnel for performing area law enforcement functions, and identification of sources of psychological stress encountered by police personnel stemming from the airborne law enforcement function (Sultan et al. 1980).

An opinion survey which these authors designed to identify problem areas and sources of psychological stress in airborne law enforcement indicated that these activities present unique stresses different from those encountered by field officers on the ground. All personnel agreed that the additional activity of flying in the air support division was a significant stressor because of the danger involved. Another unique stressor was the relative inaccessability to supervision while in the air. On the ground, an officer in a critical situation can request and receive assistance from a supervisor in a relatively short time. Airborne officers must rely on their own judgment and have only radio contact with supervisors on the ground. Finally, the potential for serious injury, and even death, as a result of a helicopter crash adds another stress for airborne personnel.

Patrol

Although patrol is not usually considered a special assignment, stress researchers have identified fatigue as one of the major magnifiers of stress in police work (Villa 1981). Since patrol officers in the field, especially during the late evening and early morning watches, are particularly susceptible to fatigue, patrol work can create stressful situations.

Fatigue is a state of weariness resulting from prolonged or intense physical, emotional, or mental effort. It tends to increase directly with the amount of time a person functions at a given task and can vary in severity from simple drowsiness to a numbing lack of awareness brought on by a particularly long or stressful tour of duty.

Villa states that administratively controlled variables, such as overtime, shift rotation, and off-duty court or educational commitments, can cause significant and dangerous levels of fatigue even in young field officers.

For many field officers, especially those who are professionally motivated, a typical work week might include the following work-related activities after normal working hours: six hours of school and two hours of study, ten hours of court appearances and eight hours of overtime due to unusual occurrence and personnel shortages. This typical 66-hour work week might easily be extended to 90 or more hours in the case of highly motivated officers working in high crime areas (Villa 1981).

Fatigue tends to increase anxiety and fearfulness, thus lowering the person's ability to deal appropriately with the many complex situations common to field experience. Fatigue also tends to lower the quality of the officer's decision making and increases the probability of a less adaptable decision than is usual. Fatigue may be a critical factor tipping the balance in a "shoot, don't shoot" situation by decreasing the officer's ability to analyze the situation appropriately. Further, the same late night and early morning hours when an officer is most likely to be fatigued are also the times when he is most likely to use force or be the victim of violence. Police administrators must control the variables contributing to officer fatigue so that this self-generating cycle, where "overtime contributes to fatigue; fatigue increases the likelihood of injuries and illnesses; injuries and illnesses create a need for overtime assignments," may be interrupted (Villa 1981).

Disasters

Disasters, whether natural or man-made, also create a special stress for police officers. Not only can disasters impact upon individual officers but they can also overwhelm whole police agencies. The crash of a Boeing 727 and a Cessna 172 over the city of San Diego on September 25, 1978 is a case in point.

Between 80 and 150 San Diego Police Department officers were involved in crowd control and body removal within the inner perimeter cornered off by the police. Davidson observed that "these individuals found themselves physically immersed in the most gruesome scene one could imagine." One veteran sergeant stated that it appeared that each victim "swallowed a stick of dynamite." Not a single body was left intact. Bodies and parts of bodies were strewn in the streets, on roofs, on automobiles parked in the area—the scene was one of horror and devastation (Davidson 1981).

Realizing that the San Diego Police Department did not have the resources within its own department to help its officers handle the stress from working on this assignment, local psychologists organized a psychological assistance program for police, fire, and paramedic workers in the area. Over thirty police officers responded to the team's offer of help and were seen in brief individual therapy. The officers reported symptoms of sleep disturbances, nightmares, loss of appetite, sex drive, anxiety, and, in many cases, anger and hostility often directed toward inappropriate targets. A major stress factor was a sense of frustration over their inability to provide lifesaving measures, since all the victims were dead. Two months after the crash, only a few officers remained in treatment. Most of the thirty officers who had participated were sufficiently symptom free.

This example shows that a carefully considered, easily implemented plan for delivering emergency psychological services to officers engaged in disaster related work can be stress reducing and can help prevent emotional dysfunction.

Police Marriages

"The dynamics of the police family are little understood as research phenomena, especially if one considers the police family to be somehow different from the normal population" (Farmer and Monahan 1980). But is the police family that different from the normal population? Niederhoffer and Niederhoffer (1978) maintain that the family relationships of the police officer are better than most and that their divorce rate is significantly lower than that of the normal population. Saper (1980) also states, "It would be a mistake to conclude that police officers have more frequent or more severe marriage problems than persons in other professions." Dr. Lester (1979) also points out that facts do not support the "myth" that police officers have an extraordinarily high rate of divorce. "Despite continued references to the high divorce among police officers, the data do not support such a conclusion. The proportion of police officers currently divorced is the same as in the general population, and the incident of previously divorced officers appears to be similar to comparable groups in the community" (Lester 1979).

This whole debate is probably best placed in perspective by Reiser, who notes that "rumors and misinformation about police divorce rates have been passed on from one generation of officers to another, but our own past surveys have not indicated a higher than average divorce rate among men on the Los Angeles Police Department" (Reiser 1978).

Whether or not police marriages have more problems than other marriages may be open to question, but no one would deny that police marriages have at least their share of problems. Here is what some police wives* (to whom the authors have talked) have to say:

*Husbands of women officers are still much less common, and as yet, little is known about the problems of this type of police family.

My husband spends all his time at the job. He seems to have no time for the children and me.

The only friends we have are his friends and these are other policemen. I have lost all my friends because with his hours, we don't have any opportunity to do things with anybody except other cops. Not only that, but he doesn't seem to be very happy going out with anybody except a cop.

My husband treats his kids like they were some punks on the street. They feel that they can't talk to him because he will not listen. He just tells them to do something because that's the way it is.

Isn't it true that a cop's most important person is his partner? Well, what if his partner is a female cop? Isn't there a danger that I'll never be able to compete with her? How can they help but form a strong emotional attachment to each other?

One wife, speaking at a seminar to the wives of other officers, said:

A subject we all can relate to, is that sometime feeling that the job is first, and all else second. To some guys, this job is a mistress, or a terrific hobby which they can do and enjoy almost everyday. How can you help but NOT become resentful? Here we are up to our necks in housework, babies, diapers, and everyday crisis while they drive away to meeting people from all walks of life. They get to talk with (are you ready for this) REAL ADULTS! What we wouldn't give some days to talk with someone over ten years old. They get to eat dinner out, while you're home dodging mashed potato fights and spilled milk. "They only get to grab a hamburger here and there," you say. Well, I'd settle for a bun with shoe leather, as long as it comes with a large order of PEACE and QUIET (Colson 1979).

What is it about police work that seems to spawn these types of complaints from police wives? Reiser (1978) states that men in police work are part of a fraternity having strong, cohesive, in-group values and pressures to conform. Because of the stresses involved in police work and the mutual interdependencies required to survive, there is a premium placed on manliness and physical adequacy. Additionally, this male fraternity places a high value on one's ability to hold liquor, to seduce women, and to be unbeatable in a fight. Extramarital sexual affairs are not only condoned but expected because of the macho image.

Barbara Bennett, in an insightful article entitled, "The Police Mystique" compiled a lengthy list of all the unwritten "shoulds" that police feel they must live up to. This list of shoulds contain five general ideas that work together to form the police mystique and serve to perpetuate its unwritten code (Bennett 1978). These five ideas are:

1. *It's us versus them.* Here the message is cops are different; at home, on the street, and after work. Cops aren't especially liked and they are misunderstood, by their wives and by the public. Cops feel most at home with other cops.

2. *Silence is security.* Here the underlying message is keep your mouth shut: accept things as they are, don't get too involved and don't take risks. According to Bennett, this results in an unwritten commitment to noncommitment.

3. *Keep your cool.* Here the facade of "don't let it show" becomes important, demanding behavior that is superhuman and unrealistic. We know that all people have emotions and need them, even cops. Like others, an officer's fight or flight response is triggered in a stressful situation. Unlike others, he usually cannot run or flee and as a result is not able to release tensions.

Another danger of the officer who "keeps his cool" is that, eventually, he begins to take this attitude home to his wife and family. As one New York officer has stated: "You change when you become a cop—you become tough and hard and cynical. You have to condition yourself to be that way in order to survive this job. And sometimes, without realizing it, you act that way all the time, even with your wife and kids" (Maslach and Jackson 1979).

When seen in a counseling office for marital problems, police officers often present the image of the tough guy whom nothing can affect. Beneath that rugged exterior is a very caring person who indeed feels deeply but doesn't know or can't remember how to let his wife know that. Often in this stage of the relationship, the wife stops seeing this hidden inside—the concerned, caring man. She no longer knows how to penetrate the shell. Eventually, she may no longer care to. In this kind of marriage the police officer is likely to go home and find that his wife has packed up and left without any prior warnings.

4. *Stay on top.* This cluster of attitudes and stereotyped behavior defines policing as a macho profession. The profile of a cop turns out to be a "Marlboro man"—rough and rugged, traveling free with a cigarette in one hand and a rifle in the other.

5. *Sex is survival.* This idea is closely related to the macho expectations that pressure most officers. It also includes archaic sexual ideas— the belief in two kinds of women (those that do and those that don't) and two kinds of sexual codes (one for husbands, one for wives). These sexual dichotomies only perpetuate game playing and one-sided sex. When human sensitivity is stifled, both sexes lose out.

These elements are part of the unwritten code of behavior and attitudes of police officers. They subtly pervade the police environment and exert influence on the marriages of these officers, often playing a role in the marital problems besetting police couples.

Other pressures on police marriages are derived from some of the stresses mentioned in the previous chapter. For example, a policeman's unusual hours may make it impossible for him to attend his daughter's graduation, a special Little League game for his son, or a birthday party for his wife. The easy availability of credit can cause financial strain if the couple does not know how to handle money correctly.

Because of the rigid structure of the police organization, an officer may carry feelings of frustration and anger home from the job and displace them onto his wife and children. Other problems may arise when he comes home because he is unable to cope with family problems after having seen nothing but problems at work all day. All he desires is peace, quiet, and a little tender loving care. At the same time, this is his family—his wife and his children—and he has a responsibility to become involved in the daily problems of family life. If communication is not open between the police officer and his wife, each may feel resentment toward the other. He sees her as nagging, and she sees him as not caring.

Drinking may become a problem in the marriage. Not only is alcohol a stress reduction device, but it also has some peer approval because it fits the macho image.

Do policemen drink harder and more often than civilians? Lester (1979) states that "data on alcoholism rates are hard to locate" and adds that "the major study of mortality in the United States by occupation shows that police officers do not have a high incidence of death of cirrhosis of the liver." However, one should not conclude from this study alone that a high incidence of alcoholism does not exist in police work. Specialists in alcohol abuse indicate that approximately 10 percent of any work force will have significant drinking problems. Considering the high stress of police work, one could conclude that the likelihood of alcoholism is greater in police work than in many other occupations.

Police organizations seem to have an ambivalent attitude about drinking and drinking-related problems. "Social drinking" is seen as a tension reducer, a catalyst to socialization, and a way of fostering camaraderie among the troops. On the other hand, the easy availability of alcohol and the frequency with which it is used as a tension reducer poses problems for police administrators who are increasingly concerned about alcoholism in the department. "The value that the male fraternity places on social drinking coupled with management's puni- tive view of drinking-related problems appear to increase the likeli- hood of contradictory messages being communciated in the organiza- tion. It is as if the police administrator is saying. . . 'don't do as I do, do as I say' " (Reiser 1978).

An alcoholic (non-police) patient of one of the authors (A.B.) said, "My worst enemies were my friends," referring to how his friends protected him and thus delayed his treatment. In a police organization, where one of the cardinal sins is to snitch on another officer, an unwillingness by any policeman to report a fellow officer for suspected or known alcohol- ism can be an even more serious block to recognition and handling of the problem than it is among civilians. In addition, supervisors are reluctant to do anything about a drunken cop—preferring either to transfer him when the opportunity arises or to let things slide—hoping that he'll quit or eventually retire. All these factors have tended to keep alcoholism among police officers a hidden disease.

Some police departments, however, are now beginning to recognize this problem (Stratton and Wroe 1980). Programs exist in some of the larger agencies for the alcoholic policeman. These programs have usu- ally been started by recovering alcoholic policemen who managed to convince an administrator of the program's value. In all cases we are aware of, treatment is based upon the principles of Alcoholics Anony- mous. The recovering alcoholic policemen form a special chapter of Alcoholics Anonymous designed to appeal to police officers, active and retired, in the community.

In alcoholic police officers, as in other alcoholics, alcoholism is only part of their problem. However, trying to help them with marital, family, financial, and other problems is doomed to failure unless the officer first completes an alcohol recovery program. Since there is al- most no chance that an alcoholic will quit drinking or will enter such a program until virtually cornered into it, we have on several occasions advised the commander to order the individual to a hospital detoxifica- tion center for treatment. While everybody including the alcoholic officer knows he can refuse this order, he cannot do so without some threat to his job. So far, we have had no refusals or even questioning of an order, probably because the alcoholic policeman at that point is, as one said, "sick and tired of being sick and tired."

Dr. Bruce L. Danto, psychiatrist for the Detroit Police Department, has focused attention on a little recognized and understood problem of police marriages: What happens to the widow and children of police officers who are slain (Danto 1974)? His study raises preliminary questions that require greater attention from police administrators. According to Danto, police wives are familiar with death expectations since they know about the danger inherent in police work, have probably seen their husbands with various injuries incurred during work, and, in association with the wives of other officers, have shared the experiences of loneliness, doubt, and fear. Nevertheless, even though she is familiar with a death expectation, the widow of a slain police officer is still the victim of a death circumstance whose anticipation she has denied. Even though she rationalizes that this is the lot of a policeman's wife and family, she still displays all the clinical features of bereavement shared by any widow in any social setting.

Significant to a police department's concern are the widows' feelings of abandonment. Many police departments offer little meaningful contact with survivors. The widows in Danto's study complained that there were few warm feelings from police officials, whom they felt should check regularly with them on an ongoing basis to show that the police department cared. The widows felt that they had belonged to a police family only to learn that they were without a family once their officer husband died. There were also bitter feelings expressed about the community, which they felt was unappreciative of the policeman's real job, expecting him to lay his life on the line for little reward and even less recognition.

Danto's study suggests that police departments should pay more attention not only to the widows of slain officers but also possibly to the widows of officers who die after retirement. Since efforts are being made by departments to encourage the feeling of the "police family" and "we take care of our own," measures designed to carry out this policy should extend to widows. FOP wives and other similar organizations can perhaps look at this area to create needed and innovative programs.

This criticism of departmental response to widows of officers does not extend to police marriages and the police family. More and more police departments realize that it is the police family, not just the police officer, which is of primary importance to the organization. Programs for spouses, such as orientation, ride-alongs, and weapons training, are becoming more frequent and extensive. However, more needs to be done to decrease the distance between the police organization and the police family.

Before concluding this section on police marriages, we should return to the myth with which we began. Both Lester and Reiser note that the belief that police marriages are doomed to end in divorce tends to become a self-fulfilling prophecy. The belief itself can create the phenomenon even though there is still a lack of hard data regarding police divorce rates. Studies that exist are contradictory. Regardless of whether police divorce rates are high, if the officer and his spouse believe that this is true, then when marital problems occur, instead of putting effort into solving these problems or seeking professional help, the couple may simply bow to the inevitable and seek the divorce they expected to experience in the first place. As anyone who has been married for longer than a few weeks knows, marriage is something that you have to work at. A successful marriage is the result of mature people compromising, understanding, and communicating with each other. This is true of police marriages as well as other marriages. They can work, they do work, they do last. They do not have to end in divorce.

Retirement

Captain Kenneth E. Johnson, Tucson Police Department, has stated that "there is an important area being ignored in the design of police training programs: that of properly preparing an officer to take and to enjoy his retirement" (Johnson 1978).

Stratton (1980) has noted the vulnerability of the retired officer to the disease of alcoholism. A recent study indicated an alarmingly high suicide rate for Detroit police retirees (*Tucson Daily Citizen* May 13, 1981). Gaska studied the deaths of 4,000 Detroit police retirees between 1944 and 1978. He found the suicide rate for these officers to be 334.7 per 100,000. The suicide rate for policemen receiving disability pensions was even higher—2,616 per 100,000. The national suicide rate is generally quoted as somewhere between 10 and 11 per 100,000. An earlier study by Labovitz and Hagedorn (1971) reported that police officers have the second highest suicide rate of 36 occupations—47.6 per 100,000 per year.

Why is retirement so stressful for the police officer? Earlier we pointed out that for most officers police work is not just a job; it's a way of life, encompassing membership in a predominantly male fraternity whose work strongly reinforces that self-image.

Suddenly, an officer completes those magic twenty years of work, when he can retire at a young age, and finds that he has nothing to retire to, or cannot find any role with the same rewards. If he is forced into retirement, either by age or by his own feeling that he should get out while he is still young enough to do something else, he goes from an active, clearly identified existence in a very familiar world to a state of identity diffusion in a very unfamiliar world. In no other occupation except the military is there such an abrupt cutoff in belonging and usefulness. There is an old expression in law enforcement: "The door hits you in the ass when you leave."

The police officer must start preparing for retirement, not the year before retirement is possible or demanded, but rather the first day he enters the academy. As Captain Johnson (1978) stated, "The orderly phasing in and out of employees helps both the individuals and the organization to continue growth in ideas and in interests. Each stays healthy by not avoiding changes in their association as an acceptable alternative to sitting around and watching the world go by."

Some departments, especially those with in-house psychologists, are already attacking this problem and setting up programs to assist officers in making the transition between active duty and civilian life. In those areas where there are local colleges and universities, a department's efforts can be assisted by vocational guidance personnel and facilities normally found in the university setting. But it is the police officer and spouse that must take primary responsibility for changing the stress of retirement into the opportunities of retirement.

Summary

In this chapter we have discussed situations and conditions of police work associated with special stress, including the use of deadly force, burnout, special assignments, police marriages, and retirement. The experienced officer can certainly think of other special stresses we have not covered.

While these last two chapters provide ample evidence to indicate how and why police officers encounter significant stress on and off the job, we also believe that police officers do a disservice to themselves and their profession by being more negative about these stresses than is called for.

As Lester (1979) has stated, "Where the facts demand it, let us be realistic. Police officers, for example, do have a high suicide rate . . . but where the facts do not demand it, let us be realistic and optimistic. Police officers appear to be psychologically healthier than civilians. Let us emphasize this. Police officers appear to be more satisfied with their jobs than office workers. Let us emphasize this."

If they emphasize the positive, the morale of police officers will improve, thus reducing the stresses caused by negative thinking.

BIBLIOGRAPHY

BENNETT, B. April 1978. "The Police Mystique." *Police Chief* 46–49.

CHAMBERLIN, C. S. March 1978. "Anomie, Burnout." *Journal of Law and Order* 20–21.

COHEN, A. 1980. "I've Killed That Man 10,000 Times." *Police* 3:4.

COLSON, D. June 1979. "A Wife's Way of Coping." *Journal of Police Stress* 15–16.

DANTO, B. L. February 1974. "Bereavement and the Widow of Slain Police Officers." *Police Chief* 51–57.

DAVIDSON, A. D. Winter 1980–81. "Air Disasters: Coping With Stress, A Program That Worked." *Journal of Police Stress* 20–22.

DOMINELLI, J. S. 1980. Quoted in *Newsletter of International Association of Chiefs of Police* 6:1.

FARMER, R. E., and MONAHAN, J. H. 1980. "The Prevention Model of Stress Reduction." *Journal of Police Science and Administration* 8:54–60.

HENDERSON, L. 1980. Quoted in "Letters to the Editor." *Police* 3:5.

HUPLER, D. 1980. "Burnout." Unpublished article.

JOHNSON, K. E. June 1978. "Retirement Counseling." *FBI Law Enforcement Bulletin* 28–32.

LABOVITZ, S., and HAGEDORN, R. 1971. "An Analysis of Suicide Rates Among Occupational Categories." *Sociological Inquiry* 41:67–72.

LESTER, D. November 1979. "The Policeman's Lot: A Postive Viewpoint." *Journal of Law and Order* 58.

MASLACH, C., and JACKSON, S. E. May 1979. "Burned-Out Cops and Their Families." *Psychology Today* 59–62.

MONROE-COOK, D. May 1975. "Stress Leads Police Officers to 'John Wayne Syndrome.'" *Police Times* 9.

NIEDERHOffer, A., and NIEDERHOffer, E. 1978. *The Police Family.* Lexington, Mass.: Lexington Books.

POWERS, M. May 30, 1980. "Hospital Workers Get Burnout Cure." *Arizona Daily Star*

REISER, M. April 1978. "The Problem of Police Officers' Wives." *Police Chief* 38–42.

SAPER, M. B. February 1980. "Police Wives—The Hidden Resource," *Police Chief* 28–29.

STRATTON, J. G., and WROE, B. September 1980. "Alcohol: A Dilemma for Some." *Journal of Law and Order* 76–79.

STRATTON, J. G., and WROE, B. October 1980. "Alcoholism Programs for Police." *Journal of Law and Order* 18–22.

SULTAN, S., SAX, S., and REISER, M. 1980. "Some Stress Factors in Airborne Law Enforcement Units." *Journal of Police Science and Administration* 8:61–65.

Tucson Daily Citizen. February 20, 1978. "Psychological Strain: Trained Lawmen Who Killed Robbers."

Tuscon Daily Citizen. May 9, 1981. "Homicide Duty: A Killer for Cops."

Tucson Daily Citizen. May 13, 1981. "Police Suicide Rates High."

VILLA, B. J. Spring 1981. "Management Control of Fatigue Among Field Police Officers." *Journal of Police Stress* 38–41.

PART VII

Conclusion

Chapter 23

The Role of the Mental Health Professional in Police Work

DURING THE LAST decade, there has been an increasing demand for mental health professionals to work with or for police agencies. This is not surprising, since police officers are so often in the role of front-line caretakers for the mentally ill in the community.

A recent article discussing the work of the San Francisco Police Department's Mental Health Unit concluded that "police may provide the most consistent mental health care in the community" (Taft 1980). This is one of the few police units in the country assigned exclusively to deal with people who are mentally ill. The Los Angeles Police Department has a Mental Evaluation Detail (MED), a three-man, round-the-clock unit that receives all reports involving mentally disturbed people, advises officers, and acts as a liaison with the various mental health and medical facilities in the city.

The extent of the problem which the mentally ill present for the police is indicated by the fact that, in 1979, the San Francisco Police

Department processed approximately 3,200 emergency detention cases in which a person was taken to a mental health center and a report was filed. In addition, there were innumerable crisis "800" calls (radio code for insane persons), family disturbances involving mental cases, and probably thousands of suspects arrested on criminal charges that stem from mental illness. In total, it is estimated that the department handled over 10,000 insane person incidents each year (Taft 1980). Further, with the recent cutback in funding for mental health services, the burden on the police is growing.

Consequently, all mental health professionals should take an active interest in how the police handle mental cases. If the police are effective, not as pseudo psychologists or psychiatrists but as police officers, then the quality of mental health care in the community will be significantly higher.

The opportunities for involvement of mental health professionals in police work are multiple and extend beyond the employment of a police psychologist. In areas where police departments do not have their own mental health resources, mental health professionals may become involved in the selection and training of police officers to insure that only emotionally stable applicants are admitted into the police academy and that, while there, they learn how to deal humanely and effectively with mental cases.

Another way that a mental health professional may become involved in working with the police is when employed to perform a certain function. For example, a psychologist may be hired to administer and interpret psychological tests and give clinical evaluations for screening purposes. In the Tucson Police Department, each applicant is given a Minnesota Multiphasic Personality Inventory (MMPI) and a clinical interview by a local psychologist in private practice who has had considerable experience in evaluating police officers. The clinical interview lasts approximately fifty minutes. If the psychologist finds that additional testing and interviews are needed, they are given, with the professional sometimes spending up to six hours with each applicant. For this service there is a set fee for each applicant, regardless of the amount of time spent.

A mental health professional may be employed by a police department to offer counseling to police officers and their families. The Arizona Department of Public Safety has contracted with a group of private practitioners in Phoenix who offer a certain number of counseling hours at a fixed price per hour to members of the department.

Nevertheless, these services provide only limited resources to police agencies. Furthermore, consultants often are inadequate because of their lack of police knowledge and their short-term involvement (Somodevilla 1978). In our judgment, the best solution is for a police agency, if possible, to hire a full-time, in-house police psychologist or otherwise qualified mental health professional. There are several advantages to this arrangement. First, the psychologist and the department will get to know each other, becoming familiar with each other's needs, expectations, and methods and building the sense of trust necessary for a successful relationship. This will be true not only in terms of the department and the psychologist, but also between the men of the department and the psychologist.

Another advantage to a full-time, in-house psychologist is availability —twenty-four hours a day, seven days a week. This availability, plus continued presence and visibility in the station and the field, develops a feeling of familiarity and trust among the officers.

We believe that there can be a more complete understanding of the services performed by a police psychologist through discussing the scope of activities performed by the senior author (H.E.R.) in the Behavioral Science Unit of the Tucson Police Department. However, first it is essential to present our basic philosophy of how a department psychologist should approach his duties and responsibilities.

In the chapters on stress, we referred several times to the belief that the police system is in many ways like the military. Like any military organization, the police department has an assigned mission. The police chief, like the military commander, is given certain resources (personnel and equipment) to accomplish this mission. The role of any technical support personnel (legal, medical, psychological) is to support the organization in accomplishing its mission, just as the role of the military psychologist is to support the command and the troops in the field. This is the identical mission of the police psychologist within the police department. Thus the primary responsibility of the police psychologist is to the department and not to the individuals making up that department. This does not preclude performing services for people, confidentiality, or having the welfare of the patient constantly in mind. In our opinion these are not mutually exclusive goals. However, the police department is not a therapeutic or rehabilitative agency. It is a law enforcement agency with a definite and restrictive function. Police departments cannot afford to throw away personnel, but neither can they afford to keep officers on the street who are ineffective and emotionally unstable.

This view is not held by all police psychologists and administrators.

Many believe that it is difficult, if not impossible, to utilize psychological services effectively for both management and clinical functions. They argue that the psychologist's involvement with management undermines the capacity to develop the rapport between psychologists and police employees which must exist if the employees are to use clinical services. They also believe that a strong relationship with employees may bias the psychologists' input to management (Morris 1980).

However, we do not perceive this as an unavoidable conflict. Those two functions are not mutually exclusive. As Morris stated after delineating these potentially conflict functions,

An effective combination of management consultation and direct services, on the part of PSU (Psychological Services Unit), does appear feasible. The same principles (autonomy, identification, avoidance of decision-making, input at the policy level) which support effective consultation also support the rapport with officers. A well-planned and regulated involvement in both direct services and management provides the psychologist with a greater comprehension of the whole range of system phenomena; both his counseling and his management input should be enhanced (Morris 1980).

We will now examine the Behavioral Science Unit of the Tucson Police Department and the function of the department's psychologist within this unit.

Scope of Activities

According to the observations of several experienced police psychologists (DePue 1979, Morris 1980, Schilling 1978, Somodevilla 1978, Stratton 1980), services provided to police departments by mental health professionals may include the following.

Psychological Screening

Mental health professionals may evaluate job applicants' emotional stability, intellectual and interpersonal skills, and suitability for police work. This evaluation may be done by a department-employed psychologist or by professionals outside the department whose services are contracted specifically for this purpose. In our judgment, the latter is preferable because a psychologist's approval or disapproval of a candidate is generally only one part of the selection process. Should the candidate who is disapproved by the psychologist still be hired by the department, potential friction between the candidate and the department psychologist may result if the candidate learns of this disapproval.

As Stratton (1980) has pointed out, the major problem with psychological screening is that few of the tests have been adequately validated for this specific population. Many, including the most frequently used MMPI, were originally devised for use with mental patients. To assume that they have validity as a selection device for police candidates may be inappropriate. Caution should be exercised in using any of the results and, in particular, relying on them to the exclusion of other available data.

Training

The department psychologist is involved in recruit training, in-service training for veteran officers, and education for specialized activities, such as handling sex crimes.

The department psychologist may also assist in evaluating the validity of certain courses taught in the police academy (for example, in determining whether a particular course is necessary or whether it is accomplishing its stated goals). The psychologist may also help students to overcome academic problems.

Criminal Investigation

The skills of the department psychologist are becoming more useful in some aspects of criminal investigation.

One relatively new and controversial area is investigative hypnosis. This technique dates back to the early 1960s when the Israeli police used hypnosis to catch terrorists, finding that witnesses to acts of terrorism could recall far more under hypnosis. For example, at first, people could not remember someone putting down an ordinary looking bag; under hypnosis, the same witnesses gave a more accurate description of who was carrying what and who sat where. Under hypnosis, some acquired a photographic memory. They were able to recall who came on a bus with them, at what stop, and what was being carried. Some even remembered the registration numbers of cars that were in the area prior to an explosion. Most important, they were able to construct composites (identity pictures) of people they "saw" while under hypnosis (Reiser).

Following the success of the Israeli police, Dr. Martin Reiser of the Los Angeles Police Department began to use hypnosis and formed an institute to teach it to other police officers and psychologists. Although investigative hypnosis remains controversial, particularly in reference to the admissibility in court of evidence obtained using it, indications are that it is here to stay. The concerns of the court, however, may result in its future use being restricted to psychologists or psychiatrists rather than police officers trained as hypno-investigators.

Another new development in criminal investigation is the profiling of suspects. From observations made at the scene of a crime, a trained mental health professional may be able to assist investigators by describing the characteristics of the person most likely to have committed a certain type of crime. For example, in the case of a brutal lust murderer who has committed a series of homicidal rapes, the investigator might learn from the mental health professional that there are only two types of people who are likely to have performed this type of crime: a paranoid schizophrenic or a psychopath. A study of the crime scene (type of weapon used, the location of the weapon, where the body was found, the position in which the body was placed when found), the type of killing (strangulation, stabbing, shooting), and other crime scene characterisitics can provide valuable psychological clues about the offender.

One of the most famous profiles of a suspect was by James Brussel, a psychiatrist who described the "mad bomber" who was plaguing New York City because of his hatred for Con Edison (the utility from which he had been discharged). Dr. Brussel was dramatically accurate in describing the then unknown suspect, telling detectives that when this person was arrested, he would be "wearing a double breasted suit with all buttons carefully buttoned" (Ault and Reese 1980).

The Behavioral Science Unit of the FBI Academy has recently published articles concerning the criminal profiling of the nuisance offender (Reese 1979), the fire setter (Rider 1980), and the lust murderer (Hazelwood and Douglas 1980). In addition, this unit is engaged in a project aimed at formulating criminal offender profiles through investigative interviews with incarcerated felons (Ressler and Douglas 1980). This study, the Criminal Personality Interview Program, is designed to identify the salient characteristics, motivations, attitudes, and behavior of offenders involved in specific types of crimes.

Counseling

One of the important services offered by department mental health professionals is counseling for police officers and their families on marital problems, sexual problems, family problems, excessive drinking, aggression, authority problems, psychosomatic problems, and problems with children (Somodevilla 1978). Crisis intervention, rather than long-term treatment, is preferred. If the psychologist sees his role primarily as a therapist, little time will be left for other duties, and his impact on the total department will be minimal. Since most communities have adequate community mental health resources that are available to all citizens, department mental health professionals should limit their services to crisis intervention counseling.

Another issue involved in providing counseling services is whether all counseling should be done by department mental health professionals, or whether sworn officers who have the background and interests to learn and apply counseling skills can also be used. In the Dallas Police Department, for example, there are three sworn officers (one sergeant, one female officer, and another male officer) who are part of the Pyschological Services Unit headed by Dr. Somodevilla and who serve as counselors. In the Tucson Police Department, a sergeant serves as a peer counselor.

Based upon our experience in Tucson and the observations of others, we believe that peer counselors are a necessary part of any behavioral science unit. Special Agent DePue of the FBI Academy (1979) has pointed out that the police experience of the officer-counselor gives him valuable insight into his client's problems and often makes him more acceptable to the client than an outside psychologist. DePue suggests that police departments set up in-house counseling programs utilizing their own officers. Officers with undergraduate degrees in the behavioral sciences and with an interest in counseling could be sent to local colleges to learn the necessary skills. DePue also suggests that courses designed to address the special problems of police officers could be established.

Liaison with Mental Health Facilities

The department mental health professional can serve as a liaison to the mental health facilities in the community. An ability to move freely between the law enforcement and the mental health systems can facilitate the referral of officers and their families to community agencies and also can assist field officers in handling difficult mental cases encountered in the streets.

With the cooperation of the various hospitals and clinics, SOPs (Standard Operating Procedures) for the police department involving the handling of mental patients and involuntary commitment can be developed. This cooperation benefits both systems and the people they serve.

Field Emergencies

The psychologist and other mental health professionals employed by the department should be available on a twenty-four-hour basis to aid officers in the field in handling subjects barricaded in defiance of authority, violent mental cases, suicides, officers involved in shootings, and other emergency situations.

Command Consultation

The police psychologist should offer consultation to all levels of command relative to the department's mental health and morale. He should be available to advise management on factors affecting police performances, such as working environment, communication, leadership, and supervisory techniques. This consultation can be offered in formal meetings and presentations or in single, informal sessions with lieutenants, captains, or sergeants. Morris (1980) notes that the effective use of the psychologist in management depends mainly on his having administrative support along with adequate autonomy, on his avoidance of a direct role in decision making, and on his involvement at the policy or procedural level.

Applied Research

As Somodevilla (1978) notes, "Research in any area of police psychology is wide open." Some of the major research currently underway involves development and validation of a physical fitness test; a study of accident proneness in police officers; personality variables associated with marksmanship; personality characteristics of officers assigned to vice, motor, SWAT; and the use of biofeedback and treatment in musculoskeletal disorders. There is a need in all police departments for applied research designed to answer pressing contemporary problems.

334

Other questions we consider important include how to select a narcotics officer, what makes a good juvenile officer, and how to evaluate an officer's performance in the prevention of violence and crime (rather than the usual evaluation of his efficiency based on the number of arrests he made and the citations he issued).

Job Evaluation

When the police mental health professional is asked to evaluate the job performance of an officer, the question is most often: "Is he fit for duty?" Stratton (1980) notes that the evaluation of personnel during their field assignments is usually conducted by sergeants. Supervision is always a difficult task, and this is even more true in police work; sergeants might be reluctant to criticize or put pressure on officers they supervise when these same officers may have been partners with whom they have worked and depended upon before they became sergeants. A sergeant hesitant to hold an officer accountable for his below-average performance may allow deterioration to such a point that the officer's performance in the field is absolutely unacceptable. Stratton (1980) states that "although it is very necessary at times for a particular officer to be psychologically evaluated for fitness, often such requests result from the supervisor's failure to hold the officer accountable for his work. Rather than discharge him, an attempt is made to 'pass the buck' to a psychologist."

The senior author (H. E. R.) has had similar experiences. Frequently, line commanders will attempt to solve administrative or disciplinary problems by using the mental health professional to "wash the dirty linen." When an officer has such problems the mental health professional should refer him back to command, noting that this officer is cleared psychologically for any disciplinary and/or administrative action deemed appropriate by command. Stratton (1980) concludes "although it seems that supervision may be complicated, often the psychologist should not be involved in evaluating how effectively the employee should do his job; rather it should be the task of the first-line supervisor, difficult though it may be."

Selection for Special Assignments

Police agencies may request the advice of the psychologist in evaluating officers for special assignments, such as SWAT, hostage negotiation teams, or sex crimes. Some police agencies have asked the psychologist to sit in on promotion boards. In our judgment, psychologists and other mental health professionals have little to offer in these cases. The best predictor of an person's behavior is past behavior. Police officers—particularly senior patrolmen, sergeants, and lieutenants—can do a much better job than most mental health professionals in selecting personnel for these assignements or for promotion.

Review of Mental Cases

One of the important duties of the mental health professional may be to go through the officers' daily reports involving mental cases in order to determine which individuals, for some reason or another, are likely to be dangerous to the officer or others. These people's names can then be placed in the computer with an appropriate notation so that the dispatcher can warn the street officer of any factors threatening his own safety or the safety of others if he is called to deal with these subjects at a later date.

Program Models

Three types of program models for the involvement of mental health professionals have emerged within the past few years. They include the Dallas Program, the Tucson Program, and the Multi-Department Program.

The Dallas Program

The Dallas Police Department operates its own psychological service unit, staffed by a civilian employee of the department and three Master's level psychologists recruited from the ranks of the sworn personnel. The budget of the unit is included in the overall police budget. Therefore all personnel are under the command of the chief of police.

The Tucson Program

The Behavioral Science Unit of the Tucson Police Department is headed by a civilian psychologist who is not an employee of the Tucson

Police Department or the City of Tucson. He is a full-time member of the staff of the Southern Arizona Mental Health Center, a bureau of the State Department of Health Services. His services are contracted for by the city from the state. He is assisted in the unit by a sworn member of the police department, a Master's level sergeant with eighteen years of service in the department.

In our judgment, the Tucson model offers certain advantages. First, since the psychologist is an independent contractor and does not report to the chief of police, he is autonomous as far as the operation of the Behavioral Science Unit is concerned. Although he must satisfy the chief of police, other command personnel, and the troops themselves, no one in the police department makes up his efficiency report or in any way has a direct bearing on whether he keeps his job. If the contract is not renewed, he is still a full-time employee of the state and will be assigned other duties. Again, since his chain of command is outside the chain of command of the police chief, he is free to advise the chief on matters within his expertise without concern for any backlash.

Another advantage to any police department considering this model is that a local mental health agency may be contracted to ascertain whether any staff member would be interested in working with the police in the role of police mental health professional. If a staff member expresses interest, a contract can be made for six months or a year. Thus, the police department can try out the new person without too much of a problem getting rid of him should he not work out. It should also be noted that the contract might call for a certain number of hours, thus making it possible for the police department to have a fully qualified professional without having to provide, in a limited police budget, a full-time salary. Further, a local mental health agency might be able to provide this service at cost, which is considerably less than the cost of employing a private psychologist as a consultant.

The Multi-Department Program

Another model that may be especially suitable for small departments is for several of them to pool their resources and hire one mental health professional to provide services to all (Chandler 1980). The psychologist can be centrally located and can provide services on an as-needed basis to the several departments that have contracted for these services. The

Law Enforcement Clarification Center in Rockford, Michigan, is located in a small town and serves all law enforcement personnel in twelve counties. The Center is located in a big white house converted for office use and not connected to any local police department. People may come and go from any department and not be noticed. It is important for small police departments to consider this model, since services involved in selection, training, and counseling may be needed more in small than large departments. If one man is ineffective in a 10-man department, it will be more devastating than if one man is ineffective in a 2,000-man department.

Referrals for Counseling Services

How do officers (and their families) avail themselves of the services of these psychological units? In the Tucson Police Department, any officer, civilian employee, or member of the family may contact the Behavioral Science Unit at any time. The confidentiality of the doctor–patient relationship applies not only to the clinical psychologist but also to the sergeant member of the Behavioral Science Unit. There are only two exceptions to this confidentiality. First, if the counselor is told that a felony has been committed, this cannot be kept confidential, since the counselor could be charged with being an accessory to a felony. This would be true even if the counselor were in private practice. The other restriction on confidentiality concerns dangerousness. Because of the badge and gun which the police officer carries, the client is told that, if at any time the counselor becomes concerned about the safety of the officer or the safety of any citizens, steps will be taken to address this issue. This may simply involve informing the officer's commander that the officer has come for counseling without revealing the details. The client is told that should any such step become necessary, he will be told exactly what the counselor proposes to say to the officer's supervisor and that he will have the opportunity to modify the counselor's proposal if he disagrees.

A person may also come in contact with the Behavioral Science Unit (BSU) through referral from a supervisor. In this situation, the officer is told that the interviews are confidential, but that some feedback will be required by the supervisor. This may consist of nothing more than telling the supervisor that the officer is coming for counseling. The officer is told that any information given to the supervisor will be with the officer's permission. In our experience this has presented no problem in the six years the unit has been in operation.

Finally, an officer may come into contact with the BSU if he is the subject of an internal affairs investigation. In this case, only the psychologist sees the officer. The officer is told at the beginning that the interview is not confidential, since he has been sent there for a specific purpose (for example, evaluation of fitness for duty or retention) and that a report will be made. The officer is further advised that he will be told the substance of the report even if it is unfavorable. It is absolutely vital to the integrity of the BSU that anything about the officer coming from the Unit be heard by the officer first from the mental health professional and not from somebody else. If the BSU has had contact with the officer in the past in a counseling relationship involving confidentiality, or if, for any other reason, there appears to be a conflict of interest, the officer should be referred to another psychologist outside the department.

Selection of the Police Mental Health Professional

If you are a member of a police agency interested in employing a mental health professional, perhaps with the objective of starting a Behavioral Science Unit in the department, how do you proceed? Since most police mental health professionals are psychologists, we will use this as our example. While employment interviews are some assistance, there are other important considerations.

First, review the educational and vocational background of the applicant. If this person has graduated from an accredited program in clinical psychology, you probably don't have to worry about professional qualifications. Ascertain whether the applicant has had experience with law enforcement agencies as an officer, employer, or consultant. If the person has worked in a military setting, this also would be favorable. Of course, you should complete a background check by contacting references and past places of employment to ascertain skills and character. The arrest record always should be checked.

The best advice we can offer is to ask the candidate to spend a week in the department, riding with some senior patrolmen who are good officers and good judges of people. Expose the applicant to sergeants whose opinion you trust and allow interaction with several commanders. After the candidate has spent several days riding and interacting with these officers, ask them questions such as, "Do you like the applicant?" "Would you trust this person's judgment?" "Would you go to see this person if you had a problem?" This approach probably will assist the most in selecting a psychologist who can relate well and who really likes to work with the police. Such a psychologist will be an asset to the department.

If you are beginning a program, it's exceptionally important that the first psychologist you select be able to perform well and to relate effectively. If the psychologist fouls up, it will be a long, long time before that negative experience will be forgotten, thus setting back by at least several years the implementation of any behavioral science program in the department.

Program Benefits

Schilling (1978) contends that experience demonstrates that a behavioral science unit returns far more than its original cost. "These units have established impressive track records for reducing the cost of internal investigations, limiting the cost of sick time benefits and decreasing the supportable grounds for liability litigation. They also produce savings in the cost of replacing employees who would be lost to the agency without rehabilitation."

In evaluating the worth of these programs, we must also note the humanistic benefits to police and their families from available counseling services and stress management programs. These services help police officers do their job more effectively and safely with fewer adverse effects upon themselves and their families. Benefits also accrue to the public, since services offered by the police mental health professional and his associates reduce the likelihood of abrasive police–citizen contacts and increase the possibility of more efficient and satisfying services to the public.

Although a cost analysis of these behavioral science units has not been done, there seems to be little doubt that the value of these services far exceeds their cost, especially when they are provided by in-house personnel.

Summary

In this chapter, we have discussed the role of the mental health professional in police work. During the last decade, there has been an increasing tendency for police departments to employ mental health professionals, especially psychologists. The in-house psychologist with multiple responsibilities is preferred over the part-time consultant who is hired on a contractual basis to provide limited counseling or other specific services. In addition to counseling services, the police mental health professional may participate effectively in a wide range of functions, such as screening, training, research, liaison with mental health agencies, consultation, and field emergencies. We have described three models for these programs that have emerged within the last few years (Dallas, Tucson, Multi-Departmental).

In the selection of a police mental health professional, the most important factor is whether the applicant will be accepted by the personnel in the department as someone they can work with, trust, and discuss problems.

Recent experiences in departments with behavioral service units indicate that these programs are cost effective.

Finally, there appears to be an increasing need to develop training programs for this new specialty within mental health—the police mental health professional. Hopefully, this need will be recognized, and graduate programs will be established in university settings to teach these programs.

BIBLIOGRAPHY

AULT, R. L., and REESE, J. T. March 1980. "A Psychological Assessment of Crime: Profiling." *FBI Law Enforcement Bulletin* 22–25.

CHANDLER, J. T. February 1980. "The Multi-Department: Police Psychologists." *The Police Chief* 34–36.

DePue, R. L. February, 1979. "Turning Inward: The Police Officer Counselor," *FBI Law Enforcement Bulletin* 8–12.

Hazelwood, R. R., and Douglas, J. E. April 1980. "The Lust Murderer." *FBI Law Enforcement Bulletin* 18–22.

Morris, H. February 1980. "Psychological Services: Clinical Service or Management Tool." *The Police Chief* 32–36.

Reese, J. T. August 1979. "Obsessive-Compulsive Behavior: The Nuisance Offender." *FBI Law Enforcement Bulletin* 6–12.

Reiser, Martin. Personal communication.

Ressler, R. K. , and Douglas, J. E. September 1980. "Offender Profiles: A Multi-Disciplinary Approach." *FBI Law Enforcement Bulletin* 16–20.

Rider, A. O. June 1980. "The Fire Setter: A Psychological Profile (Part I)." *FBI Law Enforcement Bulletin* 6–13.

Rider, A. O. July 1980. "The Fire Setter: A Psychological Profile (Part II)." *FBI Law Enforcement Bulletin* 7–17.

Schilling, C. G. April 1978. "Behavioral Science Services for Police." *The Police Chief* 28–32.

Somodevilla, S. A. April 1978. "The Psychologist's Role in the Police Department." *The Police Chief* 21–23.

Stratton, J. G. 1980. "Psychological Services for Police." *Journal of Police Science and Administration* 8(1):31–38.

Taft, P. B. January 1980. "Dealing With Mental Patients." *Police Magazine* 20–27.

Index

Abnormal behavior: defined, 42–43; of delinquents, 134–40; drug dependent, 142–55; guidelines for judging, 47–52; in military situations, 44–45, 48, 206–7, 275; misconceptions about, 44–46; paranoid, 156–62; psychopathic behavior, 103–16; sexually aberrant behavior, 117–33; stress-induced, 208–12; suicidal, 179–201 (*see also* Suicide); violent, 164–78 (*see also* Violence); *see also* Mental illness

Abraham, Karl, 95

Accidents, 49, 268; unconscious motivation and, 26

Acrophobia, 78

Adams, J. Winsted, 155

Addiction, 144–46, 150; *see also* Alcoholism; Drugs

Administration, 308, 334

Adolescence, 21, 136–37

Affective disorders, 86, 88, 94–100

Aggressive behavior: alcohol and, 165, 174–76; as a defense mechanism, 33; fear and, 56; medical conditions mistaken for, 55; in neurotic disorders, 76–77, 79; paranoia and, 158–59, 162; passivity and, 61–62; sexual aberration and, 132; *see also* Violence

Agoraphobia, 77

Aichorn, A., 141

Airborne law enforcement, 311–12

Alcohol, 33, 71, 143, 145, 232; aggression and, 165, 174–76; barbiturates and, 152; deviant sexual behavior and, 132; halluci-

nations and, 51, 148; suicide and, 187–88; *see also* Alcoholism

Alcoholics Anonymous, 318

Alcoholism, 9; affective disorders and, 95; characteristics of, 146–47; in families of psychopaths, 113; among police officers, 280, 302, 317–19; among police retirees, 320; *see also* Alcohol

Altman, H., 168, 178

Altrocchi, John, 56

Ambivalence: depression and, 99; obsessive-compulsive patterns and, 76–77, 85; suicide and, 183

American Civil War, 206, 276

American Psychiatric Association, 59, 67, 85, 100, 207, 212

Amnesia, psychogenic, 82

Amphetamines, 145, 151

Anatomy of Melancholy, 180

Andes Indian tribes, 151

Anglin, M. D., 155

Antisocial personality, 103; *see also* Psychopathic behavior

Anxiety, 61; absent in psychopaths, 109–10, 113–14; fear differentiated from, 30–31, 70; handling people suffering from, 83–84; in neurotic disorders, 69–72, 77–80, 82; paranoia and, 156–62; situational, 110

Anxiety neurosis, 70–72

Appropriateness, 47–48

Arbitration, 255–56

Archer, Peter, 10

Arizona Daily Star, 220

343